To Don

from

Dod Steiner.

Principles of Teaching for Christian Teachers

C. B. EAVEY, Ph.D.

Former Chairman of the Department of Education and Psychology, Wheaton College, Wheaton, Illinois

INTRODUCTION BY
CLARENCE H. BENSON
Secretary, Evangelical Teacher Training Association

SEVENTH EDITION

ZONDERVAN PUBLISHING HOUSE
GRAND RAPIDS, MICHIGAN

INTRODUCTION

THE four factors in teacher training are the pupil, the teacher, the lesson, and the school. In making a study of them we consider *who* to teach, *how* to teach, *what* to teach, and *where* to teach. The subjects of these studies in Christian education are generally known as Child Psychology, Pedagogy, Bible, and Church School Administration. There may be other subjects taught in a course of teacher training, such as Bible Geography, Personal Evangelism, Missionary Instruction, and Departmental Work, but these are all secondary and supplementary in place and importance.

The Evangelical Teacher Training Association has made no provision for a text-book in Bible, since in accepting the slogan of the Reformation that "the Bible and the Bible alone is the religion of Protestants," it has felt that the teacher's first requisite of Christian education was to be thoroughly familiar with the contents of the Bible rather than with what others have written about it. Text-books on Child Psychology and Church School Administration have already been prepared and in use for some years, but some difficulty has been experienced in finding a satisfactory work on Pedagogy. To supply this very important link in the chain of studies, Professor C. Benton Eavey undertook the task of writing one.

Dr. Eavey is the head of the Department of Education and Psychology in Wheaton College, which has recently added a special course in Christian Education. Wheaton College is a charter member of the Evangelical Teacher Training Association, and Dr. Eavey is chairman of

Introduction

the Texbook Committee. We are happy that both Wheaton College and Professor Eavey could make this important contribution to the approved text-books of the Evangelical Teacher Training Association.

CLARENCE H. BENSON
Secretary, Evangelical Teacher
Training Association

PREFACE

In writing this book the author has been motivated by a threefold purpose: (1) to present a view of teaching that is entirely in harmony with the evangelical point of view; (2) to give that understanding of the nature and meaning of both teaching and learning which the teacher needs in order to do effective work in the classroom; and (3) to set forth principles as a basis for right and intelligent use of methods.

For some time, there has been deepfelt need for a textbook on teaching suitable for use by Bible institutes, seminaries, and colleges that gives courses in the training of Christian teachers. While a considerable number of books in this general field are in existence, it is felt by many persons interested in the work of Christian education that these are lacking in at least two important respects: either they are too elementary or they are not up-to-date in relation to what is known about the teaching-learning process. To claim that this book meets all the requirements of an ideal treatise for the training of Christian teachers would be an unwarranted presumption. However, the author has tried to express in terms of spiritual and Biblical emphasis the best that modern psychology and education has to offer on the subject of teaching and learning and to do this in a way that will challenge the best effort of readers who are sincerely desirous of becoming efficient teachers of the Bible.

Teaching and learning are inextricably inter-related each with the other. A teacher has never taught until a pupil has learned. Apart from all teaching, comparatively little is ever learned. Teaching cannot be done well except as the teacher knows how to teach, and understanding of teaching is dependent on an understanding of the learning process. Hence, effort has been made at a thorough-going presentation of the nature of teaching in relation to learning and of the nature of learning in relation to teaching.

Method is no more than a way of doing. It is very natural and easy for teachers to place too much emphasis on method. While method is important, principles are far more so because understanding and knowledge are always essential to intelligent action. No method is good except as it is used in accordance with principles that are fundamental to teaching and learning. For good teaching, then, the teacher needs to be much more concerned with principles than with methods of teaching. Consequently, this treatise, as the title indicates, emphasizes principles rather than methods with the hope that the reader who understands the former will have a proper basis for right choice and effectual use of the latter.

The writer is so heavily indebted to the authors of such a large number of earlier discussions of teaching that recounting of the names, even if it were possible, would be tedious. Where memory and the factual data at hand availed, credit has been given in footnotes. Invariably, such acknowledgment of credit means also that permission for the use of the material has been granted by the publisher indicated. Professors Robert L. Cooke, Rebecca R. Price, and Clarence F. Stauffer read the entire manuscript and made suggestions which were stimulating and useful. For all these aids the author wishes to acknowledge his indebtedness and to express his sincere thanks.

C. B. EAVEY

Wheaton College
Wheaton, Ill.

CONTENTS

CHAPTER I

WHAT IS TEACHING?

In general, a human being's thinking is based upon certain axioms or truths assumed more or less tacitly to be self-evident. A thoughtful mind always seeks a point of departure in principles that are considered basic. Whatever is built as a superstructure rests upon a foundation; the mind must find a point of departure just as a building must have something substantial upon which to rest. And just as no building can be stronger than its foundation, so one's thinking about Christian teaching cannot be sound except as it is done consistently in terms of certain fundamental facts. Accordingly, several truths that one must keep in mind when thinking on the subject of the place of teaching in the work of promulgating Christian truth are emphasized in this chapter.

GOD IS SUPREME

The indispensable factor in the process of Christian teaching is God. The work of a teacher at best is much like that of a gardener.[1] No amount of work that the gardener can do will make a seed or a plant grow. He can fill his garden with seeds and tend the ground with

[1] R. S. Smith, New Trails for the Christian Teacher (Philadelphia: The Westminster Press, 1934), p. 236.

9

the greatest diligence, without the least result in growth so long as moisture is lacking. He can even pour much water on the seeds, and if God withholds the heat of the sun, they will not grow. No one but God can make a seed grow. His work done through the soil and moisture and sun and rain and His laws of life and growth make the apparently lifeless seed or bulb to sprout, grow, blossom, and produce fruit.

The teacher, like the gardener, works with God. It is the teacher's task to provide the necessary nourishment, the materials of instruction, and to use the proper tools, the methods of instruction, for producing growth of life implanted by God. Any true Christian teacher is without delusion as to his own importance, for he knows that his part is only to give his pupils a chance to grow. All that he can do is to serve as an instrument by use of which God may accomplish what He alone can do. Paul, who plants, and Apollos, who waters, are nothing more than means through which God gives the increase. He who plants is nothing; he who waters is nothing; only God counts.

Any life the product of many influences. Many forces combine to make a life. Every Christian has been taught by a number of teachers. He who plants and he who waters are one in that the making of the grown product is the result of their combined contributions. Who can say where the contribution of the one ends and that of the other begins? Both are laborers together with God; the bringing of life into existence and the growth of life is of God. The teacher who seeks credit for his work may find himself in the place of the minister who asked a convert in one of his services what point of emphasis in his sermon caused the decision to be made and was answered thus: "Nothing you said had anything to do with my accepting Christ. The reason I came to Him was that I saw His life exemplified in the daily living of one with whom I was in constant contact. That one taught me by his daily walk the worth and the value of union with Christ." God needs not man's labor and devices to accomplish His supreme purposes; yet He has deigned to call man into partnership with Himself in His work of reaching men and building lives for His kingdom. Man's part is to be faithful in the performance of the task given him by God; the results are of His ordering.

MAN NEEDS A PERSONAL SAVIOR

A second truth that constitutes a basis for thinking about Christian teaching is that man needs salvation. A very prevalent emphasis in religious education today considers man as inherently good. He needs, therefore, only the right kind of instruction to make him what he ought to be. Give the little child from birth onward, exponents of this view say, correct moral and religious teaching and he will grow up into sainthood in a natural way. Any person who thinks seriously for even a short time will realize that no human being can develop in any given direction or line without teaching, but no one who engages in straight, unbiased thinking will admit that any kind of mere teaching, howsoever perfect it may be in content or in method, is sufficient in and of itself to eradicate the evil of man's nature.

Teaching as the control of activity and growth. Teaching is no more than the introduction of control into the experience of a person.[2] Life means activity and activity produces growth. Any child will grow and develop whether he is taught or not taught, but growth and development will be without definite goal, direction, or

---

[2] W. S. Athearn, *The Minister and the Teacher* (New York: The Century Co., 1932) p. 1 ff.

purpose except as some sort of outer control is exercised. A child apart from all teaching will be like Topsy, one who neither came nor arrived but "jest growed." Teaching is controlling the activity of the child so that certain desired goals may be attained in growth. When a child is taught, attempt is made to stimulate and guide his experience in terms of ideas and ideals that the teacher has concerning the ends he should attain.

Contrast between religious teaching and Christian teaching. Religious education sets up goals in terms of religious ideas and ideals. Teaching religion consists in directing and guiding the activity of the learner with a view to attaining these goals. A goal or a purpose always influences both the content and the procedure used to control activity. There are those who dislike to call Christianity a religion, for, they say, it is more than a mere religion; it is a life. Admittedly this is true, and when Christianity is spoken of in any other way than that of an organized system of belief and practice, it is much more than a religion. Consequently, Christian teaching is much more than religious teaching.

Christian teaching is the introduction of control into experience in terms of the teachings of Jesus the Savior of men. Man is dead in trespasses and sins No system of nurture can bring him to life. Only the power of God brought into effectiveness through faith in the atoning merits of a Redeemer Whom God has set forth as a propitiation for sin can impart spiritual life to man. And until he is born again, there is no possibility of growth in spiritual life, for growth is an experience that begins only when life begins. Hence, the initial task of the Christian teacher is so to present Christ as Savior that he who is taught may believe, accept, and pass from death to life. Teaching that is truly Christian stands, therefore, for the reception of Christ as a personal Savior, the realization of His indwelling presence, power, and love, and a reciprocal relationship that reproduces the spirit of Christ in every-day life. To make possible this threefold development is the task of the Christian teacher. Always, however, it is God, not the teacher, who gives the increase.

THE BIBLE IS THE TEXTBOOK IN CHRISTIAN TEACHING

Religious teaching in contrast to Christian teaching finds its materials anywhere and everywhere. Hymns, prayers, poetry, paintings, and sculpture, the themes of which are religious, objects and things of beauty in the natural world, personal problems, vocational problems, social problems of every sort, political problems, economic problems, ethical problems, religious problems, and problems of every imaginable sort, are put into the curriculum of religious education with a view to making it life-centered. The Oxford doctor who said that he thought the poetry of Tennyson was inspired the same as is the Bible constitutes quite a typical illustration of a very prevalent attitude in religious education. Any product of the human spirit, no matter what realm of interest it represents, constitutes suitable material for the content of religious teaching.

Influence of secular education on religious education. Emphasis on materials of this nature is the result of several general causes.[3] First and most important, perhaps, is the impact that secular education has made on religious education. Modern educational philosophy and psychology have given teachers much better understanding of the nature and processes of learning. Atten-

[3] P. H. Lotz and L. W. Crawford, **Studies in Religious Education** (Nashville: Cokesbury Press, 1931) p. 206 ff.

tion has been called especially to the principle of self-activity as basic in learning and to the worthlessness of mere knowledge. It is recognized that the most important thing in learning is not to gather a quantity of information but to develop experience as a means to gaining power which will enable the learner to adjust himself to new situations and conditions as he meets them. Religious education has borrowed much from secular education, not being conscious of the fact that the latter is too young to be a trustworthy source from which to borrow. Secular education deals almost exclusively with the intellect while religious teaching is mostly concerned with the emotions, sentiments, and ideals which have never been studied to any adequate extent. Furthermore, it has not always been recognized that religious education has a technique peculiar to itself and that it has a content as well as a technique. In Christian teaching, technique cannot be substituted for content, for there is a gospel message. The world cannot be saved by teaching, though the teaching of Christian truth can be of tremendous help in saving men.

Emphasis on character education. A second reason for which materials such as those described are used is that search is being made for some way of getting worthwhile results in the character and the social living of those who receive religious teaching. Various tests have revealed the fact that knowledge of the Bible obtained through attendance at Sunday school does not lead to practice of some of the virtues of Christian character. In fact, very unchristian character is found some people who know much Bible, e.g., some of the world's greatest infidels and atheists knew their Bible content admirably well. And the finest kind of Christian character is sometimes found in persons who know virtually nothing about the Bible. Hence, it was concluded that something was wrong, either with the choice of passages from the Bible, since it was central in Christian instruction, or with the way in which it was taught, or with both. Along with this feeling of dissatisfaction with the results of the older manner of teaching Bible truth, there has been exerted upon the church, in recent years, a great deal of pressure for emphasis upon character outcomes. Educators have been driven more and more to the painful realization that our American education is woefully inadequate as measured by results in moral living. Consequently, many influences have combined to cause emphasis to be placed upon character outcomes in public education, and the church has felt the effect. So in the search for a content that would produce the desired results, there has been a turning toward materials that are moral and religious rather than Christian.

A third reason for the prevalent use of non-Biblical materials is found in the lessening of the authority of the Bible and the weakening of its influence on the thought and lives of men, which has been the inevitable result of modern historical study and interpretation. This has caused the Bible to be regarded as an evolutionary product of the merely human history of the Jewish people, who through the centuries developed and unfolded gradually a continually higher conception of God and of religion. This process found its culmination in the "exalted spiritual insight of Jesus and the faith of His early followers." According to this view, not all parts of the Bible are of equal value either as history or as devotional literature. It finds myths, legends, folktales, and contradictions mixed together with historical fact and lofty spiritual truth. It interprets the miracles as natural stories told in an imaginative way. It has shifted the authority of the Bible from a supernatural basis to one of purely human inclination to accept or reject as might seem fitting. With the authority of the Bible gone, it is quite natural to place its content on the same level as, or on a level inferior to, all products of the human mind and spirit.

The place of extra-Biblical material. While Christian teaching recognizes that there are sources of spiritual inspiration and guidance outside the pages of Scripture, it gives the Bible supreme place. For it, the Bible is the inerrant, inspired Word of the eternal God given to man to reveal to him his destiny, the plan of salvation, his Savior, and the will of God. By the Bible the thoughts of men will be judged, the works of men will be rewarded, and the lives of men are to be guided. It is to man what the signal light is to the locomotive engineer, what the compass is to the mariner, and what the radio beam is to the air pilot. It is the revelation of God to man. Hence, though the Christian teacher may use extra-Biblical material, the Bible will always be his point of reference and he will use such material only for the purpose of realizing the value that it may have in making clearer the truth of the Bible.

What Christian Teaching Is

Teaching is more easily and perhaps more adequately described than defined. The word "teach" comes from an Anglo-Saxon word, *taecean,* which meant "to show how to do." Perhaps the best attempt at a definition of teaching is represented by the brief sentence, "To teach is to help to learn." A fourth basic principle fundamental to all thought on the subject of Christian teaching emphasizes the nature of Christian teaching. As indicated, teaching that is distinctively Christian recognizes the relationship between God and man. It is concerned, therefore, with three indispensables: first, to bring about such consciousness within the learner of his personal need of Jesus Christ as Savior as will, through the power of the Holy Spirit, cause him to take a definite step in conversion; second, to lead the learner into a life of confession of Christ, providing the conditions under which he may grow "into a perfect man, unto the measure of the stature of the fulness of Christ" (Ephesians 4:13); third, to lead him to consecration of his life to God for service. All teaching that is truly Christian makes these three indispensables interrelated components of the process. Neither the second nor the third is possible of realization without the first, and both the second and the third are the inevitable consequence of the first.

An art demanding preparation. Christian teaching, like all teaching, is an art that demands preparation. Ability in teaching must be gained through actual experience. Teaching is a science as well as an art. As a science, it presents a body of principles basic to the art of teaching. One can know all the facts and principles of the science and not be able to practice the art; only by teaching can one learn to teach. However, knowledge of the principles of teaching is helpful and will make one a far better teacher, other things being equal, than he could be if he did not have this knowledge.

A great need in Christian education is the translation of the best in educational philosophy and science into terms that can be understood and appropriated by teachers in the church school. False views need to be corrected, technical expressions need to be reduced to familiar forms, and sound methods must be applied to Christian teaching. Teachers of the Bible must gain understanding of the learning process without becoming enslaved to a philosophy of life that banishes all Christian interpretations. Learning must be related to living just as Jesus did long before modern education devised any of its much emphasized "new" principles. Christian teachers must acquire a working mastery of the principles fundamental to learning and teaching that they may put them to the service of Christianity.[4]

It has often been said that teachers are born and not made. The statement represents a half-truth. Teachers are born, but, as someone has remarked, they are not born *made*. Heredity makes a contribution to every life; it gives the start, the potentialities, which can becomes realities. What it contributes is not something that cannot be neutralized by environment and personality. Often what is regarded as a natural gift is in reality an acquired habit. The success of any teacher is in large degree dependent upon his enthusiasm for his task, his love for his pupils, and his thoroughness in preparation. Only by dint of knowledge and pains and toil and self-sacrifice and labors most arduous is anyone made a teacher. Inspiration in presentation is largely the result of perspiration in preparation. Ask any true teacher whether he was born or made. Such an one knows what patient study, what shaping and re-shaping, what self-examination and self-criticism, what failure and re-trying, has gone into the making of him to be what he is. No such teacher is under any delusion as to the value of good, hard work as a necessity for making successful use of whatever birthday gifts he may have had when he began life.

Requisites for success. Success in teaching can be assured to almost anyone who is willing to pay the price involved in becoming familiar with the recognized principles of teaching and in making adequate preparation.

---

[4] G. S. Dobbins, **Source Book in the History, Theory, and Practice of Religious Education,** Fourth Quarter: "Principles and Methods of Teaching" (mimeographed).

While teaching is a science and an art, a psychological process, a social act, and a complex activity, it is also a simple act. Like agriculture so with teaching—there is no limit to the amount of time that may be spent in study. But again, as with agriculture, so with teaching— mastery of the entire field is not necessary for success. Putting a seed in the ground and providing the necessary conditions needed for the growth of the plant are fundamentally simple activities; planting a thought in a child's mind and nurturing the consequent growth are things that can be done effectively by one who does not have all possible knowledge in the field. Only one step at a time is required in teaching. Anyone who possesses common sense and a love for the work, who studies the Scripture and prays for enlightenment, should have no difficulty.

The laws of teaching and spiritual guidance. Does not observance of the principles of teaching conflict with the work of the Holy Spirit? Ought not every teacher who is living the surrendered life be guided and directed by the Holy Spirit? Is not the Holy Spirit dishonored by the teacher who seeks to be guided by the laws of teaching? He is not dishonored. One does not dishonor the Holy Spirit by complying with the laws of plant life. No more does one dishonor the Holy Spirit by becoming acquainted with the laws that govern the working of the human mind. There never was a teacher who was more fully led by the Holy Spirit than was our Lord Jesus Christ, and yet none ever observed the laws of teaching more consistently. So far as we know, no text on the technique of teaching was in existence in His day and He wrote no such treatise. However, it is obvious that He was a master in the art and practice of teaching. The Christian teacher of today who would be used of God could do no better than to discover and reduce to practice in his work the laws of teaching that Jesus observed.

QUESTIONS AND PROBLEMS

1. Can one think except as he starts with certain axioms or facts that he assumes to be true?
2. Indicate respects in which the work of a gardener and the work of a teacher are alike.
3. Name several influences which have combined to make you what you are today.
4. Trace the effects on your Christian life of several of your past teachers.
5. What is the work of man as a laborer with God?
6. How does straight thinking demonstrate the fact that teaching alone cannot eliminate sin from a human life?
7. Show that teaching is the introduction of control into the experience of the pupil.
8. Show how Christian teaching differs from religious teaching.
9. Cite instances of the wrong use of extra-Biblical materials. Illustrate proper use of such materials.
10. What are some things that a Christian teacher many well learn from secular education?
11. Why does knowledge of the Bible fail to produce Christian character?
12. Give illustrations of attempts to produce character through education.
13. Are you familiar with scholarly reactions against the tendency to regard the Bible as a product of natural development?
14. What is your definition of teaching?
15. With what is Christian teaching fundamentally concerned?
16. In what sense is teaching an art? A science?
17. Illustrate the necessity of relating learning to living.
18. Show the importance of preparation in the making of a teacher.
19. Name types or classes of persons who, in your judgment, could not become effective teachers.
20. Show the place of intelligent observance of laws of teaching and Holy Ghost guidance, respectively, in the work of a consecrated Christian teacher.

REFERENCES

Athearn, W. S., The Minister and the Teacher (New York: The Century Co., 1932)

Benson, C. H., A Guide for Pedagogy (Student's Manual), (Chicago: The Evangelical Teacher Training Association)

Betts, G. H., Teaching Religion Today (New York: The Abingdon Press, 1934)

De Blois, A. K., and Gorham, D. R., Christian Religious Education (New York: Fleming H. Revell Co., 1939)

Dobbins, G. S., How to Teach Young People and Adults in the Sunday School (Nashville: Sunday School Board of the Southern Baptist Convention, 1930)

Fergusson, E. M., Teaching Christianity (New York: Fleming H. Revell Co., 1929)

Freeland, G. E., The Improvement of Teaching (New York: The Macmillan Co., 1925)

Harner, N. C., The Educational Work of the Church (New York: The Abingdon Press, 1939)

Lotz, P. H., and Crawford, L. W., Studies in Religious Education (Nashville: Cokesbury Press, 1931)

Smith, R. S., New Trails for the Christian Teacher (Philadelphia: The Westminster Press, 1934)

Suter, J. W., Creative Teaching (New York: The Macmillan Co., 1924)

CHAPTER II

THE IMPORTANCE OF TEACHING

A QUESTIONNAIRE sent to twelve hundred pastors in Chicago and vicinity asked them to list in order of importance thirteen activities of the local church. The answers placed provision for teaching children in the church school near the head of the list. Pastoral calling received one more vote, but such activities as preaching, the support of missions, the maintaining of the family altar, and the mid-week prayer-meeting were considered of less importance.

TEACHING IN THE BIBLE

Old Testament statements. But the place that teaching holds in the plan of God for making His Word and will known to men is not something that was discovered only in this day. All through the years, teaching has been a chief means of bringing truth to man. If the reader will take a Bible concordance and look up the references on the word "teach," he will see what importance is given the activity by the Bible. God Himself spoke to Moses saying, "I will teach you what ye shall do" (Ex. 4:15) when He called him to go and deliver the children of Israel from bondage in Egypt. After their deliverance and after God had given them the Law, which Paul says was "our school-master to bring

22

us unto Christ, that we might be justified by faith" (Gal. 3:24), God commanded Moses to gather the people to hear His words "that they may teach their children" (Deut. 4:10). Furthermore, He commanded His people to "teach them diligently" to their children (Deut. 6:7), and to have His words and acts so in heart and mind as to be able to give their children full and clear understanding of what they had received from God. Three hundred fifty years later, when the Israelites were far away from God because of failure to heed these words, Samuel, the last of the judges and the first of the prophets, said to them, "I will teach you the good and the right way" (I Sam. 12:23). Of these people, when things were going most untowardly for them still later, it was said by Azariah under special inspiration of the Spirit of God, "Now for a long season Israel hath been without the true God, and without a teaching priest, and without law" (II Chron. 15:3). Job, afflicted sorely, made this touching appeal to Eliphaz, "Teach me, and I will hold my tongue; and cause me to understand wherein I have erred" (Job. 6:24). And Elihu, the friend of Job, exclaimed. "Behold, God exalteth by his power: who teacheth like him?" (Job 36:22). The Psalmist prayed God to "Teach me thy paths" (25:4) and he said that God will "teach sinners in the way" (25:8). Twice do we find the petition, "Teach me thy way, O Lord" (27:11; 86:11), and the Psalmist told God, after He has restored unto him the joy of salvation, he will "teach transgressors" the ways of God with the result that "sinners shall be converted" (51:13).

The books of prophecy, as well as those of law, history, and poetry, contain many statements about teaching. For example, there is the great call quoted by Isaiah (2:3) and repeated almost word for word by Micah (4:2) in which the people of the nations give recognition to the fact that in the last days God "will teach us of his ways, and we will walk in his paths." One of the most important tasks of the prophets was to teach the people the ways of God, though their work was like that of all teachers in all ages in that "precept must be upon precept, precept upon precept; line upon line, line upon line; here a little, and there a little" (Isa. 28:10). The ears of men have always been dull of hearing when the message of God comes, be it directly from Him or indirectly through the medium of those whom He has chosen to teach His truth, and an unlimited capacity for infinite patience has always been needed by him who would teach men the ways of God.

Teaching in the New Testament. In the New Testament is found even greater emphasis on teaching than in the Old. Among the Jews there was no title of honor higher than rabbi. They gave the teacher a more highly exalted position than has any other people. The Jew was taught to reverence his teacher. To dispute with a rabbi or to murmur against him was almost as sinful as to murmur against God. It was the teacher who was educated and magnified. Instead of "reverend" and "preacher," the title of distinction in Jesus' days was "rabbi" or "teacher." It was the teacher who was distinguished by the garb of a profession, who sat in the chief seats in the synagogue, and who was greeted in the market place, "Rabbi! Rabbi!"

Jesus was frequently called "Rabbi" or "Teacher." Of the ninety times the Lord was addressed, as recorded in the Gospels, sixty times He was called "Rabbi." Furthermore, the thought of the speaker in at least part of the thirty remaining cases was directed toward Jesus as a teacher, for the Greek word *didaskolos*, which refers to "one who teaches concerning the things of God, and the duties of man,"[1] is translated sometimes "teacher" and sometimes "master." Study of the Gospels discloses the fact that nearly all who addressed the Master, whether they were strangers, disciples, or critics, thought of Him as a teacher. Nicodemus, a member of the Sanhedrin, called Him a "teacher sent from God." The rich young ruler, as well as the distinguished lawyer who desired a definition of the word "neighbor," addressed Him as teacher. The disciples constantly used this term, and even the unfriendly Pharisees accorded Him this title, though it must have hurt them to do so.

The many allusions to His work of teaching, with no objection expressed by Him, indicate that Jesus regarded Himself as a teacher. "He taught in their synagogues" and similar expressions occur over and over again in the Gospels (Matt. 9:35; Mark 6:6; Luke 4:15; John 6:59). The people who heard His Sermon on the Mount marveled "for he taught them as one having authority, and not as the scribes" (Matt. 7:29). Then there is the direct statement of Jesus to His disciples, "Ye call me Teacher and Lord, and ye say well, for so I am" (John 13:13, A.R.V.).[2]

Two means by which Jesus did His work. The two great means by which Jesus did His work were His miracles and His teaching. Of these, teaching was by far the more important. As Dr. Stalker says, "His miracles were only the bell tolled to bring the people to hear His words. They impressed those who might not yet be susceptible to the subtler influence, and brought them within its range."[3] A little study shows

---

[1] H. H. Thayer, A Greek-English Lexicon (New York, American Book Co., 1889)

[2] Quoted by permission of the International Council of Religious Education

[3] James Stalker, The Life of Jesus Christ (New York, American Tract Society, 1909), p. 64

that Jesus did considerably more teaching than preaching. Only one sermon, or at most two, is recorded as
having been given by Him, whereas many instances of
His teaching appear in the record. In the beginning of
His ministry, He devoted considerable time and energy
to the instruction of individuals. During the middle
period of His public career, He addressed crowds. He
ended His mission by doing intensive teaching. This
last work was centered upon the Twelve Apostles who
were at first just ordinary disciples like many others.
He brought them into close association with Himself
by ordaining them to be apostles. He multiplied Himself, so to speak, by appointing them to be His assistants, commissioning them to teach the simpler elements
of His doctrine which He had previously imparted to
them by intensive teaching. "He educated them with
the most affectionate patience, bearing with their vulgar
hopes and their clumsy misunderstandings of His meaning. Never forgetting for a moment the part they were
to play in the future, He made their training His most
constant work."[4] Instead of a short half-hour a week,
He gave them daily instruction, which occupied nearly
all their time.

The Great Commission. Then when Jesus had finished
His work on earth, He gave His disciples a teaching
commission, "Go ye therefore, and teach all nations,
baptizing them in the name of the Father, and of the
Son, and of the Holy Ghost: teaching them to observe
all things whatsoever I have commanded you: and lo,
I am with you alway, even unto the end of the world"
(Matt. 28: 19, 20). Can this charge mean anything else
than that Jesus was recognizing teaching as the primary
method of building the kingdom of God, that teaching is
the means of building Christian character in His fol-

---

[4] James Stalker, op. cit., p. 79

lowers, and that He is present in the person of the Holy Spirit, with all who faithfully and loyally accept His teaching commission? As the Jews would have understood that charge, and as there is every reason to suppose the Lord meant it, the command was to organize schools everywhere for the teaching of the Bible as the very basis of the Christian church. Grouping scholars in classes under trained teachers for the study of the Word of God is the starting-point, as Christ intended it to be.

And it would seem as though this was the way in which the Great Commission was understood by the Apostles and their immediate successors. Every day in the Temple and in the houses, "they ceased not to teach and preach Jesus Christ" (Acts 5:42). The result was that the Word of God increased and the number of disciples multiplied greatly, even to the extent that "a great company of the priests were obedient to the faith" (Acts 6:7). The Apostles and other disciples had learned how to teach. That they realized the difference between teaching and preaching is evidenced in their frequent use of one term over against the other. Among the early Christians, the teaching ministry, as in the case of Jesus, predominated over the preaching ministry. While the word "preach" is found one hundred forty-three times in the Bible, the word "teach" is used two hundred seventeen times. Stretching from the inception of the Christian faith down to this very hour, there is an unbroken succession of teachers. Wherever preaching is at its best, the sermons, as did those of Peter, Stephen, and Paul, contain a large element of teaching content.

Paul, the teacher. Paul was the outstanding teacher of his day. As a Jewish lad of promise, he received at the hands of his well-to-do parents very superior training for this profession. When he became a Christian, he turned this training to good account for Christ and His kingdom. Far from being flying evangelistic campaigns from city to city, his great missionary journeys were teaching missions. He resided one year and a half in Corinth, two years in Rome, and three years in Ephesus. And he revisited other cities, where he did not spend long periods, for the purpose of confirming the churches by giving further instruction in the Word of God than he had been able to give during a first visit. While Paul made a few public addresses, the greater part of his ministry was devoted to the instruction of small groups in houses rather than to preaching to crowds in auditoriums.

In the brief accounts of his activities, Paul stands out as a master teacher. Educationally the best trained of all the Apostles, he wrote more books of the Bible than any other one person, and the teaching emphasis appears in every one of his epistles. To mention one example, the first eight chapters of his Epistle to the Romans disclose a teaching situation that Paul must have gone over again and again in face-to-face contacts. In presenting the theme, "justification by faith," to the distant church at Rome, the Apostle seems to imagine himself in the presence of an opponent, and the discourse is in reality a series of questions and expositions such as might have been conducted by a skilled teacher.

EFFECTS OF TEACHING IN THE EARLY CHURCH

There is no question but that the teacher was the central figure of the first century church. In this age of many books and much use of the radio, it is rather difficult to appreciate fully how successfully the Apostles and their successors carried on by means of an oral ministry. Textbooks were unknown; even the record of the words and works of the Lord Jesus were not committed to writing until thirty years after His resurrection. But the apostolic church was the burning expression of personalities who had been made new creatures in Christ Jesus and who went everywhere teaching the good news. The eminent church historian, Philip Schaff, gives tribute to the place and importance of the teaching ministry in the early church in the following words: "It is a remarkable fact that after the days of the Apostles no great missionaries are mentioned until the opening of the Middle Ages. There were no missionary societies, no missionary institutions, no organized efforts in the ante-Nicean age. Yet in less than three hundred years after the death of the disciple John, the whole population of the Roman empire, which then represented the civilized world, was nominally Christianized."

This, concludes Dr. H. Clay Trumbull, was because the divinely approved and divinely instituted plan of *child-reaching* and *child-teaching* methods of Christian activity was adhered to by the Christians who lived in the first century. "And," continues Dr. Trumbull, "the history of the church shows that in proportion as the Bible School has been accorded the place the Lord assigned it in the original plan for His Church, substantial progress has been made in extending and edifying its membership."

TEACHING IN THE CHURCH OF LATER DAYS

It is very evident that the work of the teacher was in the past, and continues to be in the present, the bulwark of the Roman Catholic Church. Both Protestant and Catholic historians agree that the religious school machinery the Jesuits set in motion as a counter movement to the Protestant Reformation arrested its triumphant advance. When Protestantism threatened to sweep Catholicism from the face of Europe, Ignatius Loyola and Francis Xavier conceived the plan of reaching the children and rearing up a new generation of lovers and defenders of Roman doctrine. The effective tools of the Jesuits were not the inquisition chambers, but their schools, and by superior teaching the Catholics soon regained whole populations that had been lost to the Church. The Catholic Church never forgot that lesson; to this day it magnifies the teaching ministry more than the preaching ministry. In practice, Catholics very generally evidence appreciation of the truth of the statement often attributed to them, "Give me a child until he is six years old and then you may have him."

Those Protestant denominations which have recognized the place and importance of teaching have also been signally successful. The Lutheran Church has always been a teaching church and it has had a remarkable and a substantial growth. Government statistics show that in the decade ending in 1926 the Lutherans added a larger proportion of pupils to their Sunday schools than any other denomination except the Southern Baptist Church.

Prior to 1900, the Southern Baptist Convention had never emphasized the teaching ministry. One of its members said at that time, "We have organized; we have evangelized; we have preached, but we have never taught." It was in 1900 that Dr. J. B. Gambrel, the president of the Convention, declared, "The time has come for us to further the teaching ministry. I believe the most significant of all modern movements is the work of teacher training." Upon his recommendation, the denomination adopted the slogan, "A certificate for every teacher" and began to concentrate all its resources upon the preparation of Sunday-school teachers for their task. Since that time, teacher training has been stressed on every platform and in every paper with the result that the Sunday School Board is now issuing more than a hundred thousand awards annually.

This measure of teacher training has been followed with a like measure of success in terms of growth in numbers. According to government statistics, the Southern Baptist organization gained one million Sunday-school pupils between 1916 and 1926, a growth by far greater than that of several of the other leading denominations combined. And in 1931, this denomination added to its membership nearly as many church members as all the other denominations put together. Truly, this church has demonstrated by its restoration of the teaching ministry the supreme importance of teaching to the life of the church.

TEACHING A DIVINE CALLING

The divine call of the teacher needs to be put on the same plane as the call of the evangelist and the call of the pastor. The ascended Christ gave gifts unto men in His church to the end that its work go forward "unto a perfect man, unto the measure of the stature of the fulness of Christ." "And he gave some, apostles; and some, prophets; and some, evangelists; and some, pastors and teachers; for the perfecting of the saints, for the work of the ministry, for the edifying of the body of Christ" (Eph. 4:11-12). The offices referred to are represented in the church of today by evangelists, pastors, and teachers. Typically, the evangelist founds the church, the pastor shepherds or governs the church, and the teacher edifies or builds up the church.

The church needs the work of the evangelist. He has a most important place in the plan of God for His church. Part of the work of any true pastor is evangelism, which, in the truly Christian church, goes on all the year round, but there may well be a time in the year when the pastor yields his place to the evangelist. Then the efforts of the entire year and the energies of the whole church are concentrated under the leadership of one man, whose burning messages may be expected to bring the final fruition of the task of many men and many months. But the success of the evangelistic campaign will depend to no small degree on the faithfulness of the teaching that was done prior to the time of the appearance of the evangelist and of that which is done after he leaves.

There can be no question as to the need for the work of the pastor in the church. He is set aside exclusively for the high calling of preaching which constitutes an important part of his work but which, quite too often in our day, tends to become the only part. Shepherding includes more than preaching; pastoral calling and personal work directed to the end of building up individuals in the faith are most essential to the work of the true pastor. He is trained in schools that exist for the sole purpose of preparing him for his task. He is ordained to the work of the ministry in a most solemn and significant ceremony. He receives a special title in recognition of his station in life. His pulpit is regarded as his throne, and his parish as his kingdom. He is acknowledged—as he should be—as the shepherd, or governor, of an ecclesiastical kingdom.

But for the teaching ministry, which exists for edifying and building up the church, there is no such adequate preparation or honorable recognition. At the same time, it is plainly taught in Scripture that the work of teaching is the divine plan of God. Surely the Protestant Church needs to awaken to the misapprehension under which it has been laboring with respect to the importance of this mighty ministry and to the tragic results of trifling with the titanic task of teaching. Why should not the work of the teacher be recognized as well as that of the evangelist or of the pastor? Why should not the claims of the teaching ministry be presented to young people? Why should the office of the teacher not be magnified? Why should not the heroic high call of the teacher receive the emphasis God manifestly intended that it should have?

Teaching and the Welfare of the Church

The importance of teaching for the welfare of the church is indicated by two sets of facts derived from statistical studies that have been made. The first has to do with the Sunday school as the feeder of the church. For some years, the Sunday school has been virtually the only institution in American life that gives Bible instruction. That it is also the recruiting ground for the church is shown by a statement of Dr. Benson, who says: "A conservative estimate indicates that seventy-five per cent of the members of all denominations come up from the Sunday school; eighty-five per cent of the church workers, and ninety-five per cent of all ministers and missionaries at some time were Sunday-school scholars." [5]

The second statistical study, reported by Squires, demonstrates that the most enduring additions to the church are gained through teaching. He says, "Of the converts brought into the fellowship of believers through the customary revival methods, eighty-seven per cent fall away in five years. Of the converts brought into the church through the Sunday school and the pastor's communicant class, forty per cent fall away in five years. In one case thirteen out of a hundred converts are to be found in the church after five years; in the other case

[5] C. H. Benson, **The Sunday School in Action** (Chicago: The Bible Institute Colportage Association, 1932), p. 37

sixty out of every hundred are still found faithful
after a like period of time. In the matter of securing
an enduring attachment to the Christian faith, the educational method is more than four times as efficient as
the revivalistic method."[6] This statement is not to be
construed as meaning that evangelism is not needed; it
simply indicates that teaching is more efficient as a
means of grounding people in the truth of God than are
revivals. Quite probably the present-day mode of conducting revivals together with the more intensive follow-
up teaching of converts would make for a change. At
any rate, whatever the truth may be concerning the
relative values of these two methods, certainly teaching
is very important.

THE NEED FOR CHRISTIAN TEACHING IN THE
SOCIETY OF TODAY

Following this treatment of the place given to teaching
in the Bible and the value that it has in winning and
holding people for the church, it may be well to turn
to a consideration of the importance of Christian teaching in the light of the educational and social conditions
of today. The forefathers in America regarded education and religion as the two cornerstones of sound
preparation for living. They taught the Bible in the
public school because they conceived that the principles
of righteousness needed to be inculcated in boys and
girls. Their position was that if the boys and girls
are taught in the way that they should go, the men and
women will go in the way they should go. They believed
with Phillips Brooks that the race moves upward or
downward on the feet of the children, and they assumed
the responsibility that was theirs for seeing that it moved

---

[6] W. A. Squires, **The Week Day Church School** (Philadelphia:
Presbyterian Education, 1929), pp. 22, 23

upward through the study of the Bible. For them, education and religious training were inseparable; they regarded as unworthy of the name any education that did not include religious instruction. The school teacher was a teacher of the Bible.

Changes in home and church life. Furthermore, the home, in the early days of American life, made the religious and spiritual life of the family the supreme consideration. The parents were the child's first and most important instructors in beginning Bible knowledge. The family altar was a very present reality in the home, and every child made contact there with the Word of God. God's command to the Israelites to the effect that His words should be taught to the children was quite literally obeyed. Along with the school and the home, the church of an early day performed a teaching ministry. The pastor was often the school teacher but, even when such was not the case, his conception of his duty was as that of one "apt to teach" the Word.

Today, however, the pastor is seldom a teacher in any formal sense. Few Protestant churches have associated with them parochial schools for the instruction of the children. In large measure, the family interest along industrial, educational, and recreational lines has been transferred to activities outside the home with the result that children too rarely have opportunity to sit in the house or to walk by the way with their parents. In other words, parents, especially fathers, have so little time for contact with their children that there is not much they could do in imparting Bible knowledge were they disposed to do so. And too frequently, the disinclination is present, for the church exerts much less influence over the home with the result that religious interests and religious practices, with their tremendous bearing upon developing child life, are conspicuous by their absence.

Changes in school life. In the school, instruction tends to be, and much of it actually is, anti-religious. The Bible has virtually no place in the modern public school. Secularization of public education has issued in a situation that is most dangerous. Only in comparatively rare instances is anything of a religious nature found in the curriculum of the public school. But all the children of all the people are brought into the public school where most elaborate provision is made for their education to meet present-day needs in everything other than religion. How could the children do else than relegate religion to a place of no importance or come to regard it as having no bearing on the affairs of this present life? Furthermore, whatever the motive of a public school may be, the inevitable consequence of the secularization of education is that it exerts an influence against religion.

What are the results? In high schools and colleges, denominational as well as undenominational, atheist societies exist and flourish because the minds and hearts of young people who have never had an opportunity to become acquainted with the Bible and the Savior Whom it proclaims constitute fruitful soil for the propagation of error. There are more children and young people in America today not receiving religious instruction of any kind—Protestant, Catholic, or Jewish—than are enrolled in all the Sunday schools. Half a million boys and girls of teen age drift out of Sunday school every year. Millions of young people and adults never see the inside of a church. Thousands of churches every year do not show a single addition upon confession of faith in Jesus Christ. It is an alarming fact that an army of criminals, most of whom are under twenty years of age, exists in this country. Corruption and violence are rampant throughout the land.

The need of the hour. Faced with these conditions, one is impelled to say with Roger Babson: "The need of the hour is not more factories or materials, not more railroads or steamships, not more armies or navies, but more education based on the plain teachings of Jesus." The outstanding development of the past hundred years is the amazing degree to which man has gained control over the material world. The invention of machinery, improvement in methods of manufacture, and increase in facilities of transportation and communication have made society a vastly different thing from what it was even one hundred years ago. Man's genius has soared to great heights in the field of the material but his development of power over nature has increased the complexity of many social issues and brought into existence a host of social problems. The result is that in social living attempt is made at social reform. Man strives mightily to bring about marvelous changes in social life without recognition of the fact that the Bible is just as sufficient for the complex issues of modern living as it was for the simpler living of an earlier day.

The question of the times. "Talk about the questions of the times," exclaimed William Ewart Gladstone, "there is but one question: How to bring the truths of God's Word into vital contact with the minds and hearts of all classes of the people." What America needs is not more advancement along material lines, not more development in social reform, but more knowledge of the Bible, the change of heart and life which this knowledge should bring, and the application of Bible truths to daily living. Great in magnitude is the work of the different organizations and societies which are laboring to distribute the Bible; it is estimated that the various agencies throughout the world engaged in circulating it distribute more than thirty million copies per year. But Bible distribution, apart from Bible study, means little. The mere purchase and ownership of a Bible means nothing; it must be read and its truths reduced to experience and practice to avail anything. On every side we see exemplified the truth expressed in the words of Theodore Roosevelt when he said, "People educated in intellect and not educated in morals and religion will become a menace to the nation." And we see, also, the need for what he emphasized in these words, "To every man who faces life with a real desire to do his part in everything, I appeal for a study of the Bible. No book of any kind ever written has so affected the whole life of a people."

TEACHING THE BIBLE TO MEET THE NEEDS OF MAN

The Bible read and studied aright will commend itself to any person as the Word of God because he will find in it the key to his own heart, his need, his happiness, and his duty. What is needed is an army of teachers to undertake the task of teaching the millions of youth who are growing up with no knowledge of the Bible. If it seem to any person that reading and study independently of a teacher should be sufficient, such an one should remember, first of all, that few people, especially young people, will ever receive much from the Bible in this way. The sharing of experience between one who has received and one who has not received is an essential, almost everywhere in life, to the development of the immature. What hast thou that thou hast not received? No one can attain much without the contribution that comes from some other who has what one does not have.

This truth has strong force in the realm of the spiritual, for God, in His chosen way of working, has made acquaintance with Himself and His Word quite dependent upon the instrumentality of those who have come to know Him. As has been seen earlier, a chief method used by Jesus was that of calling out twelve men and teaching them to present the truth of God to others. And when His mission on earth was completed, He commanded them and all followers to go and teach all nations. The Apostle Paul tells the Corinthians that he delivered unto them that which he had received. When the Ethiopian eunuch was reading the Word of God, the Spirit drew Philip away from the work of ministering to the citizens of many villages and directed him to go interpret the Word to the eunuch. The question of this seeker is one that echoes and re-echoes from the hearts of multitudes today: How can I understand what I read except some man should guide me?

The Bible is very much a meaningless book to a reader until the living Spirit of God acts upon the content read through the heart, life, and lips of some person who has become acquainted with its Author. The spirit of the learner must meet with the spirit of the teacher, and the Holy Spirit must impart eternal truth to the one through the other as a medium. "Wonderful is the privilege of the teacher! Great is the challenge of the teaching ministry to everyone who bears the name of Christian! Certainly nothing is more important than the spiritual life of the child, and nothing is more necessary than consecrated teachers—teachers who are leading holy lives."

QUESTIONS AND PROBLEMS

1. What is the most important activity that is carried on by a local church?
2. Find in the books of the Pentateuch references to teaching other than those given in the text.
3. Show what place teaching had in the work of the prophets.
4. Do you believe that it is at all irreverent to think of Jesus as a teacher?
5. Try to ascertain how much the work that He did while on earth was dependent on teaching.
6. What is the twofold emphasis on teaching in the Great Commission?
7. Emphasize the importance of teaching in the work of the Apostles as recorded in Acts.
8. What training did Paul have for teaching as compared with that of the other Apostles?
9. Would the apostolic church have prospered as it did had there been no teaching?
10. Can you cite concrete evidence from personal experience or observation which would indicate that a local church or a denomination would be less successful if it did less teaching?
11. Is a teacher called by God the same as a preacher or a missionary?
12. Do you think that church school teachers should be consecrated or dedicated publicly to their work? If so, why? If not, why not?
13. In your own estimation, what is the relative importance of the teaching method and the revival method?
14. Is there more or less need for Bible teaching in church schools today than was the case one hundred years ago? Give reasons for your answer.
15. On the basis of the quality of the teaching in public schools and in church schools, what would you expect the attitude of children toward the Bible to be?
16. Of what importance is the work of Bible distribution as it is carried on by the various organizations engaged in the task?

17. Just how much do you conceive that it is possible for anyone to get from the Bible with no teaching whatsoever?

18. Did you ever hear, on well-authenticated evidence, of any person's coming to know God's saving grace apart from all teaching?

References

Athearn, W. S., **The Minister and the Teacher** (New York: The Century Co., 1932)

Bitting, W. C., **The Teaching Pastor** (Philadelphia: The Judson Press, 1923)

Cady, M. E., **The Education that Educates** (New York: Fleming H. Revell Co., 1937)

De Blois, A. K., and Gorham, D. R., **Christian Religious Education** (New York: Fleming H. Revell Co., 1939)

Fergusson, E. M., **Teaching Christianity** (New York: Fleming H. Revell Co., 1929)

Horne, H. H., **Jesus—the Master Teacher** (New York: The Association Press, 1920)

Kent, C. F., **The Great Teachers of Judaism and Christianity** (New York: Eaton and Mains, 1911)

Kuist, H. T., **The Pedagogy of St. Paul** (New York: Geo. H. Doran Co., 1925)

McCoy, C. F., **The Art of Jesus as a Teacher** (Philadelphia: The Judson Press, 1930)

Munro, H. C., **The Pastor and Religious Education** (New York: The Abingdon Press, 1930)

Price, J. M., **Introduction to Religious Education** (New York: The Macmillan Co., 1932)

Richardson, N. E., **The Christ of the Classroom** (New York: The Macmillan Co., 1931)

Squires, W. A., **The Pedagogy of Jesus in the Twilight of Today** (New York: Geo. H. Doran Co., 1927)

Stalker, Jas., **The Life of Christ** (New York: The American Tract Society, 1909)

Verkuyl, Gerrit, **Christ in American Education** (New York: Fleming H. Revell Co., 1934)

CHAPTER III

AIMS IN CHRISTIAN TEACHING

A CURSE that blights much of human activity is aimlessness. The fable of the grasshopper and the ant illustrates vividly the necessity of purpose. The ant was diligent in business, working constantly toward the accomplishment of a predetermined end. The grasshopper spent time aimlessly, having nothing to do but to enjoy the thrill of passing through the air under the impetus of self-propelled activity directed toward the accomplishment of nothing in particular. The ant attained results in terms of what her activity was intended to accomplish; the grasshopper reaped the consequences of having no end in view, for he perished as an outcome of his own aimless activity. The world is full of very active people who hop about hither and thither but who never accomplish anything worth while because they have never taken time to obtain the wisdom they could have were they to give careful consideration to the possible ends and goals of activity in which they engage. One who enters upon any course of action without such consideration is like a man who starts upon a journey without knowing where he is going; both will get nowhere in particular.

The Need for Aims that Are Clear and Definite

Life is cursed not only by aimlessness but also by lack of clear and definite aims. Many people go on their way with only hazy ideas as to what it is all about; they have some perception as to the purpose of their activity but do not have it clearly in mind. In end effect, the results are the same in both cases, with the exception that in the latter case, there is greater possibility that the goal may be reached accidentally. One is somewhat more likely to arrive in Rantoul if he starts out with knowledge that Rantoul lies in a certain general direction than he is if he starts out oblivious of the fact that there is any such place as Rantoul. In the former case, he would not know where he was going, but he would be on his way; in the latter, he would simply be going around in circles. If a gunner aims at a target and hits an object a few feet to one side, one cannot say that he failed to aim, but one can say that he failed to aim accurately, or, other things being equal, he would have hit the target. He who would have definite success crown his efforts must have a clear and definite aim before him while he works.

But do these statements apply to Christian teaching? Is the work of God so dependent on human effort as to necessitate that a human being's aims be the factor that determines success? If God does the work, need the worker be concerned about aims? Can he not simply resign himself to being used of God as God sees fit to use him? In short, are the aims not God's rather than man's aims? When the ant engages in busy activity, she is not conscious of any end or goal. Likewise, the grasshopper is without consciousness of lack of goal; yet both fill a place in the plan of things. Should not a Christian teacher be under the unseen and uncomprehended guidance of God as the ant is under the blind dominance of sheer mechanism which propels her she knows not where but yet in the direction of ultimate results that are entirely satisfactory in the great world?

Man not a machine but a co-worker with God. If man were a mere mechanism, an affirmative answer would have to be given to this question. But since man is a human being endowed with consciousness, will, and power to think, the answer must be negative. A machine functions only in terms of the levers, the cogs, and the parts that make it the kind of machine it is. The ant, under the rule of instinct, does without consciousness of end that which the mechanism within her impels her to do; she has no choice of will or power of action to do otherwise. The stone, as it lies on the ground, as it rolls about under the control of physical forces, or even as it is thrown, cannot be said to have any aim or purpose. Where it lies, where it comes to rest, the path it takes as it flies through the air, are all definitely determined by forces outside of itself, subject to the limitations of weight, shape, and other characteristics of the stone, or to the limitations of environing circumstances. But God does not use men as machines or stones. When He created man, He breathed into his nostrils the breath of life, and man became a living soul. As such, he is endowed with will, with power of conscious control, and with capacity for living a God-guided life. It is true that the supreme God does His own work, but He does it through man as His agent, who, far from being used merely as a stick or a stone, has been exalted by God to be a co-worker with Himself (I Cor. 3:9).

Aim in the New Testament. Certainly, he who plants must plant for a purpose, and he who lays a foundation has in view a building to be put thereupon. Jesus, when great multitudes were flocking after Him without definite

aim or purpose, called upon them to consider what
they were doing because one who follows Him must
have a purpose firm (Luke 14: 25-33). Paul, speaking
of his personal spiritual living, says, "I therefore so
run, not as uncertainly; so fight I, not as one that beateth
the air" (I Cor. 9:26), thus emphasizing the fact that
he was moving in the direction of the accomplishment
of a set aim. What was true of Paul in personal life
was true, also, of him in his life of service. He said
to these same Corinthians, "I determined not to know
anything among you, save Jesus Christ, and him crucified" (I Cor. 2:2). He told the Thessalonians that he
was gentle among them, "even as a nurse cherisheth
her children" (I Thess. 2:7). A nurse, like a hus-
bandman or a builder, must have an aim in view,
or the nursling's growth and training will be quite
imperfect. Over and over again in the pastoral epistles,
Paul exhorted and admonished to definiteness of aim.
To Timothy, he wrote about warring "a good warfare"
(I Tim. 1:18), about being an "example" (I Tim. 4:12),
about following "after righteousness, godliness, faith,
love, patience, meekness" (I Tim. 6:11), concerning
holding "fast the form of sound words" (II Tim. 1:13),
concerning his aims as a "workman that needeth not to
be ashamed" (II Tim. 2:15), and about watching, enduring afflictions, and making full proof of his ministry
(II Tim. 4:5) These few citations are only random
samples from a much larger number in Timothy and
Titus which are used by a great teacher to emphasize to
younger teachers the importance and the necessity of
aims in carrying on their work.

THE NATURE OF AIM

An aim implies activity directed in an orderly manner toward the accomplishment of some end. The word

is commonly used to refer to the direction in which an arrow or a gun is pointed for the purpose of shooting to hit an object. If the bow or the gun were to be fired in the air at random, the arrow or the bullet would land somewhere. There would be a result, but no end. An end is more than a result. When the ant proceeds in an orderly manner to build her house, to gather her food in harvest, and to perform all the complex acts that her instinctive mechanism prompts her to do without conscious intention, the outcome is more than a result; it is an end. Each act grows out of the other and becomes a link in an unbroken chain of events that move toward the consummation of something. That which the ant lacks to make the end an aim instead of a mere end is imaginative foresight. An aim, then, is the direction of activity toward a foreseen end. One who aims sees in advance what he wants to do and directs his series of actions in an orderly way so that he may accomplish what he has in mind.

The aim is, therefore, the major influence in controlling procedure in any great undertaking. Teaching that lacks aim is poor teaching even if it is characterized by the presence of many good qualities. Teaching that is indefinite in aim is poor teaching, for indefiniteness in aim is bad aim.[1] Too much teaching has been aimless; few of the major activities in which men have been engaged have been so lacking in clearly defined aims as education. Yet education is essentially a matter first of aims and then of procedures. Before a teacher can use principles and methods aright, he must have clearly and adequately in mind the ends to be attained. The better he knows where he is going , the more intelligently can he provide the means for getting there. Being sure of the aim of his endeavors, he can make good use

[1] S. L. Roberts, **Teaching in the Church School** (Philadelphia: The Judson Press, 1927), p. 31

of his knowledge of truth, of pupils, and of principles and methods in the direction of that aim. Learning is never an activity engaged in for its own sake. It is always a means to an end, and the clearer the conception of that end, the better can the means be chosen for the realization of the end.

FUNCTIONS OF AIM IN TEACHING

Some of the functions of aim have been suggested in the preceding discussion but it may be helpful to state these functions in a more specific manner and to consider some details in connection with each function. Right aim in teaching serves at least six important purposes.[2]

1. *Gives direction.* Aim gives direction to thought, activity, and the processes necessary for effecting desirable changes. Considering the last of these three first, it must be observed that the very essence of education is the bringing about of changes in the pupils taught but that change in itself is no virtue. Mere modification is not learning; change can be wrong as well as right. The change wrought in the pupil must be in a given desirable direction. Teaching with an aim implies that the teacher has thought through, with definite purpose in view, both his own activity and the probable activity of his pupils, and worked out a careful plan, determined upon a starting point, considered the successive steps along the way, and decided upon a destination that is to be reached for a given lesson or a series of lessons.

As a consequence of such aiming, the entire teaching situation is enriched, and those taught reap the results in terms of realization of the true outcomes of effective education. It may be that many good Christian teachers do not know really what their aims are and at the same

---

[2] S. L. Roberts, *op. cit.,* pp. 40-44

time they accomplish worthwhile results, but, if they do, it is by chance or by the overruling power of a gracious God. They could accomplish much more if they had clearly and adequately in mind the most thoroughly Christian aims. One must know the direction in which he is going if he wishes to accomplish right results. A teacher without aims is like an architect without a blueprint or a ship's captain without a compass. It will be difficult for him to get from "whar he is to whar he ain't" if the latter is some place to which he desires to go.

2. *Makes for orderly continuity*. Right aim gives continuity to the process of teaching. It enables the teacher to put various parts of the work in proper order; it helps him to discriminate between major and minor points of emphasis; it keeps the mind from getting so lost in a maze of details that the task of reaching an adequate solution of problems is abandoned or left to some impatient, tired guesswork. It is an aid, if not a necessity, in keeping first things first. Learning is always a continuous process, a going from the known to the unknown, a building up on previous foundations. The aimless teacher runs counter to this process, teaching as if each lesson were a disconnected unit. On the other hand, the existence of a well-defined aim makes for connected experiences, unity of mental life, and integration of the pupil's personality. It enables the teacher to link truth to truth, activity to activity, in orderly, continuous, and progressive movement toward a predetermined goal.

3. *Provides a basis for selection of materials and activities*. Proper aim makes possible the selection of better types of materials and activities. All formal teaching is concerned with subject matter and with methods of stimulating and guiding pupil experience

in relation to this subject matter. When no aim exists, a teacher is without means for making a choice of content and pupil response thereto. When aim is not clear and definite, one's prejudices and incomplete analyses of pupil needs and how to meet them have no check. Selection of material depends entirely upon what is proposed to be done; only as the right aim is clearly conceived is it possible for selection of right materials to be made. Pupil activity leads to proper learning only as it is directed in the light of different alternative consequences resulting from the things pupils do in given situations.

4. *Gives a sound basis for measurement.* Aim makes possible the measurement of progress in a rational manner. The mind can make evaluations only according to the degree to which an aim is maintained—according to results in terms of some standard. An aim provides the norm by which to determine how effectively the desirable activities have been performed. The teacher with an aim is not one who is merely on his way, ignorant as to where he is going; his movement is in a direction set by his ends, or purposes. He is moving away from something to something; he is making progress, not merely moving. To ascertain whether or not improvement has been made, comparison of results attained must be made with results sought. Without clear aim, there is no basis for measurement; there can be no continuing improvement. Right aim is most important for rational measurement of desired progress.

5. *Encourages right aims in pupils.* Right aim on the part of the teacher helps the pupil to make aims for himself. A teacher who, very manifestly, does not know where he is going, provides a pupil with no incentive to go to the same place. A scatterbrained teacher will make for harum-scarum pupils. If the

teacher does not know what he expects a class to learn, how can the pupils in that class know what they are to learn? And if they do not know what is expected of them, how can they direct their activity toward definite and effective accomplishment? The test of right aim is not the worthiness of the teacher's purpose but the degree to which results in terms of that aim are achieved in the life of the individual pupil. One of the most fundamental principles of all teaching is that the teacher must provide right motivation for the pupil, that he should so guide and direct the pupil that he will have right aims for his self-activity. The greater the degree of clearness with which the teacher perceives his aim, the more will the pupil develop clear, definite, and effective aims for his learning activity.

6. *Keeps the teacher courageous and energetic.* Right aim inspires the worker. Nothing succeeds like success, and no success brings such thrill as results from earnest effort directed toward the attainment of a high and lofty end. One who is possessed with a purpose experiences constant lack of satisfaction until the gap between desire and successful accomplishment is closed. The aim sets a limit to a unit of purposeful activity; then, when this unit is completed, the worker experiences the satisfaction of well-earned success. And when the reaching of a subordinate aim is seen to further the larger movements of activity in the direction of the attainment of an inclusive aim, the teacher is incited to work on in spite of difficulties, discouragements, and distractions until this final aim is reached. As the mountain-climber keeps his eye fixed on the distant peak he purposes to conquer, he has the heart to pass through the intervening valleys and to climb the lower elevations he meets on his way. So the teacher, with his gaze fixed on an aim inclusive enough in breadth, time, and em-

phasis to make possible the subordination to it of all other aims, as well as all procedures and further factors involved, has courage and energy in the face of the greatest obstacles to press on until final success crowns his efforts.

THE INCLUSIVE AIM OF THE CHRISTIAN TEACHER

After this somewhat lengthy discussion of the nature of, the need for, and the functions of aim in teaching, it should be evident that the teacher must have a clear and well-defined aim and hold tenaciously to it until its attainment can be fully realized. A question the Christian teacher may well ask is: What should constitute this clear and well-defined aim?

Sources which have been used for discovery of aims. In answering this question, a second inevitably arises: Where shall we seek for an adequate aim? Many and various have been the sources to which inquirers have turned when dealing with it. Some have turned to philosophy and attempted to build an aim based on logical reasoning and serious consideration of social privileges and duties. Others have sought in psychology for an answer in terms of "changes and conditions involved in the progress from what people now are to what we wish to make them," emphasizing such aims as happiness, service, morality, complete living, natural development, knowledge, discipline, and culture. Some say that improvement of society is the ultimate goal. Then there are those who find the solution in consideration of the more practical issues of the day: conditions under which life is lived, the customs to which all must conform, and the need for getting the most out of life as it must be lived at the present time establish their aim. And there are those who take the self-activity of an awakened personality, enriched by many personal

52 *Principles of Teaching for Christian Teachers*

and social experiments, as the last word in respect to aim.

Some concrete statements of aims. The intelligent Christian teacher, examining all these sources of aim, finds in them something of value, but yet he realizes that they are inadequate.[3] As he continues his search, he will discover many concrete statements of aims that are excellent. Dr. Herman Harrell Horne says, "The objectives are, that all pupils should act rightly, think rightly, and feel rightly; all as in the presence of God, and all as Christ would have us." Dean Goodrich C. White says that the aim should include a threefold purpose:

1. To lead a pupil to a knowledge of God's will.

2. To lead each pupil to an acceptance of Jesus Christ as a personal Savior.

3. To develop a Christian character, which will be expressed through worship, right living, and efficient service.

Dr. H. E. Carnack also expressed a threefold aim in these words:

1. Bring the pupil to Christ.

2. Build him up in Christ.

3. Send him forth to work for Christ.

Dr. Theodore E. Schmauk, who defines teaching as instructing "the pupil in the Word of God and in the things that a Christian ought to know," says, "The purpose of the teacher is to make the Word of God clear and cogent," thus emphasizing the important fact that exact knowledge of what the Bible says is of greater importance to both teacher and pupil than is any implied inference of what it may say.[4]

---

[3] G. S. Dobbins, **How to Teach Young People and Adults in the Sunday School** (Nashville: Sunday School Board of the Southern Baptist Convention, 1930), p. 77

[4] C. H. Benson, **A Guide for Pedagogy, a Student's Manual** (Chicago: The Evangelical Teacher Training Association), p. 17

The Bible the true source of aim. While the Christian
teacher recognizes the value in these various statements
of aim, he is careful not to lose himself and go drifting
among them. He realizes how imperative it is that his
aim be closely allied to the study and use of the Bible.
In the Scriptures are to be found the only aims that
can stand the test; from the Bible it is possible to con-
struct for every man and every group of men a series
of aims sufficient for every demand of life, individual
and social. "The way of man is not in himself." What
man devises is not sufficient for direction of self or of
others. Only the truth revealed in the Bible has power
to transform life and build Christian character. The
aim of the Christian teacher is found in the Bible, the
revelation of God to man concerning his state, his need,
his salvation, and his destiny.

Knowledge of the Bible not the inclusive aim. Perhaps the most frequent answer one would receive to the
question, "What is the purpose of Christian teaching?"
if he put it to teachers in Sunday school and to other
Christian teachers, would be "To teach the Bible." But
subject matter is never an end within itself; it is always
a means to an end. Pupils use subject matter as a basis
for activities so that they may grow and develop. What
the learner becomes as a consequence of the use of that
which he learns is, therefore, of far greater importance
than knowledge of content learned. Even the Bible is
but a means to an end, never an end in itself. The
great purpose of the Christian teacher is not to teach
the Bible merely but so to teach the Bible that the content taught may have its intended effect in the lives of
those whom he teaches. Knowledge is of no worth
except as it can be applied and used in fruitful ways.
Knowledge of what is in the Bible does not guarantee
that the one who possesses that knowledge will apply

it to his life and its need. So the teaching of the Bible cannot be the aim of Christian teaching. The Pharisee of Jesus' day knew it well; many an infidel, agnostic, and atheist of past and present have been masters of Bible content; and hosts of Sunday school pupils have known much Bible that never found application to their lives.

The perfect man of God the inclusive aim. A Christian teacher is a human being who has been made a new creature in Christ Jesus. His absorbing purpose is to glorify God; this is the end in view for his life. His teaching and all that he does is the direction of activity for the attainment of this end. To him, the Bible is the inspired Word of God and, with intelligent conviction, he turns to it to find an inclusive aim for his teaching. As a teacher, he has aims subordinate to his inclusive aim as a Christian, i.e., to glorify God. But as a teacher again, he has one inclusive aim which, in turn, has within it subordinate aims. The practical question which remains after all that has been heretofore expressed is put together is: What is a clear and definite aim for Christian teaching that is sufficiently inclusive for all other aims to be subordinated to it? The direct answer to this question is, *The inclusive aim of the Christian teacher is "that the man of God may be perfect, throughly furnished unto all good works"* (II Tim. 3:17). All of Christian teaching is directed to the one final and only aim of the upbuilding of those taught in perfection of godly character.

THE INCLUSIVE AIM IN RELATION TO STATEMENTS OF AIM BASED ON SOURCES OTHER THAN THE BIBLE

Subordinate to this inclusive aim are the various minor aims, the attainment of which result in the attainment of the final inclusive aim. But before these are

considered, it may be helpful to examine this inclusive
aim in relation to other expressed aims and in relation
to our Lord's objectives. With reference to its relation
to other aims of the day, it may be pertinent to observe,
first of all, that man is God's creature and never finds
the purpose of his existence in himself. The highest
ideals, aspirations, and attainments of his nature find
their completion only in God. All aims from other
sources, then, be they philosophical, psychological, educational, social, ethical, or whatsoever they may be,
leave one with a sense of inadequacy not felt when the
mind contemplates the perfect man of God who, while
the true, the genuine, the complete man, is thoroughly
human. And, being human, he ever needs the Word
of God "for doctrine, for reproof, for correction, for
instruction in righteousness." In other words, so long
as he is a man in this world, the ultimate, inclusive
aim of absolute perfection and complete furnishing
will never be an actual reality. This is equivalent to
saying that man will always need to be subjected to
Christian teaching.

THE INCLUSIVE AIM IN RELATION TO THE AIMS OF JESUS

Consideration of this inclusive aim in the light of
aims of Jesus as revealed through careful examination
of the four Gospels indicates that His objectives were
comprehended within it. His teaching objectives were
as follows:[5]

1. *To reveal God's gracious and glorious plan for all
who accepted Him.* He declared, "I am come that they
might have life, and that they might have it more
abundantly" (John 10:10). "Fear not, little flock; for
it is your Father's good pleasure to give you the king-

---
[5] C. H. Benson, **op. cit.,** pp. 18-20

dom" (Luke 12:32). "In my Father's house are many mansions: if it were not so, I would have told you. I go to prepare a place for you" (John 14:2).

The life about which He was concerned and of which He taught was eternal, not temporal. For Him, it was not a matter of the achievement of Christian personality but one of passing from death to life. He never sought to impress His disciples with the benefits of earthly knowledge, culture, and personal development, but ever held before their eyes the vision of a timeless eternity and the necessity of man's being prepared to enter it. To Him, it was not a question of being educated, cultured, and refined, but one of having been born again as a new creature into a different kingdom. This temporal life, with all its questions and interests, was so unimportant in comparison with the eternal plan of God the Father for His children that Jesus posed the unanswerable questions: "What shall it profit a man, if he shall gain the whole world, and lose his own soul? Or what shall a man give in exchange for his soul?" (Mark 8: 36, 37).

Again, the life with which Jesus was concerned and of which He taught was spiritual, not material. He never instituted social reforms; He did not attempt to secure better legislation; He did not advocate the building of better tenements; He did not try to get His disciples elected to worldly positions so that they might exert a wholesome influence over men; He never advocated a system of old age pensions with a view to making material existence more satisfying. Why did He do none of the things the natural man regards as being so highly desirable? Because His emphasis was upon the things that are infinitely more important. The soul is of incomparable value in relation to the body; the **kingdom of heaven is of infinitely greater worth than**

the kingdoms of earth. He told His followers, present
and future, that in this world they would suffer hunger,
imprisonment, persecution, punishment, and martyr-
dom. He gave them no promise of material ease and
temporal satisfaction but admonished them to rejoice in
the reward that would be theirs in heaven (Matt. 5:
10-12).

2. *To win them to active faith in Himself as the
Savior of men, the promised Messiah, and the coming
King.* The offer by God of eternal life was dependent
on the acceptance of His Son by faith. He came into
the world to die for the salvation of men (John 3:16).
Jesus made this truth central in His teachings from the
beginning to the end of His ministry, telling Peter that
He would build His Church upon the confession of it
by men. The very center of His teaching was Himself.
He often spoke of the work He had come into the world
to do. The practical issue of all His teaching was the
invitation to come to Him, to learn of Him, to follow
Him. "Come unto me, all ye that labor and are heavy
laden, and I will give you rest" (Matt. 11:28) is the
welcome He sounded forth frequently in spirit if not in
word. A very common phrase in His teaching was "the
kingdom of God." He spoke many a parable setting
forth the nature of the kingdom of which He is King.

What did this teaching signify? It meant that the
kingdom predicted by prophets and looked for by saints
through the years was being ushered in, and He who
brought it was the promised Messiah and the coming
King. "The main drift of His preaching was to set
forth this conception of the kingdom of God (one in
which God ruled in the loving heart and the obedient
will of surrendered lives), the character of its members,
their blessedness in the love and communion of their
Father in heaven, and their prospects in the glory of

the future world." All, from the lowest to the highest, were invited into the kingdom. He ever persuaded men by loving appeal and winning manner to forsake the vanity of wealth, the pomp of circumstance, and the illusion of temporal satisfaction to seek first the kingdom of God and its righteousness, making promise after promise of what glories would be the portion of all who would accept Him as Savior from sin and Lord of their lives.

3. *To teach the Christian way of life as opposed to a dead, dry system of theology.* His Sermon on the Mount is an outstanding example of the emphasis He placed upon the things that are truly worthwhile. No hair-splitting arguments find expression in His teaching. Instead of mere repetition of thought, He expounds the Scriptures with life-giving power. Instead of setting forth ritual, He presents God as truly pictured in the sacred text. And instead of talking about superstitious practices of dead leaders, He points His listeners to God, the source of life and power. Christianity is presented to us as the way of life. God the loving Father is presented as a very present and real Being. Small wonder that "the people were astonished at His doctrine."

4. *To prepare and train His followers to be His witnesses.* At various times Jesus commanded those who received Him to go and witness to others of the blessing received. However, from the total number of disciples, He chose twelve whom He called to give up their ordinary activities of life and be with Him constantly. These twelve He appointed as His assistants, so to speak. He sent them out to teach and to evangelize under His oversight after having first given them training in close association with Himself and thus reached many people with His teaching who otherwise would never have been

reached. "He educated them with the most affectionate patience, bearing with their vulgar hopes and their clumsy misunderstanding of His meaning." He gave them teaching which the larger body of followers and people in general could not receive, thus preparing them to carry on His work after His departure.[6]

Unswerving devotion to aim. It may be a source both of encouragement and of admonition to Christian teachers to notice how unswervingly the Master-Teacher adhered to His objectives. No temptation, no threat, and no appeal sufficed to cause Him ever to give up, even for a moment. When the people would have made Him a king, He taught them that the work of God was to "believe on him whom he hath sent," and not to place emphasis on temporal values. When the Jews threatened to slay Him, He said, "I am not come of myself, but he that sent me is true, whom ye know not but I know him: for I am from him, and he hath sent me." When one of His hearers, with a view of getting his rights, requested Him to judge in the division of an estate, Jesus told the story of the rich fool to impress the fact that a man's life consists not in the possession of earthly things. In answer to criticism made because the alabaster box of costly ointment was used to anoint Him instead of the money's being given to the poor, our Lord approved the act as a testimony of faith in Him as the appointed Savior of mankind. Replying to the request that He rebuke His followers because they heralded Him as a King on His last entry into Jerusalem, Christ declared that if men were silent even the stones would cry out in testimony to His authority. After His resurrection, when it was suggested that the time was ripe for Him to set up His Messianic kingdom,

---

[6] James Stalker, *The Life of Jesus Christ* (New York: American Tract Society, 1909), pp. 77 ff

He reiterated that the divine program was for His followers to be His witnesses unto the uttermost parts of the earth.

Aims Subordinate to the Inclusive Aim

Having observed the great objectives of our Lord's teaching and the tenacity with which He held to them, it may be well to apply them to the inclusive aim of the Christian teacher. These objectives of Jesus may well be considered as aims subordinate to the inclusive aim of Christian teaching because as each of these is realized, progress is made in the direction of the attainment of the inclusive aim. In order "that the man of God may be perfect throughly furnished unto all good works," the Christian teacher must:

1. *Bring the pupils to understand God's gracious and glorious purpose for His children.* "Eye hath not seen, nor ear heard, neither have entered into the heart of man, the things which God hath prepared for them that love Him" (I Cor. 2:9). It is the privilege of the Christian teacher, under the guidance and help of the Holy Spirit, to open to the view of his pupils the undreamed glories of an unseen existence. The more abundant life concerning which Jesus taught His disciples is the marvelous theme of every Christian teacher. Those things which God, in infinite wisdom, saw fit not to reveal in times past, things which angels desire to look into, can now be presented by the humblest servant of the Lord. The unsearchable ways of God, the depth of the riches of His omniscience, and the inscrutability of His wisdom, once kept, as it were, behind a veil, can be seen and understood by a Christian teacher. When such an one has had revealed to him a real conception of the priceless value of one immortal soul and a vision of the far-reaching happiness which is the portion of every

child of God, he is ready to bring to his pupils some understanding of what God has in store for sin-cursed men who will forsake the evil of their ways and turn to Him for pardon and cleansing.

2. *Lead each pupil to receive and confess Jesus Christ as Savior and Lord.* A human being, seeing God's glorious provision and his own worthlessness in God's sight, may well say as Peter said to Jesus, "Depart from me; for I am a sinful man, O Lord." As the pupil is brought to a realization of the righteousness of God and the sinfulness of man, the teacher can then present Christ and His atoning work as meritorious for the sinner in order to make him accepted by the righteous God. Only as one is convicted by the Holy Spirit and brought to a sense of his inadequacy is it possible for that one to lay hold on the sufficiency of Christ. As truths along this line are presented by the Christian teacher, he will not fail to make clear the way of salvation as revealed in God's Word, to pray earnestly for each pupil, and to seek by tactful, sympathetic means to bring him to a definite acceptance of Christ as personal Savior. Such decisions must come voluntarily and spontaneously, often as the culmination of a period of careful preparation. They must be free from artificial stimulation and from the force of high-pressure methods.

Acceptance of Christ as Savior will be only the first step. The Christian teacher will lead the pupil on until he has made a complete surrender to Christ as Lord of his life. It is one thing to be saved from sin; it is another thing to be saved from its power. If Christianity be anything, it is as much the one as the other, for He who atoned for sin's penalty died also that the atoned soul might be made free to live for Him who died. So the Christian teacher will not rest content until he has led each pupil to consecrate himself—body, soul and spirit, to Him who must be Lord of all if He is to be Lord at all.

3. *Build each pupil up in the Christian life, establishing him in the things of God and guiding his growth.* After the pupil is brought to Christ, his need of teaching is even greater than it was before he became a Christian because he now has a new life that must be nourished and sustained. He needs thorough and correct understanding of his position in Christ and of his relationship to the end that he may grow and develop in the Christian life. An appropriating knowledge of the purpose and work of the Holy Spirit will enable him to live in daily possession of the victory given him in Christ. Comprehensive instruction in what the Bible teaches, its rules and standards for living a healthy Christian life, the provisions made for the fulfilment of these, and understanding of the purposes of God through the ages will prepare the young Christian for a sane and balanced Christian life. Wholesome Christian attitudes toward the individual Christian's place in society and in the church, as well as in regard to government, political life, social problems, other races, etc., should be developed. In a very true sense, the Christian teacher must be a life-builder as well as a soul-winner, heeding the Lord's commission, "Feed my lambs." Only as pupils are nurtured by instruction in the Scriptures can they grow spiritually.

MEANS OF SPIRITUAL GROWTH

Spiritual growth will find expression in and will be advanced by

1. *Worship.* Through worship, the Christian experiences the reality of God's nearness and realizes a sense of fellowship with Him. Worship develops proper atti-

tudes of the soul toward God and toward one's fellowmen; it induces spiritual moods and gives them stability;
it provides the atmosphere in which great life decisions
are made. In short, worship makes it possible for God
to work more definitely in the life. Hence, an essential
task of the teacher is to cultivate the devotional life of
the pupil. The class sessions and the services of the
church as a whole provide opportunity for training with
the purpose of cultivating reverence, gratitude, love, and
faith. As a basis for good training, instruction should
be given in the use of songs and stories and the types
of prayers best suited to different classes, departments,
and occasions. Effective training requires that pupils be
given opportunities to worship. Exercise and participation in worshiping and in praying lead to development
in these activities.

The teacher should also give instruction in the value
of daily devotional reading and private prayer. Under
the teacher's stimulation and guidance, each pupil
should form daily habits of reading the Bible and com-
muning with God. For the forming of these, pupils
should be taught how to read the Bible for devotional
purposes and how to pray effectively. The spirit, not
the routine of worship, is what counts; hence the former
should be emphasized. Devices such as pledges secured,
records kept, and rewards given, may be of some little
worth in obtaining the desired results, but the use of
these should always be subordinated to the cultivation
of the spirit of worship and devotion.

This training in worship needs to be given apart from
worship itself; hence it is distinctly a part of the educational work of a church to give such training. Since the
home is much less a center of religious life than it
once was, a greater burden falls upon the Christian
teacher in this as well as in many other phases of Chris-

tian training. The teacher should see that familiarity with and appreciation of the best in worship materials are developed in the pupils.

The Word of God provides most adequate content for instruction in worship. The spirit, the forms, and the principles of prayer may be studied in the Bible. The Lord gave His followers definite instruction in prayer in addition to being a living example of prayer. In the Bible are recorded prayers of various other Bible characters as well as many statements about prayer. The Book of Psalms, especially, abounds in expressions that are most acceptable forms of devotion. The most beautiful and worshipful verses of the Bible should be studied, memorized, and understood. Proper instruction in the Word of God bears a most vital relation to worship, and the spirit of true worship may be developed on such instruction as a basis.

2. *Character*. The constant aim of the Christian teacher is the development of Christian character, the man of God perfected in good works. Unless the truths taught find lodgment in the hearts of pupils and expression in their daily lives and conduct, teaching is done in vain. "Faith without works is dead." If pupils have faith, evidence of its existence will be manifest. It is the teacher's responsibility to link up the truths taught with the daily lives of the pupils so that they may be "doers of the word, and not hearers only."

After all, if Christianity is not practical, it is of no value; so the pupils need to "learn to maintain good works for necessary uses, that they be not unfruitful" (Titus 3:14). To a great extent, Christians are judged by the way they treat others. Therefore, the Christian teacher should strive to teach pupils how to deal with others who are or who are not Christians. For such teaching there is one perfect pattern, the Lord

Jesus Himself, many examples in Bible characters of what should or should not be done, and much by way of command and exhortation in the Bible. Until one's faith is consistently manifest by his actions, one is of little value as a witness, for to the world inconsistency must ever appear as insincerity. If Christians possess the truth as well as profess it, the world will see evidence of it in their lives.

"Sow an act and you reap a habit; sow a habit and you reap a character." Christian habits result from Christian instruction. Every recitation and every lesson affords the Christian teacher opportunity to build Christian character. If pupils are not forming right habits of good attention, interest, proper behavior, and politeness, they are inevitably, every time the teacher meets them, forming habits of inattention, heedlessness, wrong behavior, and rudeness. Schools are habit factories, and a Bible class where pupils are permitted to be noisy, disobedient, discourteous, and irreverent may be doing its members more harm than good. Every act of life constitutes the base for the development of some habit, good or bad, and character is nothing more than a bundle of habits. The teacher's opportunity and responsibility is to see that everything in the class tends to the formation of right instead of wrong habits in the pupils.

3. *Service*. A growing Christian is an active Christian, ready and eager to serve his Lord. Such an one is not so much concerned with visions of service in the distant future that he cannot see present opportunities. It is the teacher's privilege and obligation to instruct the pupil and guide him in the perfection of his Christian character and the accumulation of good works so that he may be ready for effective service. Then the teacher has the further responsibility of suggesting opportuni-

ties for the pupil's activity. Such opportunities may be found in home, school, church, and everywhere in life. Once the pupil becomes a member of the church, he should be in line for the many opportunities for service which this institution affords. The well-organized Sunday school can use many people as officers, teachers, and substitute teachers. The young people's society presents large scope for much active service. Tract distribution, jail work, visitation of the sick, meetings in missions, hospitals, or on the street, are forms of work which are carried on in many churches and afford much opportunity for active service. Everyone can do something when the church sees its opportunity.

The training in service should include not only the giving of time and energy but also the giving of money. Every Christian should give cheerfully, liberally, and systematically as unto the Lord, Who gave Himself for us. Happy is the Christian who acquires early the habit of giving, and great is the service of the teacher who so teaches and guides as to form this habit.

The Christian with no vision of service in reaching and bringing others to Christ may easily become "stagnant" and a dead weight in the advancement of the kingdom of God. The furnishing of the man of God for all good works has inherently the ideal that in the midst of the world man is obliged to carry to others the message of reconciliation. Hence the Christian teacher should so present Christ's teachings, the need of the unsaved, and the believer's debt of love and gratitude to his Savior that the pupil will be constrained by the love of God to seek and save the lost. The responsibility of making Christ known rests upon every believer. Every Christian is an ambassador to those who know Him not, and some of these are found in every Christian's daily contacts.

QUESTIONS AND PROBLEMS

1. Does one ever do anything without an aim?
2. Which is worse in its effects, aimlessness or indefiniteness of aim? Give reasons for your answer.
3. Show the necessity for clear and definite aim in Christian teaching.
4. Can you give illustrations from the Bible, other than those given in the text, of aim in teaching?
5. What is aim?
6. State the six functions of right aim in teaching.
7. From what different sources may one draw in order to formulate aims for religious teaching? For Christian teaching?
8. Which of the concrete statements of aims do you prefer, and why do you prefer it?
9. Why is the aim of teaching of the Bible inadequate?
10. What is an inclusive aim?
11. Do you agree with the statement of the inclusive aim for Christian teachers? If not, what would you give?
12. Can man ever reach a place where he will no longer be in need of Christian teaching?
13. What were the teaching objectives of Jesus?
14. Comment on the opportunities which He had to forsake them.
15. State the subordinate aims of Christian teaching. Can you add others?
16. In what ways, other than those named, may spiritual growth be advanced?
17. How can a teacher help pupils to form daily habits of Bible reading and private communion with God?
18. Emphasize the importance of training in Christian character.
19. Explain the statement, "A growing Christian is an active Christian."
20. How may a teacher train pupils in the grace of giving?

REFERENCES

Benson, C. H., A Guide to Pedagogy, a Students Manual (Chicago: The Evangelical Teacher Training Association)

Betts, G. H., Teaching Religion Today (New York: The Abingdon Press, 1934)

Brederveld, Jacob, Christian Education (Grand Rapids: Smitter Book Company, 1928)

De Blois, A. K., and Gorham, D. R., **Christian Religous Education** (New York: Fleming H. Revell Co., 1939)

Dobbins, G. S., **How to Teach Young People and Adults in the Sunday School** (Nashville: Sunday School Board of the Southern Baptist Convention, 1930)

Horne, H. H., **Jesus—the Master Teacher** (New York: The Association Press, 1920)

Lotz, P. H., and Crawford, L. W., **Studies in Religious Education** (Nashville: Cokesbury Press, 1931)

McKibben, F. M., **Intermediate Method in the Church School** (New York: The Abingdon Press, 1926)

Moore, M. A., **Senior Method in the Church School** (New York: The Abingdon Press, 1929)

Price, J. M., **Introduction to Religious Education** (New York: The Macmillan Co., 1932)

Roberts, S. L., **Teaching in the Church School** (Philadelphia: The Judson Press, 1930)

Schmauk, T. E., **How to Teach in Sunday School** (Philadelphia: The United Lutheran Publishing House, 1920)

Smith, R. S., **New Trails for the Christian Teacher** (Philadelphia: The Westminster Press, 1934)

Vieth, P. H., **How to Teach in the Church School** (Philadelphia; The Westminster Press, 1935)

Objectives in Religious Education (New York: Harper & Brothers, 1930)

CHAPTER IV

THE CHRISTIAN TEACHER

IN a very true sense, the New Testament standard is that all Christians are expected to be teachers of the gospel they have received. The divine plan is that the one who has received should pass on to others the glorious story of redeeming grace. "Go ye therefore, and teach all nations," is the perpetual command of our Lord to all Christians, and the further command is that, after those taught have received Him as Savior, teaching is to continue so that they may know to observe all things that He has commanded. Thus teaching is an ever-continuing process so great and challenging that each member of the church of Christ is needed in some capacity. Every Christian is under personal obligation to his Lord to teach the gospel as God may open the way and to seek such openings, counting every use of them a joy. To be a Christian means being a Christian teacher. When one is cleansed, to go home to one's friends to tell and show what the Lord has done is an unescapable obligation.[1]

WHAT TEACHING IS

But what is it to teach? Just what does the expression, "the Christian teacher," mean? Dr. Trumbull says,

---

[1] E. M. Fergusson, Teaching Christianity (New York: Fleming H. Revell Co., 1929), p. 31 (Used by permission)

"It is obviously true that a man *may* be called 'a teacher' without being a teacher." He goes on to say that being designated to the office of teacher by the authorities of a school does not make a person a teacher. "That makes him a 'teacher'—by the record; but it does not make him a teacher in fact. Nor does his *acceptance* of the position tendered him, make the selected 'teacher' a teacher."[2] In other words, it is one thing to be called a teacher and quite another thing to be a teacher. To understand what a teacher is, one needs to know what it is to teach and it is not easy to obtain a clear understanding of the term "teach." Dictionary definitions are vague and unsatisfactory. Technical treatises are quite generally characterized by use of the term with the assumption that its meaning is understood.

Perhaps as good a dictionary definition as any is, "to give intelligence concerning." Jacetot said that "to teach is to cause to learn." This statement is in harmony with what seems pretty generally to be the present day tendency, viz., to define teaching as stimulating, guiding, and encouraging learning. It would seem, then, that teaching means learning, that no teaching has been done except as something has been learned. "Unless there is learning by a learner there can be no teaching by a teacher!" "There is no such thing as teaching by a teacher unless at the same time there is learning by a learner." From this, it follows that a teacher is one from whom, through whom, or with whom pupils learn. The last phrase of this triplet is the best, for, as will be seen later, a real teacher always learns with his pupils.

What a Christian Is

It now remains to consider what the word "Christian" means, for, quite obviously, one must be both a teacher

---

[2] H. C. Trumbull, **Teaching and Teachers** (Philadelphia: John D. Wattles and Co., 1897), p. 7

and a Christian in order to be a Christian teacher. Though it is not easy to define this term in an objective manner, it would seem that one might well start with the observation that a Christian is a follower of Christ. And in order to be a follower of Christ in deed and in truth, one must, as a sinner, have met Christ, accepted the atonement made by Him for sin, and passed from death unto life. The natural man, being dead in trespasses and sin, cannot follow Christ as a Christian though he may, in a self-effortful way, follow Him as an example. Christ is the Savior of men, and one who follows Christ as a Christian is one who has been saved. As is the case with "teacher," so it is with "Christian": that men say or that the individual says he is a Christian does not make one a Christian. It is one thing to be called a Christian and quite another thing to be a Christian. By way of summary, then, it may be said that a Christian is a human being who has met and accepted Christ as a personal Savior and who, as a consequence of this experience of grace, has become a follower of Christ.

A Christian Teacher

Therefore, a Christian teacher is one who, having experienced a personal relationship with God through faith in the atoning merits of Christ the Savior, brings to others things new and old in such a way that they cannot gainsay the fact that he is speaking the things that he has seen and heard. What is true and central in his life because he himself has experienced it is imparted to others. Speaking most reverently, we may say that the message of the true Christian teacher causes hearers to marvel as did those who heard Jesus because He spoke with authority. Teaching that is truly Christian comes with the authority of personal experience and is so received by pupils, whatever they may do with the message or the messenger.

TEACHING IS A MATTER OF LIFE, NOT OF BOOKS AND OF SCHOOLS

The association of teaching with books, lessons, classes, and school is quite artificial. Education does not consist in something to be learned from books; it is wholly something done to the learner. Far from saying things to a class, teaching means that he who teaches engages in activities that induce pupil experiences such as produce certain results in the lives of the pupils. Teaching is a necessity everywhere in life. The parent in the home, the tradesman in the shop, the storekeeper in the store, the businessman in his office, the engineer in his building, the expert in his laboratory — every person who engages in any activity that maintains a standard of performance and uses more than one worker at a time finds teaching a necessity. And in the degree that true teaching is done, the primary concern of him who teaches is, not what the taught one knows in terms of being able to state facts, but what his needs and problems are, what can be done to and for him in terms of these, and of what value the teaching may be in helping him to become different than he is, as measured by the educational objective. In short, true teaching is concerned always with the effecting of desirable changes in the one taught.

The minds and thought of men, educators as well as others, have been influenced by a narrow academic conception of education dependent upon formal work in a school situation which, all too frequently, fails to meet the needs of the child. To think of the teaching process, one must think of needs felt, situations faced, and experiences shared leading to the development of the learner.

In terms of Christian teaching, life is just one situation after another, and every situation affords opportunity for both new teaching and new learning. Everywhere a Christian finds himself, therefore, be it in the church or in the world, at home or abroad, in house or in field, in school or in factory, in hospital or in jail—wherever he is in such contact with others that they and he must associate together, there he may be a teacher for Jesus Christ. To him, opportunity for work is never lacking so long as there is a human being whom he can approach.

Jesus taught constantly. The earthly life of our Lord was characterized by such constant teaching. A sentence most vividly and accurately descriptive of His earthly ministry might read thus: He spent the years walking up and down the land, teaching people, individually and collectively, wherever and whenever He came into contact with them, the things concerning the kingdom of God. Did a Pharisee impressed by His teaching come to visit Him at night? He taught him the necessity of a new birth. Did He meet a sinful woman at the well? He taught her the elements of true worship of a holy God. Did His disciples feel that He needed food? He taught them concerning the true satisfaction of a life devoted to the service of God. When censured for working a miracle on a lame man, He taught carping Jews the love of a kind Father in heaven and the way to that love through Him whose act they were criticizing. When the multitudes were hungry, He gave them food to eat and told them of the bread of life that came down from heaven to feed their souls. Everywhere and at all times, He was about His Father's business. Every social occasion, every temporal event, every need, spoken or unspoken, every experience of life, presented Him with an opportunity to convey to men the truths of the Christian life.

THE CHRISTIAN TEACHER IN THE CHURCH SCHOOL

But while it is justifiable to say that all Christians are teachers in one way or another in matters concerning the presentation of the gospel message and the building up in the faith of those who receive that message, interest here is with teaching and teachers in a somewhat more concrete or practical sense. From Paul's statement in the third chapter of his Epistle to the Ephesians, one learns that the risen Christ calls some Christians apart for the special ministry of teaching. It is with these that the present treatise is more particularly concerned; therefore examination will be made of what a Christian as a Sunday-school teacher, a week-day Bible-school teacher, a vacation-school teacher or a teacher in any other form of Christian service, should be like. Be it said in passing that no person engaged in any special phase of Christian service has greater need of certain outstanding qualities of character, personality, and life than has the average Christian except for the fact that the former is charged with responsibility for a special work. Being set apart for that work, he should exemplify in marked degree the qualities of Christian character.

ESSENTIAL MARKS OF A TRUE CHRISTIAN TEACHER

A very short answer can be given to the question, "What should a Christian teacher be?" by saying, "He should be a perfect person and a perfect Christian." However, since lack of perfection both in persons and in Christians is always with us as finite human beings, such an answer is not very satisfying. Furthermore, one would like to know what constitutes perfection.

So, though it be hazardous to attempt description of
either human or Christian perfection, a few ideas will
be set forth as a basis for further thought concerning
the characteristics that a Christian teacher should have.

He is a leader. A teacher has much more to do than
to teach. In fact, teaching is not always the most important work of the teacher. What a teacher is counts
for much more than what he says. "What you are keeps
ringing in my ears so loudly that I cannot hear what
you say," is a statement that applies with vivid force
to a Christian teacher. The impress of a teacher's personality and character, the influence of his life, which
are brought to bear on his pupils' lives, may leave most
indelible marks long after the effects of what he said
and what he taught have been lost forever. Teaching a
Bible lesson is one thing; influencing a life is another
thing. While either may be done without the other, the
ideal Christian teacher does both together, but does the
second even when he is not doing the first.

Again, the Christian teacher is a leader from another
point of view. The best conception of a class is that of
a group of people working together to accomplish something that no one of them working alone could accomplish. Teaching is a coöperative enterprise directed
toward some goal or end. As the teacher teaches, the
pupils learn; as the pupils learn, the teacher teaches.
Wherever a group is working coöperatively there must
be leadership. True it is, first one and then another,
may lead in different phases of the common undertaking,
but, in general, there needs to be one who has the
maturity, the vision, and the experience necessary for
intelligent planning and wise direction of the total
movement.

The effective teacher, while he will need at times to
prove his coöperative spirit and helpful attitude as a

follower and as a co-worker, will be in general charge of the activity of the group.[3] A teacher is usually older, the pupils younger. A teacher is one who has gone the way over which he is leading his pupils. He has had the experiences into which it is now his purpose to lead them. The task of the teacher is not merely to impart facts and ideas. He is the leader, stimulating, directing, and guiding the learner as he goes on before.

He is a learner. The coöperative enterprise of education implies that all the members of the group are learning together. Someone has said, "It is a poor teacher who does not learn more from a class than he teaches it." While the statement may not be true as given, it contains important truth, for it is a poor teacher who does not learn something when he teaches a class.

In the first place, no one can teach a lesson effectively unless he makes specific preparation for doing so. This is true no matter how long he may have taught or how much he may know about the lesson, or at least it is true that one can teach a lesson more effectively if he makes specific preparation for the teaching. And as he studies, he learns.

Second, the teacher who has a proper sense of responsibility is not satisfied with merely enough content to meet the issues of teaching a series of lessons to succeeding generations of classes. Instead, he is constantly reading, studying, and seeking larger understanding of truth and life so that he may become more and more effective as a teacher. The command of Paul to Timothy finds literal exemplification in the practice of a truly Christian teacher: "Study to shew thyself approved unto God, a workman that needeth not to be ashamed, rightly dividing the word of truth" (II Tim. 2:15). The call to be a teacher, to one who takes the

[3] N. L. Garrison, **The Technique and Administration of Teaching** (New York: American Book Company, 1933), p. 19

call seriously, means that he must strive ever to learn more and more of the content he is to teach his pupils.

Third, a true teacher gains knowledge from the classes he teaches. The individual reactions of his pupils, the responses they make, the questions they ask, and the interpretations they give make for larger comprehension of and deeper insight into the meaning of the materials. How often does a chance remark of even a very small child open up to a mature adult a vista of truth which he had never seen nor understood before! The alert teacher learns much from even the youngest pupils, for each class is composed of individuals whose reception of the truth is different from that of all other pupils in all past classes.

In the fourth place, a teacher is a learner because he feels his inadequacy and makes constant attempt to improve. Self-sufficiency in respect to what he knows is a trait which is conspicuously absent in a truly good teacher. Such an one, far from being proud that he knows so much, is very humble that he knows so little. Feeling his inadequacy, he works away constantly, trying to improve. From every possible source — personal study, learning from other people who study or who have studied, the contributions of his pupils, reading, meditation, prayer, the Christian teacher who has an adequate conception of his calling learns more and more of the facts and the truths he has been called to bring to the minds and hearts of his pupils.

Finally, the teacher is a learner because the very act of effective teaching compels one to learn. No one ever masters content so well when he studies it with the attitude of a learner as he does when he studies it with the feeling of responsibility for bringing that content effectively and adequately to others. This feeling of responsibility, the effort to see relationships, the thought of how this fact or that truth may be presented most helpfully, consideration of how each pupil will likely respond, and many other things that he who would really teach must do as he studies, give him such vistas of truth, visions of heights, and grasp of depths as only a teacher can get. To be a teacher means to be a learner.

He is a growing personality. What a teacher is as a person as well as what he is as a Christian is most potent in determining the effectiveness of his teaching. Phillips Brooks made a statement about preaching that applies equally as well to Christian teaching. These, with "teaching" substituted for "preaching," were his words: "Teaching is the communication of truth by man to man. It has in it two essential elements, truth and personality. Neither of these can it spare, and still be teaching. . . . The truth must come really through the person, not merely over his lips. . . . It must come through his character, his affections, his whole intellectual and moral being. . . . I think that, granting equal intelligence and study, here is the great difference which we feel between two teachers of the Word. The gospel has come over one of them. . . . The gospel has come through the other."

The greatest single human factor in any teacher's success, then, is *himself,* for the elusive thing called "personality" is nothing more than the quality of being a person. The term means all the factors in a person's being that exert influence over others. Christian teaching is essentially the interaction of personality with personality, the influencing for God and righteousness of one person by another whose personality has been touched and transformed by Jesus Christ. So the one indispensable element in all Christian teaching is personality—personality that Christ has possessed, that is under the power and direction of the Holy Spirit, and that is being transformed into the likeness of Christ. Leadership ability, learning power, knowledge of content, equipment, and methods are essential to teaching, but they are of little worth except as they are used by a teacher through whose personality they can be made means for the transmission of truth that will transform the personalities of those taught. The teacher may teach a little by what he says; he teaches more by what he does, but most by what he is.

A Christian teacher who realizes the important place which personality has in teaching success or failure will immediately become concerned with the problem of the improvement of his personality. As emphasized, the true teacher is a learning companion. As such, he has personal goals of advanced attainment toward which he is striving. He is not one who, having met the Lord in definite experience, is at present resting under the blighting influence of felt superiority of advanced spiritual standing and relationship. Instead, he is, as was the Apostle Paul, pressing "toward the mark for the prize of the high calling of God in Christ Jesus." Knowing that he is not "already perfect," he is "reaching forth unto those things which are before," being careful lest by any means, when he has taught others, he himself "should be a castaway." So the earnest teacher's problem is: How can I improve myself?

To get a helpful answer to this question, three other questions need to be considered: (1) What are the sources of personality? (2) What are the constituent elements of good teaching personality? (3) How may one get these elements into his being?

THE SOURCES OF PERSONALITY

Many people think of personality as something that comes with one when he enters the world and about which nothing can be done. Either one has it or one has it not, and that is the end of the matter. There is some truth in this thought, for heredity is one source of personality, and a person can no more increase native endowment of personality than he can add to his stature. Everyone has many characteristics of body and mind because he came from a certain family and a certain race and because he belongs to a certain sex. But what comes from heredity is only a part of the total personality. There are few inherited characteristics that are not modified sooner or later by environment. While one cannot increase his native endowment, he can, by thought and rightly directed effort, add markedly to the effectiveness of what heredity gave him. He can develop what he has; personality depends in large measure on what one does with the talents heredity has given him. It is something that is constantly in the process of being made. It grows by what it feeds on, changing in accordance with the experiences the individual undergoes.

So the first step in the improvement of personality is intelligent recognition of the fact that while personality is fundamentally inborn or inherited, it is also acquired. To the extent that it is a matter of acquisition, it is subject to cultivation and improvement. One should accept himself at face value, recognizing his strong points and his weak points, whatever be their source. He does well to discover as definitely as he can just what tendencies he has from original inheritance. He needs also to explain as well as he can how traits have been modified by influences that have surrounded him from early childhood until the present moment. In this self-study, one should be most careful to trace the influences of early years, for these often make such profound impressions as to induce belief that they are a part of original inheritance. With the results of this kind of discriminative study and thoughtful scrutiny as a basis, one is ready for the self-discipline and the hard work without which improvement of personality cannot be made.

THE CONSTITUENT ELEMENTS OF GOOD TEACHING PERSONALITY

It has already been stated that an ideal Christian teacher is one who is perfect as a person and as a Christian. When the mind wanders in contemplation of what constitutes good teaching personality, it is impressed with the truth of this statement. To make a complete list of the constituent elements of good teaching personality would be to list all the desirable traits that should be found in a human being.

A suggestive, but not at all exhaustive, list may be given in the form of an acrostic of the word itself:

P—patience, peace, perseverance, personal appearance, physique, politeness, poise, posture, practicalness, promptness, punctuality, purity, purpose

E—earnestness, education, efficiency, endurance, energy, elasticity, enthusiasm

R—reliability, resourcefulness, respect, responsibility, responsiveness, reverence

S—sacrifice, scholarship, self-control, sense, sensibility, sensitivity, serenity, service, sincerity, spirituality, strength, surrender, sympathy

O—objectivity, openmindedness, optimism

N—neatness, nerve, nobility, knack, knowledge

A—accuracy, action, achievement, adaptability, address, alertness, altruism, ambition, approachableness, aptness, attractiveness

L—leadership, liberty, little things, love, loyalty

I—ideas, ideals, imagination, impartiality, initiative, insight, inspiration, intelligence, interest, intuition

T—tact, temperance, tenderness, thought, thrift (in time, money, energy), tolerance, truthfulness

Y—yourself at your best[4]

---

[4] W. E. Raffety, **The Smaller Sunday School Makes Good** (Philadelphia: The American Sunday School Union, 1927), p. 160

To make clearer the path to improvement, it may be well to think of the different phases of personality.[5] Broadly speaking, there are six phases under which the many traits may be grouped: (1) physical life; (2) mental life; (3) temperament; (4) conduct or social behavior; (5) character; and (6) spiritual life. Improvement of the total personality is obviously a matter of improving each of these phases in balanced relationship with all the others.

I. What physical traits and characteristics are of greatest importance to the Christian teacher? A few outstanding ones upon which all would probably agree are:

1. Good personal appearance
2. Physical endurance
3. Sound health
4. Abundant energy
5. Physical vigor
6. Physical strength
7. Good carriage and posture
8. Physical control
9. Correct personal habits
10. Good voice

Fortunate is the teacher who has the asset of a striking physical appearance. A person of good physique commands the attention and draws the interest of others in the very beginning no matter how disappointing the later impression may be. Therefore, a teacher who attracts by physique has an initial advantage which, other things being equal, will greatly enhance the effectiveness of his work. This is something in which no improvement can be made, for one is born as he is so far as general physical appearance is concerned. The short person will be short; the heavy person will be heavy; the one who is mean and unprepossessing in physique can often do nothing about that factor in itself.

However, untoward effects of physique may be minimized by definite attention to dress and matters of

[5] G. S. Dobbins, **How to Teach Young People and Adults in the Sunday School** (Nashville: Sunday School Board of the Southern Baptist Convention, 1930), pp. 19-26

personal appearance. While all teachers cannot be perfect specimens of physical manhood or womanhood, all can dress attractively and in good taste. Untidiness in the person and extremes in dress can be avoided as can also dowdiness or undue monotony in dress. Every person can present a clean, well-groomed look which gives evidence of reasonable regard for the details of personal appearance based upon proper respect for self and for others. The effectiveness of a teacher's personality can be so greatly increased by reasonable attention to appearance that no one need feel discouraged because of what he does not have in the way of physique.

Furthermore, improvement of other factors in physical life will help an individual to overcome to a remarkable degree any deleterious effects of general lack he may have. From every point of view, sound physical health is of the greatest significance in the work of the teacher. Without it, the buoyancy of spirit so essential to effective work with young people especially is very likely to be lacking. Many troubles, such as poor discipline, lack of interest in the work, and want of sympathy between teacher and pupils have their source in the defective physical condition of the teacher. It is most difficult for a teacher who is not well physically to be at his or her best in mental life and spiritual outlook. And every teacher can promote good physical health by following a definite recreational program, by observance of careful habits, and by constant effort to keep himself at his best.

But possession of perfect health does not guarantee that the teacher will express himself in such a way as to suggest vigor, energy, and vitality. There are outward indications of health and strength that have much to do with the way in which personality exerts its influence. The impassive countenance of one who never smiles and the face that never lights up in sympathetic response to the feelings of pupils are liabilities in teaching. Evidences of fatigue, real or unreal, awaken within pupils unconscious sympathetic responses not favorable to learning. Good carriage and posture, important by way of example, have even greater importance in the suggestion of physical and mental control they convey. "Assured and confident physical control as expressed in the erect posture and the alert movement suggests mental strength and mental alertness just as clearly as the slouchy posture and the slow, uncertain movement suggests a lazy mind; while jerky, nervous, and useless movements suggest undirected or 'flighty' mental activity." Even if the suggestion be deceptive, its effect is no less real. So in addition to keeping health at the very best, the teacher owes it to himself and to his work to be careful to maintain the best in physical expression. For this, constant self-scrutiny, supported by careful observation of effects upon pupils of his actions, constitute a good basis for making improvement.

Another factor in the physical features of personality which is of much importance is the teacher's voice. A good voice results from a combination of various qualities, all of which may be greatly improved by attention and practice. The voice that is too high, too low, harsh, indistinct, unpleasant, shrill, rasping, complaining, or lacking character, is a severe handicap. The quality of the teacher's voice is most potent in its effects upon the spirit of the classroom. The teacher's voice should be pleasing in quality, distinct, intense, and emphatic. Many teachers talk too loud; some talk too low; some talk too fast; others do not enunciate clearly. Shortcomings in voice can be improved to a marked degree by determined effort.

II. What mental factors are important for success in teaching? From the many that might be named, the following are selected as being among the most important:

1. Genuine interest	7. Ability to see ahead; foresightedness
2. Accurate knowledge	
3. Clear thinking	8. Ability to concentrate
4. Sound judgment	9. Mental alertness; openmindedness
5. Power of decision	
6. Scholarly attitude; will to learn	10. Constructive imagination

As already emphasized, it is a poor teacher who is not also a learner. Genuine interest in the pursuit of learning, therefore, is a prominent trait of a good teacher's mental life. Seeking to know and to understand will make him a careful reader of good books and magazines. "A vigorous mental life does not result from haphazard newspaper reading and the perusal of cheap fiction." The mentally alert person reads according to a definite plan for definite purposes, and, as he reads, he meditates, compares, contrasts, imagines, and asks questions. Truly to read involves much more than grasping the thought of the author and even more than thinking with the author. One who truly reads, goes beyond and adds to the thought of the author from the store of his own experience. Every teacher who "is instructed unto the kingdom of heaven," far from being one who merely passes on to others what he has read, is one who brings "forth out of his treasures things new and old."

The key to the improvement of one's mental life, then, is to plan intelligently and to work perseveringly the plan made. One should ask himself what reading he should do, how effectively he reads, how well he thinks, how much he can rely on the soundness of his conclusions, whether or not he makes decisions accurately, and how steadfastly he executes decisions made. On the basis of his answers to these questions, he can formulate a plan for definite growth in mental life which, carried out, will result in the overcoming of weaknesses and the strengthening of his strong points. The teacher who keeps himself ever in hand along this line will reap definite rewards in increased satisfaction from work well done.

III. What are the factors of temperament and disposition that affect teaching personality? The following list is suggestive:

1. General good health
2. Good cheer, joy, optimism
3. Sympathy, tenderness, love
4. Patience, perseverance, objectivity
5. Sensitivity, responsiveness, serenity
6. Sense of humor, enthusiasm
7. Self-control, peace, caution
8. Kindliness, courtesy, politeness
9. Poise, attractiveness, purpose
10. Zeal, reverence, exaltation

Temperament is the sum total of one's emotional qualities. It stands between each person and his surroundings. Through his individual temperament, each must experience the world about him. Each reacts to stimulation according to his individual temperament. One person may have a gloomy outlook, another a buoyant, cheerful outlook; one may be very responsive to certain stimuli, while another may be most stolid in his reception of the same or similar stimulation, and so on. Again, the state of the same person's affective life at different times may make for different reactions to the same sensation.

General good health, physical and mental, is the primary requisite for right disposition and temperament. Anything that affects either physical or mental health in a deleterious manner is very likely to disturb the affective life and make for bad disposition and the wrong kind of temperament. So he who would be at his best in temperamental character does well to take heed to the condition of his physical body and the health of his mental life. Over-eating, lack of needed rest, excesses of any kind, anxiety, worry, and all departures from sane, normal, healthy physical and mental living will be taboo with him.

Improvement in this phase of personality, however, is much more a matter of positive emphasis than of negative. Definite cultivation of a buoyant spirit, a joyful outlook, serenity, love, friendliness, sympathy, courtesy, etc., will accomplish far more than will the perpetual attempt to kill off the undesirable traits. But to start with, one need face himself squarely, accepting his liabilities as well as his assets at their true value. Then, seeing the blemishes, one should concentrate on the development of the opposite traits. No one who goes at the task intelligently and continues persever-ingly, trusting in the grace of God, will ever fail to grow in the direction of better temperament.

And such growth is of greatest importance in the work of Christian teaching, for the affective qualities of personality are most potent in their effect. A teacher may have the finest kind of intellectual equipment and fail because of temperamental difficulties. On the other hand, one who lacks much along intellectual lines may accomplish very creditable results if he has a bal-anced and effective emotional life. "Intellect is more or less of a luxury, and a high intelligence is of less importance than a stout heart—a vigorous, balanced, and harmonious, effective life—the 'springs of action.' "

IV. What qualities of social behavior does the effec-tive Christian teacher need?

1. Address, understanding
2. Tact, sympathy
3. Leadership, attractiveness
4. Resourcefulness,
5. Punctuality, practicalness
   responsibility

6. Reliability, sincerity
7. Truthfulness, honesty
8. Tolerance, respect

9. Altruism, unselfishness
10. Ambition, dependability

The way in which one meets people is a most important element of good teaching personality. Courtesy, deference, and sincere interest based on real understanding of the other person's point of view are essential qualities of a good address. It is a teacher's duty to develop the ability to meet people graciously and pleasantly. This may be done through careful, sympathetic observation of others and through practice in meeting people. Taking thought to be agreeable, to refrain from making pointed, sarcastic statements, and wide reading of good literature will also be found valuable by one who is seeking to improve. Much association with people from various levels in society will be of further help.

As a basis for self-improvement, one may ask himself a host of questions on the topic of social behavior. How dependable am I? To what degree do my own interests have place in my motives? Do I understand my pupil's needs? Have I the necessary tact to deal aright with them? Do I get their point of view? Am I punctual in meeting all my obligations, moral as well as legal? Do I ever bluff? Can pupils believe what I say or have I so often said and did not that they do not know when I am speaking the truth?

In short, thorough and complete self-examination by the teacher of his social qualities should reveal himself in the crystal-clear gaze of himself as his pupils see him. If, then, there are things he would not have them see, he is ready to improve in those respects. Every social contact with pupils or with other people affords opportunity for exercise of those social graces and qualities necessary for successful Christian teaching. These can be developed only by dint of the hard work of continual exercise.

V. What traits of character or moral life should a Christian teacher have? A few are:

1. Purity
2. Respect
3. High moral standards
4. Sensitivity
5. Unflinching devotion to the right
6. Fairness
7. Impartiality
8. Loyalty
9. Earnestness
10. Dignity

It might seem unnecessary to say that any Christian worker should be impeccable in moral character. However, the statement, "It is just too bad that so many good people have so much bad in them," and a second statement, "One cannot understand why some people are as bad as they are unless it is to show us how we should not be," indicate that moral standards, or moral practices, are not always what they might be among Christians. The aim expressed in the previous chapter emphasized the fact that the Scripture is given to make the man of God perfect, "throughly furnished unto all good works." And the Biblical injunction in another place exhorts that those who believe should be careful to "maintain good works." It is a sad fact that Christian workers have sometimes brought blemish upon the cause of Christ by indulging in the wrong kind of moral practices.

Character education does not make anyone a Christian; only an act of God's grace can do that. But a Christian, and especially a Christian teacher because of his greater influence by way of example, should be a person of good moral character. Impurity, compromise with wrong, lack of sensitivity to fine distinctions, low moral standards, and indulgence in questionable practices should be far from the life of a Christian leader. Another Biblical admonition fits in here: "Abstain from all appearance of evil." And yet another comes to mind, "Let your light so shine before men, that they may see your good works, and glorify your Father which is in heaven."

The sincere, earnest Christian teacher will walk carefully through the maze of this world's evils. He will ever strive to maintain a conscience void of offense toward God and toward men. He will eschew all evil; he will take himself severely to task for any dereliction from moral duty that he may make; and he will do his utmost to be a pattern of good works by which his pupils may mold themselves with confidence and assurance.

Character has to do with one's attitude toward right and wrong. Morality is concerned with right relations with our fellowmen; religion is concerned with right relationship with God. Without religious sanctions, morality and character have a very inadequate basis. From the Christian point of view, morality and personal relationship with God are inseparable. This brings us face to face with the question of the spiritual phase of personality.

VI. What are the qualities of spiritual life which must be possessed by a Christian teacher? From a very great number, the following important ones are chosen:

1. Absolute surrender to God
2. Vivid sense of the reality and presence of God
3. Recognition of Jesus Christ as the only way to God
4. Whole-hearted dependence on the Holy Spirit
5. Keen, deep interest in the salvation and the spiritual welfare of others
6. Humble, growing sense of victory over selfishness, worldliness, and sin
7. Intelligent and genuine conviction concerning great fundamental truths

8. Willingness to serve and to give without thought of recognition
9. Given to importunate, effective prayer
10. Deep, sincere love of God and of pupils

This list but emphasizes the fact that spirituality is the dominant trait in the personality of the Christian teacher. His confidence and his life are so permeated with and integrated in the power of God, the love of Jesus Christ, and the power and the work of the Holy Spirit, that for him to live is to be occupied with spiritual, not with material things. He recognizes himself as belonging to God, his work as being done in the power of the Holy Spirit, and his goal as the perfecting of the pupils in the grace of God through the Lord Jesus Christ. As a teacher, his highest desire, that for which he will pour out his life in service, sacrifice, and interceding prayer, is that the souls of his pupils may prosper.

Such spirituality is dependent upon the deepest heart-searching and the closest walking with God. With the Psalmist, the teacher will pray, "Search me, O God, and know my heart: try me, and know my thoughts: and see if there be any wicked way in me, and lead me in the way everlasting" (Ps. 139: 23, 24). And his attitude will be that of the Apostle Paul, "With me it is a very small matter that I should be judged of you, or of man's judgment: yea, I judge not mine own self. For I know nothing by myself; yet am I not hereby justified: but he that judgeth me is the Lord" (I Cor. 4: 3, 4).

When the teacher has examined himself and has been subjected to the searching power of the Holy Spirit, the view of his insufficiency and need will drive him to God for grace and strength to supply his need. His trust will be in God Who said, "My grace is sufficient

for thee: for my strength is made perfect in weakness"
(II Cor. 12:9).

HOW PERSONALITY MAY BE IMPROVED

Along with consideration of some of the constituent
elements that enter into the six phases of personality,
some bases for improvement have already been noted.
In further consideration, the essentials for improvement
may be reëmphasized in more definite and specific
manner.

Undoubtedly, the great majority of Christian teachers
have sufficient native endowment to do excellent work.
But many are not letting the force of their personality
be felt or are allowing inexcusable weakness, bad habits,
and unnecessary attitudes to destroy the effectiveness
of their work. So often it is said of the Christian
teacher, when he has made a poor impression or has
not been successful in his work with others, "Oh, he
meant well," or "That is just his way." Even more
frequently, perhaps, the teacher excuses himself in such
cases with the thought that what he is has been irrevoc-
ably determined by the past.

It is very true that personality is largely a matter of
heredity and early training. Nature and nurture give
one, by the time he arrives at maturity, a cast which
is not easily changed. What one has been "becoming"
through years of life cannot be changed during minutes.
Persons differ widely in personality. Some people, it
seems, just naturally have all or nearly all the qualities that make for a strong and winsome personality;
others, and most people belong with the others, have
noticeable deficiencies. But personality is something
that can be cultivated and developed. He who will set
himself determinedly, assiduously, and intelligently to
the task of self-improvement is bound to make progress. It is a law of life that one grows in the direction

in which he exercises. Repeated practice of good carriage and manner, mental alertness, truthfulness, courtesy, faith and prayer, or any of the other innumerable
traits of a perfect person results inevitably in increase
of perfection in the personality of the one who thus
practices.

So the task of the teacher is to study himself in
order to strengthen his weak points and to improve the
desirable qualities that his birth and training have established. Self-scrutiny is needed. An occasional self-
analysis should be made by every teacher. But the
self-analysis needs to be the opposite of the kind in
which one beholds oneself and goes his way, straight-
way forgetting "what manner of man he was." One
must see himself as he is and, on the basis of this
view, set himself on a course aiming at the definite
improvement of his personality. Dr. Dobbins lists
several very practical suggestions that have possibility
of value to the Christian teacher who has discovered
the strong and the weak points of his personality and
who is earnestly desirous of making improvement.[6]
Their worth is so great as to merit quotation bodily:

"1. Take courage because of the strong points—fall back on
them, capitalize them, utilize them.

"2. Go to God in prayer concerning your manifest deficiencies. Claim His promise that if you ask it will be given
you, if you seek you shall find, if you knock it shall be
opened unto you.

"3. Go to God's Word for passages that bear on these
weaknesses, and study them with great care. Note how
men and women of the Bible overcame similar weaknesses with God's help.

"4. Set yourself determinedly to strengthen yourself at your
weak points by stern self-discipline and unceasing practice. Read the best books, seek the counsel of your pastor

[6] G. S. Dobbins, op. cit., pp. 26, 27

and a few intimate, trusted friends, set out on a program of self-mastery for Christ and for His cause.

"5. Refuse to become discouraged. Look to Christ, not self, for the victory. Assert with Paul, 'I can do all things through Christ, who strengtheneth me.' Claim the promise of Jesus, 'Lo, I am with you.' If some thorn in the flesh persists, accept it humbly and go on, saying, 'Thy grace is sufficient.' By and by Christ will shine through your personality, making you a radiant, capable, effective witness and teacher of the Word of God."

The Christian teacher who will reduce these helpful suggestions to careful, consistent, persistent practice need never despair because he will find himself growing in power to render effective service as a worker for God.

QUESTIONS AND PROBLEMS

1. Justify the statement that all Christians are teachers.
2. What does one do when he teaches?
3. How do you explain the fact that there is no teaching except as there is learning?
4. Explain the statement, A teacher is one with whom pupils learn.
5. What is a Christian?
6. Do you agree with the thought that a Christian teacher teaches with authority?
7. Give examples of teaching that is done outside of a class-room.
8. What is the one thing that true teaching always does?
9. Have you, as a Christian, been zealous in buying up your opportunities to teach?
10. Should a Christian teacher be superior in personality?
11. In what senses is a teacher always a leader?
12. How can a teacher be a follower and a co-worker as well as a leader?
13. Can you suggest further respects in which a teacher is a learner?
14. What is personality? A growing personality?
15. Show the place of heredity and of environment, respectively, in the making of personality.

16. Determine, if you can, what is the most important trait of personality in each one of the six different phases.
17. Can a teacher be too much concerned with the improvement of his personality?
18. Can anyone improve his personality?
19. What is, basically, the most important thing to do in respect to the improving of one's personality?
20. Criticize the suggestions of Dobbins.

REFERENCES

Almack, J. C., and Lang, A. R., **The Beginning Teacher** (Boston: Houghton Mifflin Company, 1928)

Barclay, W. C., **The Adult Worker and His Work** (Chicago: The Methodist Book Concern, 1914)

Betts, G. H., and Hawthorne, M. O., **Method in Teaching Religion** (New York: The Abingdon Press, 1925)

Dobbins, G. S., **How to Teach Young People and Adults in the Sunday School** (Nashville: Sunday School Board of the Southern Baptist Convention, 1930)

Fergusson, E. M., **Teaching Christianity** (New York: Fleming H. Revell Co., 1929)

Horne, H. H., **Jesus—the Master Teacher** (New York: The Association Press, 1920)
    This New Education (New York: The Abingdon Press, 1931)

Raffety, W. E., **The Smaller Sunday School Makes Good** (Philadelphia: The American Sunday School Union, 1927)
    Religious Education of Adults (New York: Fleming H. Revell Co., 1930)

Richardson, N. E., **The Christ of the Classroom** (New York: The Macmillan Co., 1931)

Sherrill, L. J., and Purcell, J. E., **Adult Education in the Church** (Richmond: Presbyterian Committee of Publication, 1936)

Suter, J. W., **Creative Teaching** (New York: The Macmillan Company, 1924)

Thomas, F. W., **Principles and Technique of Teaching** (Boston: Houghton Mifflin Co., 1927)

CHAPTER V

THE CHRISTIAN TEACHER PREPARING
TO TEACH

THE first task of this treatise was to present certain
principles that must be considered basic in all Christian
teaching; next, the importance of and the necessity for
Christian teaching were stressed; then, the aims of the
Christian teacher were discussed. In the previous chapter, consideration was given to the subject of what the
Christian teacher should be, especially as a person. The
task now at hand is to advance some thoughts on the subject of the teacher's preparation for teaching. In a sense
this represents a continuation of the subject because
development of good teaching personality is one of the
most important forms of preparation that can be made
for Christian teaching.

But there are other forms of preparation that he who
would teach effectively must undergo. Emphasis has
been placed on the fact that the teaching process is a
twofold one, including both learning and teaching. It
has also been seen that whenever teaching is done, there
is a person who is to learn, a person who is to stimulate, guide, and direct the learning, and a content to
be learned. It would seem to be obvious, then, that
the effective teacher would need to know the one taught,
what to teach him, and how to teach. And logically it

would seem also that to teach aright one would need to know the school in which he is teaching.

This gives knowledge as one essential for good teaching. An art as intricate as teaching can be learned best by observing how others do it; hence observation is a second essential. And without practice, one could scarcely hope to attain any high degree of success no matter how much he may know or how much he may observe; therefore, doing becomes a third essential. The effective teacher must know, observe, and do.[1] Obviously, preparation for teaching is important, as is also the means available for the training of teachers. The subjects that will be discussed in the present chapter are, then: (1) the need for teacher preparation; (2) learning to know: (a) the pupil; (b) subject matter; (c) how to teach; (d) the school; (3) observing as preparation for teaching; (4) doing in preparation for teaching; (5) means available for teacher preparation.

1. THE NEED FOR TEACHER PREPARATION

The teacher is the all important factor in any school. Quite evidently, every single thing that has any bearing upon the pupils in a school affects the quality of the teaching. Thus, the type of building, the equipment and materials, the organization and administration of the school, the conditions of home life, the ideals of the community, and everything else that affects the life of the pupil exerts influence on the teaching of Christian truth in the church school.

The teacher is the most important factor in a school. But the factor that looms highest in importance is the teacher. Of what avail is it if the school is housed in the finest building equipped with the best in material things if the teaching is not done well? Of what worth

---

[1] W. E. Raffety, **The Smaller Sunday School Makes Good** (Philadelphia: The American Sunday School Union, 1927), p. 154

is a good curriculum and expert administration if the teacher in the classroom does not know how to teach? What can ideal home life and good public sentiment accomplish, so far as the work of a school is concerned, if the teacher in that school is so poorly prepared that he cannot teach efficiently? In fact, poor work in the classroom, as was pointed out in an earlier chapter, can do much to inculcate wrong habits and attitudes in children. On the other hand, one truly and fully prepared to teach may do very effective work without the aid of these external advantages, valuable as these may be for the accomplishment of worthwhile results.

Teacher training is necessary. Effectiveness in teaching depends largely upon the adequacy of preparation. Well-trained teachers make good schools where pupils learn what they are taught. But if preparation has been superficial, haphazard, or misdirected, pupils cannot learn well, if at all. This fact is recognized in secular education. No public-school teacher can come to his task without specific preparation for the particular work he is to do. Then he does his teaching in buildings designed for educational purposes with all the equipment and materials necessary for effective accomplishment. And the public-school teacher works under conditions intended to make for definite improvement in teaching.

Training of Christian teachers must be adequate. Why should children of today be denied the right to as much opportunity to learn Bible truth as they have to learn history, science, arithmetic, and the other subjects commonly taught in the public school? And if children have a right to Bible knowledge, do they not have the further right to efficient teaching of the Bible? Is it true that just anyone, whether he has had training or not, is sufficient for impartation of knowledge of the Bible while only the highly trained are permitted to teach secular subjects? Does the putting of names such as "Sunday," "Sabbath," "Bible," or "Church" in front of the word "school" mean that some mystical occurrence will make it unnecessary for the teachers in that school to be prepared? Certainly any person who is at all interested in the highest welfare of children and who has any conception of relative values and eternal verities would not hesitate for a moment to say, "It is the right of every child to have teachers of Bible who can present the Word in the most effective manner."

The Christian teacher of today unprepared for his specific work is at a tremendous disadvantage, and his being at a disadvantage reflects discredit not only upon him but upon the cause for which he stands. How can a boy or a girl who attends public school five days a week where he gets the very best instruction from a well trained teacher have much respect for an unprepared or a poorly prepared Sunday-school teacher under whom he or she sits for an hour of undirected or misdirected activity on Sunday? How much value is such a boy or a girl likely to attach to that which the Sunday-school teacher is supposed to be teaching? And how much respect can he or she have for a church that perpetrates upon him the outrage, having the audacity to call the work "Christian education"? Any normal boy or girl makes the comparison between the work done in the public school and that done in the church school as inevitably as he would make the comparison between riding behind an ox-team and riding in the latest model of automobile, were he required to use the former means of transportation in this modern age. That the comparison is less striking because it is perhaps less conscious does not make the attitude formed without the most untoward results.

Dr. Walter S. Athearn has spoken words in this connection the truth of which may well be pondered and weighed by all:

> Society protects its *land* from the ravishes of unskilled tenants; it insists that justice be not thwarted by untrained jurists; it guards the bodies of its citizenship from the untrained "quack"; it excludes the charlatan from the schoolroom that the *minds* of our children may not be maimed and crippled by unskilled workmen; but the souls of children have been left unprotected from malpractice at the hands of well-meaning, but untrained workers in the field of religious education.
>
> It is strange that the last resource that society has attempted to conserve is the spiritual life of the children. It is just now beginning to dawn upon Christian people that there is such a thing as *spiritual malpractice,* and that the pious, well-meaning church-school teacher may ignorantly pull up by the roots and destroy the very elements which enable the soul to bring forth the fruits of the Spirit. . . .
>
> We give all honor to the faithful men and women of the past who gave of their best to the cause they loved more than life itself; but a new day has come, and new demands must be made of those who serve in the Lord's House. To sincerity, devotion, noble Christian character, we must add that technical skill which comes from instruction and training.

Obligations for obtaining thorough preparation. The conscientious Christian teacher will, therefore, feel very keenly the obligation to God, first of all, for the specific command is, "Study to shew thyself approved unto God." He will feel it is an obligation to his pupils also because, as a Christian teacher, he has responsibility for their spiritual and eternal welfare. One unguided, careless, or superficial act of a single teacher may determine the unhappy future destiny of a pupil or of pupils. Finally, the teacher will feel that he owes it to himself to prepare in the best possible manner for his great task. Teaching, like all other work, yields its greatest rewards to those who take its responsibilities most seriously and who make most diligent effort to fit themselves to do the work well. Consequently, the teacher who is willing to pay the price of hard study, increasing devotion, and holding a fixed determination to master a difficult art is the one who will realize greatest satisfaction from his teaching. Such an one will find himself "a workman that needeth not to be ashamed."

2. The Knowledge Needed for Adequate Preparation

As was mentioned, knowledge is one essential to preparation for good teaching. It is fundamental to the other two essentials, for one must know before he can observe intelligently or do effectively. Also the more completely, accurately, and fully one knows, the better he can observe and do. To be well-prepared, the teacher should aim at the mastery of four kinds of knowledge: (a) knowledge of pupils; (b) knowledge of content to be taught; (c) knowledge of the technique of teaching; (d) knowledge of the school in which the teaching is done.

a) *The Teacher Learning to Know His Pupils*

Regardless of how good a teacher may be, he is not prepared to teach a class until he knows the members of that class. He cannot study the lesson properly or decide intelligently upon his aims and the methods he should use unless he knows whom he is to teach the truth of that lesson. Nor is it sufficient that the teacher study the class or the children in general; he must know the individual boy or girl whom he is to teach. Of course, these two kinds of knowledge overlap somewhat: the better a teacher knows children the more easily he can understand a child, and as he learns to know the individual child, he gains better understanding of children in general.

Specific study of pupil traits. Before the teacher begins to teach, therefore, he should learn all that he can about his pupils. He should understand their nature and needs in their particular stage of development; he should know their capacities and attainments, their interests and their normal experiences, their attitudes and their modes of thought, their problems and their difficulties. If he is teaching primary children, he will need to make a particular study of children of that age; if he is teaching young people, he will need to learn all that he can about young people. In other words, specific study of the characteristics of the particular age level being taught is an essential preparation for good teaching.

Study of physical life. Upon this study as a foundation, the effective Christian teacher will find himself able to make particular study of the pupils in his class. To understand them aright, he must know something about their heredity and environment. He should understand that the influences of environment are being exerted continually, modifying what the child received from heredity. He will study the physical characteristics of each pupil, learning his rate of physical growth and observing the factors that influence growth and physical development. He will ascertain whether or not he has defects that will mitigate against effective learning and he will gain appreciation of the particular conditions that affect the physical life of the individual pupil.

Mental, social, and personal life. The thorough-going teacher will also study the mental life of each pupil to learn his level of mental ability, the kinds of reaction and the modes of response that are peculiar to him, and the outlook he has as a consequence of his type of mental life. He will acquaint himself with the major interests, physical, mental, spiritual, and social, of each pupil. He will learn something about his companions, his recreations, his home life, and his religious views. He will also be concerned about and interested in the problems and difficulties of each pupil. His careful, persistent, individual study will enable him not only to detect these but to be quick to bring to bear the emphasis necessary for correct solution of problems and adequate meeting of difficulties.

Recognition of individual differences. An alert teacher will recognize individual differences among his pupils. A principal of a school once said that if he had a class of fifty scholars, he would try to be fifty different teachers, as he turned from one to another of those scholars to instruct them. A very successful teacher of boys maintained that his practice was to teach only one boy at a time; he left to one side, as it were, all the other pupils in the class while he centered his attention upon one. These teachers were doing what every teacher must do—teaching individuals. There is no other way to teach; pupils never learn as a class. No teacher can teach intelligently until he knows the ways in which each pupil is different from every other.

It is utterly impossible to make wise adaptation of either subject matter or technique unless the teacher understands the peculiarities of each pupil. If a pupil is tender and loving, appeal must be made to him in a way different than would be used with a pupil of cool, calculating disposition. One pupil likes to delve into the depths of abstruse thought; another delights in stories and illustrations that require little thinking on his part. One lives in his feelings; another reasons out everything. This pupil is living in conscious fellowship and communion with God; that one is harrassed by doubts and fears. Each has his individuality, and the teacher must understand his ways of reacting before he can hope to be of any service to him.

Knowing the language of pupils. To teach aright, the teacher and the pupil must speak a common language.[2] In other words, the teacher must be able so to speak that the pupil understands what he says. The greater the difference between the ages of the teacher and the pupils the more likely is the former to use language which the latter does not comprehend. As one becomes well acquainted with a field or subject and the words in it, he is quite likely to assume that others are as well acquainted with either or both as he himself is. For example, a mature, enthusiastic, devoted Christian teacher might use terms such as "knowing the Lord," "being saved," "the coming of the Lord," etc., the meaning of which his pupils who are unfamiliar with Christian and Biblical terminology could not grasp without explanation. To the end that the language used in teaching may be common to teacher and pupil, the teacher need study constantly and carefully the conversation of the pupils so that he may express himself as far as possible in terms that are comprehensible to them.

In addition to making unwarranted assumptions about the language understood by pupils, the teacher may assume too much concerning the state of the child's knowledge. The teacher of the man who was surprised to learn that "Dan and Beersheba were places" because he always thought "they were husband and wife like Sodom and Gomorrah" would be quite ineffective in teaching him facts of the Old Testament geography so long as he thus thought. Perhaps it was Coleridge who said, "We cannot make another comprehend our knowledge, until we first know his ignorance." So long as a

[2] H. C. Trumbull, **Teaching and Teachers** (Philadelphia: John D. Wattles & Co., 1897), p. 38

teacher assumes that a pupil knows what he does not know, he will be severely handicapped in teaching him in that connection. The prepared teacher knows the attainments, general and specific, of each of his pupils and thus is able to bring to them new knowledge in terms of what they already know.

b) *The Teacher Learning to Know His Subject Matter*

When the teacher knows the pupil, his nature, needs, interests, characteristics, attainments, etc., there comes the question: What shall I teach him? In seeking to answer this question, it must be kept in mind very definitely that what a pupil is taught is never an end in itself. Not what he knows but what he is as a result of coming to know is the acid test of teaching. The teacher uses subject matter as a means to the end of bringing about results in the life of the pupil. In terms of our aims, it may be said that Christian teaching uses the content for the purpose of bringing the pupil to Christ, building him up in Christ, and sending him out for Christ. So the test of the effectiveness of the Christian teacher's work is not how much the pupils know about the Bible and related subjects but how fully the knowledge of these becomes effective in the lives of the pupils.

The Bible the subject matter of the Christian teacher. The last sentence suggests what the subject matter of the Christian teacher is: "the Bible and related subjects." The Bible is the revealed Word of God given to man that he may know whence he comes and whither he goes, that he may be perfected for the eternal destiny which a loving God intended for him, and that he may be completely furnished for living the life which God wishes him to live. The Bible, therefore, is basic content for Christian teaching, and it is not the Bible as a book, nor as a piece of historical literature, nor as a presentation of social Christianity that is basic; it is the Bible as God's Word, as the Word of life. What the truly Christian teacher finds in the Bible "is not merely a record, or a series of documents, or a depository of truth, nor a treasure house of fine art and good morals, but God's powerful living Word, which enters the soul, to bring it to repentance and faith, to transform it and to build it into Christ."

"Related subjects" comprise things the teacher needs to know in order to make the Bible message clearly understood. In addition to a thorough knowledge of the textbook, the teacher should be familiar with the geography of Bible lands, ancient history, antiquities and customs of Bible lands, and missionary principles and progress. Other fields of knowledge which may well form part of the equipment of the most thorough-going teacher are: knowledge of church history, especially the history of his own church, understanding of the principle doctrinal tenets of his church, familiarity with the great social and political movements of the day, and current events of every-day life. Acquaintances with great masterpieces of literature, music, and art will also be found very helpful.

The teacher's two kinds of study. In learning to know subject matter, the study of the teacher will assume two forms: (1) general, directed toward making himself complete and well-rounded in his knowledge of what he is to teach; (2) special, directed toward thorough preparation of the particular lesson. Since the material in bulk for the Christian teacher is his Bible and since he must know it better than any other book, the remainder of the treatment of this topic will be devoted to consideration of how the teacher should study his Bible.

(1) *The teacher learning to know the Bible.* The effective teacher is always a student of that which

he is teaching. To teach intelligently and practically any portion of the subject, he must be familiar with the whole. Without thorough understanding of the whole subject, the material to be taught cannot be organized and used to meet the needs of the pupils. No matter what the subject is, the teacher must be engaged continually in study, keeping fresh his gained store of knowledge and ever expanding in his field. This is the price he must pay in order to be a good teacher.

What real study is. Every teacher needs, therefore, to understand the meaning and purpose of study and to stimulate himself to the love of study, investigation, research, and problem-solving. *"All real study involves investigative thinking*—problem solving, mental exploration, a quest for truth. Letting the thoughts of another pass uncritically through one's mind, meditating upon what one already knows, memorizing what someone else has said, may be valuable aids to study, but they are not essentially study. Study, in the true sense of the word, occurs only when the mind is confronted with a difficulty, a problem, a novel situation. The initial step in the process of study is to recognize the difficulty and proceed to define it; after which possibilities of solution are suggested by reasoning based on experience—one's own and that of the race; conclusions thus reached to be carefully checked by observation and verification."[3]

Some practical suggestions for one who wishes to stimulate himself along the lines of effective study are: maintain a good physical condition; provide conditions favorable to study such as light, temperature, ventilation, absence of distractions, etc.; have a regular time and place to study; form systematic habits in study;

[3] G. S. Dobbins, **How to Teach Young People and Adults in the Sunday School** (Nashville: Sunday School Board of the Southern Baptist Convention, 1930), p. 64

maintain an attitude of interest and attention; determine the purpose of study; assume a problem solving attitude; make careful notes and outlines; and have a sufficient motive for study.

Why the Christian teacher studies the Bible. The motive of the Christian teacher in studying the Bible is to gain thorough knowledge of the whole Bible—not knowledge which will make him a Bible scholar but such knowledge as will enable him to interpret the truths aright to the minds and hearts of his pupils. His aim is to get a reasonable understanding of its contents, not necessarily an exegetical understanding. Although detailed knowledge may be most helpful, it is not necessary to master the technicalities to gain a working knowledge of the Bible. No one can teach a portion of the Bible to advantage until he has a knowledge of the sixty-six books. Without a comprehensive understanding of the whole, preparation for the teaching of separate lessons becomes most burdensome and ultimately fruitless. The teacher, therefore, must study the Bible as a book, not in little, isolated fragments.

Conditions of effective Bible study. There are certain fundamental conditions for most profitable Bible study. Anyone who meets these conditions will get more out of the Bible while pursuing the poorest method of study than will the one who does not meet them even if he uses the best method of study. First, he who would really know the Bible must be born again. The natural man receives not the things of the Spirit; one must have spiritual perception to be an understanding student and a competent teacher of the Bible. Second, to know the Bible one must have love for the Bible. It must be studied with real appetite, not from a mere sense of duty. Third, he who would know the Bible must be willing to do hard work. Its hidden treasures cannot be found without digging. Study means the putting forth of diligent effort. Fourth, the student of the Bible must have a will absolutely surrendered to God. Without such surrender, he will lack that clearness of vision and that teachableness of heart necessary for the revelation of truth by the Holy Spirit and no one can understand the Bible without this revelation. Fifth, he must be obedient to revealed light. "Be ye doers of the Word and not hearers only." Every duty which one fails to perform obscures some truth he should know. Sixth, a child-like mind and spirit are essential. Simple, trusting faith, meek teachableness of spirit, and unbiased acceptance of the truth must characterize him who would know the Bible. Seventh, it must be studied as the Word of God. This involves unquestioning acceptance of its teachings, absolute reliance upon its promises, and wholehearted obedience to its commands. The Bible is not a book of magic but a revelation of the will of God. Eighth, the Bible must be studied in the spirit of prayer. Simple, trustful looking to God, asking Him to reveal His meaning, must accompany intellectual effort on the part of him who sincerely desires to know its message.

For the general mastery of the Bible as a whole, several fruitful forms of study may be used. The Christian teacher who is desirous of attaining to the best working mastery of its content will find it worth while to study in all these ways at one time or another. However, each individual may wish to follow predominately that particular method of study toward which his personal disposition and past experience incline him most favorably.

The synthetic method of Bible study. By beginning at Genesis and going on to Revelation, one gets a view of the Bible as a whole. Such a mode of study gives unity, helping to prevent onesidedness and partial views of the truth. It also makes for a perspective in which overemphasis on particular teachings and portions have no place. To avoid the tendency to monotony and consequent lack of interest due to the reading and study of the same type of content too long at a time, the user of this method can study the Old Testament and the New at the same time. One can read the Bible through in a year by reading six chapters daily. A simple plan is to read two chapters daily from each of three portions: the Old Testament, beginning with Genesis, the portion beginning with Psalms, and the New Testament.

The study of the Bible by individual books. This is a very good method. The beginner should choose a short book, one that is comparatively easy and one that is especially rich in content. The first step in such study is to master the general content of the book. Reading it through at one sitting without stopping to deal with difficulties is a good way to begin. A certain preacher who used this method of study very effectively said that he read a book through one hundred times as a preliminary to intensive study. Preparation of an introduction to the book, the making of an outline of the book, and the marking of the great passages are further steps. Finally, each verse should be studied and pondered, the results of the whole study classified, and the findings of the process meditated upon and digested. Bible study of this kind is very rich and satisfying to both mind and heart.

The study of the Bible by topics. This is a very systematic, thorough, and exact method. Topics such as "God," "faith," "salvation," "prayer," "Christ," "The Holy Spirit," and the like, studied with the aid of a good concordance or even with the aid of a reference Bible constitutes an interesting and very profitable exercise. One of the helps often found in Bibles is a subject-index, in which the references to many of the great subjects treated in the Bible are presented in outline form. With the aid of such an outline, a student may make an intensive study of important topics.

Biographical study of the Bible. To use this method the student selects one great character after another, collects all passages dealing with the person studied, and analyzes his character. Strong and weak points should be noted, and the lessons can be summarized. Thus glimpses of God's ways in dealing with men and men's wrong and right attitudes toward God can be learned. All of the lessons can then be applied in the teacher's own spiritual development as well as to the lives of the pupils. This is an interesting method and one which yields very worth while results.

The study of the Bible by types. By use of this method the student can gain good understanding of the message of the Bible. The Old Testament sets forth in shadow and figure the reality which the New presents. The law had a "shadow of good things to come and not the very image of the things" (Heb. 10:1). To study by types necessitates looking up all Scripture references dealing with that which is being studied and getting full meaning of names and places under consideration. One who uses this method must ever be on guard against the fanciful and the making of interpretations not warranted by the Scriptures. Rightly and carefully used, the method can be most helpful in getting an accurate understanding of the teachings of Scripture.

The study of the Bible for practical usefulness. This method yields rich returns. The Bible was not written to be used as a book of culture but as a book of spiritual guidance. To study it for practical purposes gives the student a vision of how perfectly it is adapted to man's need. The teacher who uses this method of study will catch constantly new meaning of the Bible in relation to the needs of men—his own as well as others. In seeking food for others he himself will be fed. Whatever the

problem, difficulty, burden, or perplexity that confronts
one, the Bible has a message that throws light upon it
and gives safety and comfort.

(2) *The teacher learning to know the lesson.* Knowledge of the pupils to be taught and general knowledge
of the Bible to be taught these pupils are two things
the teacher must know. Next comes a knowledge
of the special truth to be taught. The study of
a lesson in preparation for its teaching is an art
that should be mastered thoroughly by every Christian
teacher. However well a teacher may know his Bible
and however long he may have taught, the diligent
preparation of each lesson is a necessity for most effective teaching. Marion Lawrance said, "The greatest
need in our church work today is trained teachers who
will put their whole mind into their preparation, their
whole soul into their presentation, and their whole life
into their illustration." No teacher who values success
or who has a sense of responsibility for his pupils will
enter a classroom to teach, relying on his general knowledge of content or depending on a few minutes of
hurried preparation for the teaching of the lesson.

The materials for study. An important factor in the
preparation of a lesson is the source of the materials.
Obviously, since the Bible is the textbook of the Christian school, it should be the teacher's first study. While
good lesson helps may be a valuable aid, a teacher
should not depend on these primarily. Lesson helps
should be used with the Bible and never apart from it.
Furthermore, helps should be used for the purpose of
getting light on the meaning of the Bible text. A true
teacher will study the Bible text and the Bible context
before he uses helps, for he knows that the Bible is its
own best interpreter. The best way to get light on ob-
scure passages is to compare Scripture with Scripture.

In this connection, it may be well to recognize that

there are various kinds of Bibles. For instance, there
is the Bible that has in the back many valuable, historical, geographical, encyclopedic, and other kinds of
helps. Some of these have considerable value but most
of that which is given can be found in other volumes.
Then there are Bibles that have notes and comments on
various passages; in other words, a sort of commentary on the text is provided. While such explanations
are valuable for certain purposes, especially to a beginner, they have the effect of discouraging independent
thinking, for the natural tendency of the student is to
accept the opinion of the commentator as his own without having investigated its foundation. The best kind
of Bible for the teacher to use is a good chain-reference
Bible so that parallel passages may be independently
investigated and passage compared with passage. One
great thing the teacher should do for his pupils is to
make them independent investigators of truth and this
he cannot do unless he himself is an investigator. One
form of help the teacher's study Bible should have is
good maps.

Other sources of material the teacher should have
are: an English dictionary; a good Bible dictionary;
a concordance such as Strong's, Young's or Cruden's
complete concordance. A good Bible commentary may
well be used for the purpose of ascertaining what interpretations and explanations have been given difficult
passages by Bible scholars. Gray's Christian Workers'
Commentary is a good one-volume work. A complete
set of Jamieson, Fausset, and Brown is recommended
for those who desire a more exhaustive commentary.

The plan of study. A second important factor in the
teacher's preparation of a lesson is a plan of study. To
be successful, study must be pursued according to a
system. The spending of much time is to no avail if the
teacher is not prepared to teach after he has spent the

time. He will not be well prepared if his study lacks a plan. So each teacher should formulate and follow a plan such as will enable him to accomplish the best results of which he is capable. No plan is alike desirable for and helpful to all teachers.

In studying the lessons from the Bible, the teacher will, first of all, need to get an understanding of the words. Then he will find it necessary to ascertain their connected meanings. Next he will wish to make practical applications of these meanings. In other words, the first thing is the simple text of the lesson, the second is the plan for teaching of the text, and the last is the application of truths taught. The teacher wants to know what is said, what is meant by what is said, and what the bearing of all this is on his pupils.

Studying in terms of pupil needs. As he studies, the teacher does well to keep in mind the individual members of his class. His constant study of individual pupils and their needs will reveal ways in which help may be given under the guidance of the Holy Spirit. Then he will look for and recognize in the lesson those special portions that should be chosen for each of the pupils. This will be true not only of instruction that may be imparted but also of guidance of pupils in their personal research or direction of them in their work. In all his study, the Christian teacher will be tapping reservoirs that enrich his own life. Like Chaucer's pastor, he will be teaching others in the way he himself has first followed.

Knowing more than can be taught. A warning that may well be sounded for the benefit of a hard working teacher is that there is much more in every lesson than he can hope to teach. One who has made most thorough preparation sometimes becomes discouraged when he finds that time is too short to present all his gathered material. It is a poor teacher who teaches on the fringe of what he knows; everyone should know much more than he can present. Goethe says, "Nothing is worse than a teacher who knows only as much as he has to make known to the scholar." For the work of true teaching it is not so much a question of how much the teacher knows about the lesson as it is of how much change he is able to bring about in the pupils. If he knows a great deal more than he can teach, the teacher can select here and there from his stores to suit the needs of those taught. Not what the teacher could teach but what has happened to the pupil because the teacher has taught is the test of the worth of the teaching.

Dependence on prayer. Finally, it may be said that all the study of the Christian teacher is done in dependence upon the power and guidance of the Holy Spirit. In prayer, he approaches the lesson, through prayer he obtains understanding of the lesson, and by means of prayer he brings the lesson to bear on the lives of his pupils. Fervent prayer helps him over the greatest obstacles, and with prayer he conquers for Christ. Whatever he may have by way of training and whatever he does by way of effort in study are only instrumental forces which, taken and used by God, bring to pass spiritual results in the lives of pupils. Christian teaching is not done in the power and strength of human effort.

c) *Knowledge of How to Teach*

One may know his pupils, one may know his Bible, and be well prepared in knowledge of the lesson and yet be unable to teach effectively. Everything that is done must be done by some method. Both experience and observation teach that there are some ways of doing things that are more effective than others. There can be no teaching without some kind of method. As in everything else, so in teaching, he who knows how will get best results. The fact that the work being done is Christian teaching does not make it any less important that he who does it should know how to do it. No one is ready to teach until he knows what to teach, but, in addition, he must also know how to teach.

Knowledge of a subject is one thing, but ability to make that knowledge available practically and effectively to others is quite another thing. Who would want to be treated for some physical ailment by a doctor who knew much about medical science if he was not able to reduce what he knew to practice in treating a particular case? Of what worth to a person who wants a house would an architect or a contractor be if he knew all about the different styles of architecture but could not arrange the building material so that part fitted to part? Likewise, the teacher who knows his pupils ever so well and who has thorough mastery of what he would teach is not prepared for his work unless he can effect changes in the lives of those pupils through the right use of what he knows about his subject. So far as any Christian teacher is concerned, the Bible will be a dead book to his pupils until he is able to make it live in their lives.

All teaching is done by some method. All teachers use some method of teaching. The method used may be faulty, careless, ineffective, even weak or harmful, or it may be strong and very effective. To succeed in his work, any teacher must have understanding of the way in which learning takes place, and with this as a basis, he must use ways of organizing, presenting, and handling content, materials, and activities to meet pupils' needs, interests, and abilities. The Christian teacher trained and consecrated to his work will need to guard against two dangers; careless, haphazard method or such dependence on method as will hinder the Holy Spirit in His operation. There need be no conflict between careful, well planned teacher activity and the work of the Holy Spirit. On the contrary, it is reasonable to think that the Holy Spirit can use a teacher better in choosing a proper method and good plans than He can use a teacher who attempts to teach a class without preparing carefully and intelligently to do so.

Principles and method. There are various methods of teaching, and no two teaching situations are ever exactly alike. More accurately, it may be said that there is no set "method" of teaching, but a variety of "methods" basic to which are certain principles of teaching that must be mastered by him who would be successful. Then, when he teaches, he will make use of this, that, or the other mode of procedure as may be best for achieving the objective in mind. Not all lessons can be taught in the same way. One pupil will have to be handled this way and another in some other way to accomplish the same results. One teacher can use most successfully a technique which, used by a fellow teacher, would result in dismal failure. For the achievement of a certain aim, it may be advisable to use one method while the attainment of another outcome may necessitate the employment of a very different method. Factors such as the age and the maturity of the pupils, the attitudes and interests of the class, the physical equipment and facilities, and the materials for study will also have a part in determining what is the best way for the teacher to present the materials of instruction.

But, let it be reiterated, in order to make this choice, the teacher must know the principles basic to good teaching. What are these principles? They have been stated in various ways by many writers, but it seems that the following seven principles should be studied by any teacher who wishes to know how to teach. Some of these have been dealt with earlier in this treatise and some will receive consideration in later pages. Briefly stated, they are:

There is no teaching without learning. Consequently, the teacher must know how learning takes place and how to direct the activities of pupils so that desired growth and adjustment result. What is learned by the pupils is a test of the effectiveness of the technique used.

The pupil does the learning. All learning comes through self-activity. No amount of teacher-activity in and of itself produces learning. Telling is not teaching; lecturing is not teaching; doing is not teaching. Only as the teacher gets reaction of individuals to certain items in the total situation will pupils learn and be able to recall those things.

The motivation of the pupil determines what he will learn. Interest must be sought and maintained; attention must be won and held. The learning activities of pupils should be adequately motivated and guided toward definitely conceived learning outcomes.

The mental set of a learner at a particular moment is most potent in determining the nature of the learning response. The teacher should do everything within his power to secure the most favorable conditions, physical, mental, and emotional.

Various ways of learning make variety in teaching necessary. The intelligent teacher, far from becoming enamored with any formal mode of procedure, will be concerned primarily with the problem of how to get the work done rather than with what kind of tools to use. Tools, like subject matter, are a means to an end.

The teacher needs to plan most carefully and thoroughly for the teaching of each separate lesson. The objectives need to be very clearly perceived, the subject matter arranged in terms of the steps taken in learning, and provision made for every step in the learning process.

Every teacher should be improving his method constantly. He needs to be analyzing the total process of teaching and rating himself without ceasing. He should maintain an alert, experimental attitude in all teaching situations. Without self-criticism there can be no growth, and a teacher who is not growing is a poor teacher.

d) *Knowing the School*

To be most effective, the teacher needs an understanding of the school in which he teaches. Any school is an organization. To fill his place properly, a person who is part of an organization must know something about the manner in which that organization functions. A church school exists for the purpose of making Christian teaching possible. Instructing and training pupils in the things of God to the end that they become mature Christians is the function of the church school. It must therefore be a *school*. It must be administered like a school. Each member of the organization has certain responsibilities for the work of the whole, and each should know and keep his place.

The teacher stands central in any school, for no matter how large or how well organized a school may be, it is the work of the teacher in the classroom that determines whether or not the function of the school is being fulfilled. If the teacher fails, the school fails. Regardless of outward show, a school is only as good as the teaching done in it. Good teachers make good schools. The position of teacher is, therefore, the most important position in the school.

But the church school must be administered with

proper responsibility all along the line from pupil to teacher, from teacher to superintendent, from superintendent to minister. The superintendent should realize that his major charge is to protect and promote the teaching ministry. The teacher should understand what his responsibility is to the other members of the organization so that he can work harmoniously with all for the accomplishment of the great purpose for which the school exists. Only as each person in the church school discharges effectively the task that is his to do can the work of the whole go forward to successful conclusion.

3. Observation as Preparation for Teaching

Mere knowledge acquirement, however complete and thorough it be, is inadequate for fulness of preparation for teaching. In the performance of any kind of activity, one should be guided by a model, or mental pattern, representing what he is trying to do. For the Christian teacher, the best means of acquiring such a pattern is through observing teaching. Keen observation of the good teaching of public-school teachers of children of the same age as those whom he is teaching and of other teachers in church schools gives him opportunity to study specific teaching situations and to take account of just how particular desired reactions can be secured.

For observation to be most effective, certain conditions should be met. In the first place, the observer should have made sufficient study previously of some phase of the work to be observed to enable him to form intelligent judgment as to the effectiveness of what is seen. Second, the inexperienced observer should limit the number of topics of observation to a few and make preliminary study of the essential features of each. Confusion will result from an attempt to note too many things. Third, the observer should maintain an attitude of openmindedness with respect to the teaching he sees. There is a very strong tendency for one to be prejudiced greatly in favor of teaching as he was taught. The point of view of the pupil in the class is so different that he cannot gather worth while intelligence of what is best in the classroom, particularly as regards instruction. And even if they were completely appraised, methods that are current in the best schools even of the present day may not be so good that they can be safely imitated. The observer should be openminded to the degree that he can see what is actually done and be able to accept or reject in terms of what is commendable or condemnatory in that which is seen.

4. Doing in Preparation for Teaching

No one can develop skill in teaching without practice; one can learn to do only by doing. Mere practice, however, never makes perfect. Unless it is practice of the right procedure, practice will be clumsy, wasteful, and imperfect. If one practices on the basis of accurate knowledge, sound theory, and wide observation, with adequate provision for constant correction and improvement, whenever and wherever these are required, he will improve. Constructive criticism by another, especially if he be experienced in teaching, will be of great value in connection with practice. However, the individual who practices should have the information and know the standards needed for self-criticism. In the last analysis, all criticism must become self-criticism, for only as one accepts the criticism and gives it meaning in the light of standards he apprehends does it become effective for him.

5. Means Available for Teacher Preparation

Where there is a will, there is a way. A teacher who wants to secure good training can secure it somehow, some way. Universities, some colleges, some seminaries, and a few Bible institutes offer courses emphasizing various phases of religious education. To those who cannot avail themselves of the privilege of attendance at such institutions, there are afforded various other opportunities. Conventions and camp conferences often present opportunities for intensive study for ten days or two weeks and sometimes for longer periods. Teacher-training classes can be organized either in the local church or community. Such a class can meet once a week for ten or twelve weeks, two hours a week for five or six weeks, or two hours an evening for five or six evenings in one week. Usually the first of these plans is best.

A teacher or a few teachers who feel the need of training, or a superintendent who first realizes the need, can gather together some interested workers and form a class, select a teacher, and arrange for a time of meeting. With this group as a nucleus other teachers and officers may be drawn into the class. Persons not in active service who give promise of usefulness in the work of Christian teaching may also become interested and thus obtain preparation for future activity. Along with study of the principles of teaching, frequent visits to classes may be made for the purpose of observation. Members of the class who are teaching at present have a chance to test the truths of their lessons and others can occasionally assist, or substitute for an experienced teacher, though inexperienced persons should not be given too heavy responsibilities lest they become discouraged.

Every Sunday school might well have a normal class or a teacher-training class composed of young people in training as prospective teachers. This class could meet during the regular Sunday school hour and take up some definite work that would fit its members for teaching. Thus there would be kept before the minds of youth the possibility of their serving by teaching. From the membership of this class, past and present, recruits may be drawn for the teaching staff of the school as need arises from time to time.

The individual who wishes to prepare to teach or to become effective in teaching, who cannot avail himself of any of these means of preparation, need not despair. For such an one there are good books and departmental magazines. Every teacher should read each year a few books bearing on his teaching field. A magazine offers fresh material from month to month. Another form of training open to the individual teacher is correspondence courses that are offered by many denominations and some colleges and universities. The individual teacher in service can subject himself to continual self-supervision by keeping a record of his work and criticizing himself objectively. Thus he can greatly improve his own teaching.

In short, he who is impressed with a sense of responsibility to God and to others for getting needed preparation will secure it. Such an one will not rob self, nor others who could profit by his expenditure of energy and time, nor be unfair to God whom he serves. The challenge of these words comes to every Christian teacher:

> *There is no chance, no destiny, no fate*
> *Can circumvent, or hinder or control*
> *The firm resolve of a determined soul.*
> *Gifts count for little; will alone is great.*
> *No man can place a limit on thy strength,*
> *All heights are thine, if thou wilt but believe*
> *In thy Creator and thyself. At length*
> *Some feet must tread some heights now unattained.*
> *Why not thine own? Press on. Achieve!*

QUESTIONS AND PROBLEMS

1. What kinds of preparation should a Christian teacher make for his work?
2. Emphasize the need for preparation on the part of the teacher.
3. Does a Christian teacher need to prepare any less than a teacher in a public school?
4. To whom does the Christian teacher owe obligations?
5. What four kinds of knowledge are essential to adequate preparation for teaching? Which do you think is most important?
6. For what reasons does a teacher need to know his pupils?
7. What should the teacher know about his pupils?
8. Why must the teacher understand individual differences?
9. Can a teacher teach a group or is teaching always an individual matter?
10. Do you think that teachers often assume that their pupils know more than they really do?
11. What is the one test of the effectiveness of teaching?
12. Enumerate things other than the Bible that a Christian needs to know. Why should he know these?
13. Which of the two forms of study of subject matter is more important? Why?
14. What is real study?
15. Name conditions essential to effective study.
16. Enumerate conditions essential to profitable study of the Bible.
17. Comment on each of the methods of Bible study suggested, emphasizing the particular merits.
18. Have you found other methods that are helpful?
19. Outline a good plan for the study of a particular lesson.
20. What materials, other than the Bible, may be used to good advantage in the study of the lesson?
21. Emphasize the importance of the teacher's keeping individual pupils in mind as he studies.
22. What is method?

23. Which is more important for a teacher to know, method or principles? Why?
24. Give the essence of the seven principles of teaching.
25. For what reasons is it important that a teacher know the school?
26. State the conditions for most effective observation.
27. How can a teacher use doing as a means of preparation for teaching?
28. What are the means which a teacher can use to secure training?
29. Show the importance of a teacher-training class.

References

Betts, G. H., Teaching Religion Today (New York: The Abingdon Press, 1934)

Burton, W. H., Supervision and the Improvement of Teaching (New York: D. Appleton and Co., 1922)

Crawford, C. E., How to Teach (Los Angeles: Southern California School Book Depository, 1938)

Dobbins, G. S., How to Teach Young People and Adults in the Sunday School (Nashville: Sunday School Board of the Southern Baptist Convention, 1930)

Fergusson, E. M., Teaching Christianity (New York: Fleming H. Revell Co., 1929)

Fiske, G. W., Purpose in Teaching Religion (New York: The Abingdon Press, 1927)

Harner, N. C., The Educational Work of the Church (New York: The Abingdon Press, 1939)

Lotz, P. H., and Crawford, L. W., Studies in Religious Education (Nashville: Cokesbury Press, 1931)

McLester, F. C., Our Pupils and How They Learn (Nashville: Cokesbury Press, 1930)

Myers, A. J. W., Teaching Religion (Philadelphia: The Westminster Press, 1930)

Plummer, L. F., The Soul Winning Teacher (New York; Fleming H. Revell Co., 1934)

Price, J. M., Introduction to Religious Education (New York: The Macmillan Co., 1932)

Raffety, W. E., The Smaller Sunday School Makes Good (Philadelphia: The American Sunday School Union, 1927)

Roberts, S. L., Teaching in the Church School (Philadelphia: The Judson Press, 1930)

Schmauk, T. E., How to Teach in Sunday School (Philadelphia: The United Lutheran Publication House, 1920)

Smith, R. S., **New Trails for the Christian Teacher** (Philadelphia: The Westminster Press, 1934)

Vieth, P. H., **How to Teach in the Church School** (Philadelphia: The Westminster Press, 1935)

Teaching for Christian Living (St. Louis; Bethany Press, 1929)

CHAPTER VI

HOW PUPILS LEARN

To TEACH is to stimulate, encourage, and direct learning. Nothing is ever taught until something is learned. The teacher must know the subject-matter, for this constitutes the materials that he uses to bring learning to pass. The teacher must also know educational principles and educational methods, for these are the tools that he must use intelligently in order to stimulate and encourage learning. In addition to mastery of subject-matter and understanding of the technique of instruction, the teacher needs knowledge of the mental activity of the pupil. He must know how the pupil learns in order to use subject-matter aright, and only as he understands the learning process can he choose the method suitable for proper direction of that learning.

No teaching without method. All good teaching follows some method that experience and research have demonstrated to be good. To teach without method, to teach unmindful of method, or to teach by use of some poor method are three sure means of bringing about failure. Zeal without knowledge, enthusiasm apart from understanding, devotion to duty with ignorance of correct procedures, even consecration to God unaccompanied by rightly directed effort—none of these singly

nor all of them in combination will bring the desired
results in Christian teaching.

Principles basic to techniques. Beneath techniques
lie principles. In order to choose method aright and
to use properly the method chosen, a teacher must know
the principles of learning. These, when rightly understood, will be found to rest upon laws that inhere in
the mind itself. Knowledge of how the mind operates,
how the laws of mental life express themselves in the
principles of learning, and how these principles determine methods of teaching, are, therefore, essential
to success in teaching. To spray pupils with ideas regardless of what is going on in their minds is to use
the method of stupid ignorance. He who understands
the learning process, as well as lessons, has insight to
make adaptations where they should be made for most
effective results.

Knowledge alone not sufficient. As emphasized in a
previous chapter, the inclusive aim of the Christian
teacher is so to teach the Word of God that his pupils
may be perfected in Christian character for the doing
of Christian works. This involves more than mere
knowing. To inform the mind is one thing; to enrich
the soul is quite another thing. The Christian teacher
must know how to enrich the soul. His teaching must
grip the pupil in three phases of his life: knowing,
feeling, and doing. Merely to know facts does not make
for Christian character nor is one a Christian because
he feels certain things in certain ways. A Christian is
one who knows the truth of God, feels the power of
God, and does the will of God. Until the teacher has
so taught that the pupil knows, thinks, and feels aright
and reduces to practice what he knows, the teaching
must be considered ineffective.

Teacher must know how the pupil learns. In so far
as perfecting of pupils in Christian character and good

works is dependent upon teaching and consequent learning by the pupils, to that degree it is imperative that the nature of learning be clearly understood. The teacher must be master of the means of control by which the learning of the pupil is started, directed, changed, or stopped. This mastery will enable him to get pupils to do what is best at the time it should be done and in the way that is most effective. Knowing how learning takes place, the teacher will be able to direct pupil activity in such ways as will bring about the desired outcome—Christian character issuing in Christian conduct. It is as essential for a Christian teacher to study the nature of the human mind and to work in harmony with the principles of learning as it is for a gardener to know his plants and to work in harmony with their nature. A gardener who works contrary to the laws of plant life will likely waste his energy to no purpose; a teacher who ignores the principles of learning will likewise arrive at the destination of nowhere in his teaching.

THE PHYSICAL BASIS OF LEARNING

Though much contention has taken place over the proper description of learning, there can be no controversion of the truth of the statement that the nervous system constitutes the physical basis of learning. A child at birth is a bundle of potentialities; he knows nothing and can do little. But if he is normal, he has the physiological mechanisms essential to learning. The nervous system is composed of billions of neurones representing a considerable variety of functions. Mechanisms essential to learning are:

a) Receptors—the end-organs of the senses which receive stimulation from without. The most important senses are those of sight, hearing, smell, taste, and touch.

b) Conductors—the nerves, or neurones, that carry the nerve impulses from place to place; and
c) Effectors—the muscles that receive and use the currents sent.

The action of the nervous system. Nerve impulses aroused by the reception of stimuli are carried from the receptors, which are located in all parts of the body, to the central system, which includes the brain, the midbrain, and the spinal cord. The function of the central system is to switch the nerve impulses into certain motor neurones that run to the effectors. These are stimulated into greater activity or depressed into less or no activity, depending on the character of the nerve impulse received. The activity of the nervous system resembles the functioning of a telephone system. The stimulus received by a receptor corresponds to a call made in a telephone in a home or in an office; the nerve current aroused by the stimulus passes along the nerve as the electrical current passes along the telephone wire. The message is received in the nerve center, the brain or the spinal cord as the telephone call comes to "central"; and the message goes out to effectors akin to the way in which the telephone message is sent out to the receiving instrument with which connection is made through the central switchboard.

A switchboard is most necessary in both cases. Without "central" in the telephone system, the system would be impossible; if there were no "switchboard" in the human body, the current generated by stimulation would always go to the same muscles with the result that reactions to any and all stimuli coming through a given sense organ would always be the same. Examination of a nerve center by microscope shows immense numbers of nerve endings that seem to be a hopeless tangle of tiny fibers. However, the chaos is only apparent, for

the ends of nerves that carry the impulse into the center
are so located that they can very conveniently discharge
their impulses into the nerves leading to the muscles
which are to make final use of the current.

The structure of the nervous system. Knowledge of
the way in which the nervous system is built is required
for an understanding of nerve action. The unit of structure is the neurone. A neurone is a nerve cell with
its branches. The branches are of two kinds, called
dendrites and axons. Dendrites are short branches that
spread out into numerous, tree-like processses. An axon
is a long, slender branch which, on ending, breaks up
into a tuft of much finer branches called the end-brush.
The end-brush of the axon is always in close contact
with the dendrites of another neurone. A nerve is composed of a number of axons any one of which may be
several feet in length. The "white matter" of the brain
and the spinal cord is composed of axons.

The axons afford the means of communication between the nerve centers and the receptors, between the
effectors and receptors, and between one nerve center
and another. The meeting place of an axon and the
dendrites is the synapse. The end-brush of the axon
does not, apparently, actually grow into the branching
processes of the dendrite but the two come close enough
together to make contact possible. The dendrite carries
the nervous impulse received across a synapse into the
cell body, and the axon carries it away from the cell
to another synapse, where it is received by the dendrite
of another neurone. In other words, the axon may
stimulate the dendrite, but the dendrite never stimulates
the axon.

Three levels of action. The course an impulse will
take in its passage from neurone to neurone through
the central system depends upon the resistance offered
at the synapse. The various pathways may be grouped

in three levels. The first level is the reflex level. When the degree of relationship is so close that a given impulse brought in over a certain neurone to a specific end-brush always goes to the same dendrite, the result is reaction on this lowest level. For the most part, connections in the spinal cord are involved. An example of reaction on this level is the involuntary closing of the eye when some object approaches suddenly. The second level is that of the so-called instinctive reactions. This type of action results when the relationship at the synapse is not so close or so simple, yet enough so that the general character of the automatic reactions will always be the same. The connections involved are more complex ones in the mid-brain. The tendency to seek food when hungry is an illustration of this level of reaction. The third level of reaction is the level of acquired connections. There are literally millions of possibilities of synaptic connections. Quite probably, the connections involved in reactions on the two lower levels are all native, but reactions on the third level are typically learned or acquired through the brain. Reactions on this highest level are usually less prompt, less variable from person to person, and easier to modify. "Capacities" is the name generally given to these weak connections, which function only when trained to do so.

It is with these that the teacher is concerned, for the most part. When a nerve impulse has once crossed from a certain end-brush to a particular dendrite, there is established a tendency for a second impulse of the same kind to follow the same pathway. When this connection becomes so strong that a given impulse is almost sure to cross in this way and result in a certain definite reaction, the person is said to have learned that reaction. Learning, then, is a matter of getting connections in the nervous system, particularly the brain, into such a close degree of relationship that the impulse from a desired stimulus will take a desired course across the synapse and produce the desired reaction. And the task of teaching is, in essence, a matter of choosing appropriate stimuli, guiding activity in desirable directions, and producing such strength of connections, or bonds, as will result in certain definite reactions. Thus some of the millions of the potentialities of the child's nervous system can become actualities in his life.

While all this seems comparatively simple, it must be recognized that the functioning of the nervous system is actually a very complex activity. All behavior is the result of stimuli acting upon receptors. But neither these stimuli nor the action of the receptors determines the character of the behavior. All that they do is to excite activity in neurones. These transmit the impulse aroused to other neurones in the central nervous system. In turn, this activity is transmitted to muscles and glands. Thus we have a process known as a sensory-motor response. But the organism is so very complex that it is practically impossible to stimulate a single receptor. Furthermore, the interconnections among neurones are affected whenever a stimulus is experienced. So the very simplest response is actually quite complex. No reaction of the human organism is simple in the sense that it may be attributed to direct connection between receptor and effector.

How the Mind Operates

A response, or reaction, is more than a physiological process. It is true that the total response includes certain physical and chemical processes in the tissues of the body. These physical and chemical processes are sometimes called the physiological part of the response. However, along with the physical and chemical processes, there is conscious response, which is more than a matter of mere chemical and physical response or process. Conscious response includes *being conscious*. When consciousness is a part of the response, something beyond the physical and material is present.

Knowledge exists only in the mind. The nervous system is the medium of connection between the physical, or material, on the one hand and the mental and the spiritual on the other. From a great variety of sources, myriads of sensations come from the receptors to the brain. Here they undergo a change. As experienced on the physiological level, they are physical forces, merely things of the physical realm. They can be measured and dealt with in all essential respects the same as are other things that are physical or material. An instant later they have undergone a radical transformation, which has changed them in every essential aspect. No longer do they have material qualities; they have taken unto themselves meaning in terms of consciousness. They are no more things of the nerves and of the brain; they are now things of the mind. They have passed from the realm of the physical to the realm of the mental.

Great is the mystery of this transformation. No one knows how it is wrought. Here, at one moment, are the raw materials of sensation, the stimuli impinging upon the organism from many sources; there, at the next moment, are the meaningful products of learning. In some marvelous way the former have become the latter. It cannot be said that knowledge has entered; knowledge exists in neither brain nor nerves. There is no knowledge in books; there is no knowledge in spoken words. Nowhere outside of the mind is there any knowledge.

The only things that have any existence outside the mind are stimuli. A thing comes within the range of the special senses; it is seen, heard, felt, or experienced through some other medium of contact. The impulse resulting from the sensation experienced is carried through the nervous system to the brain, which is constantly receiving a multitude of sensations. Only a few of the many can be transformed into products of learning. If the particular sensation is one that undergoes mysterious transformation, the result in the mind is knowledge or some other product of learning. A thing is not learned when it is presented to the senses; it is not learned when sensation is received by the brain. Learning takes place only when that which is received by the brain is worked upon by the mind and made a part of consciousness.

Teaching is guiding. What is the task of the teacher in the process whereby the raw materials of sensation are made over into the elements of mental life? Obviously, since the structure of the sense organs is mostly a matter of heredity, teaching has little to do with the manner of their functioning. Sensation is something that cannot be cultivated except in limited degree. But much can be done by way of controlling the environment from which stimuli come and by way of selecting those stimuli that should come. Furthermore, the teacher can do much in the preparation and the use of methods and instruments by which sensation may be stimulated and directed.

But the teacher can do something that is of far greater importance than is the selection, stimulation, and direction of the sensory experiences of the learner. As indicated previously, the process whereby the material things of the world become meaningful to a person is a process that goes on in the mind of a conscious being. The power that he has to take sensations and make them into mental products is called perception, and the mental products themselves are called percepts. A percept may be defined as a sensation which, through the self-activity of a conscious being, has taken on meaning in his consciousness. The meaning given a particular sensation depends upon experience. Only the first sensation can be a pure sensation, and it can never become perception without further sensation. The greater work of the teacher, then, is that of guiding the experience and the interpretation of sensations that come to the mind of the pupil. The cultivation of interpretation is almost unlimited. As the learner is led to see the meaning of the sensations that impinge upon his brain, patterns of perception may be produced that greatly facilitate sensory and motor response and thus increase manyfold the value of the sensory apparatus.

The unlearned tendencies of the pupil. In the first section of this chapter, it was pointed out that there are three levels of activity in the functioning of the nervous system, viz., the reflex level, the so-called instinctive level, and the level of acquired connections or conscious response. It was also indicated that the work of teaching is mostly concerned with the third of these levels. As the teacher arranges the environment, selects stimuli, and directs and guides the learner in the interpretation of the sensations that come, he is dealing with activity on this highest level. Very little or none of the work of teaching is concerned with the activity on the lowest level. But no teaching can be done without recognizing and using the instinctive equipment of the learner.

Every child has inborn urges, or drives to action, which are most dynamic in nature. They are the unlearned tendencies to act in certain ways. A very large proportion of his energy is expended upon these reactions, which early in life become fixed in patterns. While the mind does not direct the responses of these innate mechanisms, its operation is very much influenced by the habits built up through their recurring expression, for habits are basic in educational procedure.

Teaching, therefore, is concerned with selecting for

the awareness of individuals who receive knowledge and experience not only in terms of their intellects but also in terms of fundamental drives and urges, those things which will result in growth of the kind desired. In other words, learning involves the modification of inborn urges and drives as well as the selection and interpretation of stimuli. Teaching, then, is the art of so arranging environment as to occasion self-activities which will change the learner from what he is to what he should become.

Inasmuch as the mind operates under the influence of these drives, they cannot be ignored in teaching. Certain ones can be used, others have to be controlled in their functioning, and still others need to be guided into different channels of expression. The task of the teacher with reference to the unlearned tendencies of pupils to act in certain ways is, therefore, a three-fold one:

1. To use them for the formation of habits, the planting of ideas, and the building of ideals.

2. To control them through strengthening some tendencies and eliminating others. The first is accomplished by exercise with pleasurable results, while the second is achieved by so managing the environment of the learner that the impulse does not find expression, with the consequence that it will atrophy through disuse.

3. To redirect them toward the goals which have been set up for attainment. Each impulse has an outlet for itself in terms of crude human nature. For the attainment of the desired goal, the activity must be guided into channels of expression that are better than the natural ones.[1]

---

[1] J. M. Price, **Introduction to Religious Education** (New York: The Macmillan Co., 1932), pp. 108, 109 (Used by permission.)

How Learning Takes Place

Acquisition of knowledge. Learning may be studied from different points of view and defined in various ways. A very common definition states that learning is the acquisition of knowledge. If a person knows many facts from various fields or if he has wide and accurate knowledge in a particular field, he is thought to be a learned person. Obviously, this definition leaves something to be desired, for one can know much and be no different for the knowing. Jesus said, "If ye know these things, happy are ye if ye do them" (John 13:17). Paul includes the having of "all knowledge" among those possessions which make one nothing except as he has charity also (I Cor. 13:2). And James says that the "doer of the word," not the "forgetful hearer," is the man who "shall be blessed in his doing" (James 1:25). The scribes and the Pharisees of Jesus' day knew much about the teachings of God, but they had learned nothing about the ways of God.

While learning includes much more than mere knowing, it does include knowing as a component part. One cannot do what he does not know how to do. Merely to know in the sense of having factual knowledge that is put to no use is one thing; to know so as to feel the force of the known in a way that causes it to be reduced to practice in the life is quite another thing. Knowledge as acquisition and mastery is worthless, but knowledge that brings about desirable changes in the life is invaluable. "The only kind of knowledge worth having is the knowledge that can be used in solving the important problems of life. All other knowledge is excess baggage."[2] So learning as the study and intellectual mastery of factual materials of

---

[2] H. N. Wieman, **Methods of Private Religious Living** (New York: The Macmillan Co., 1929), p. 96

knowledge is worth while only as the truths contained therein grip the springs of action within the being of the learner and move him to express these truths in concrete living.

An aspect of mental development. Learning is, in the second place, an aspect of mental development.[3] Two conspicuous things about learning are the inward change and the outward improvement. When the pupil learns, something takes place within his being. As emphasized in the previous section, the raw materials of physical and sensory life become the materials of mental life, the possessions of a self-conscious being, through mental activity. There can be no learning without mental activity and whenever learning results from mental activity, the learner develops mentally by so much. Underlying mental activity are physiological processes that constitute the basis for the transformation by means of which physical stimuli became elements of learning. The functioning of the mental processes involved in this transformation constitutes an aspect of the whole of mental development. He who has learned is recognized as one who has ability to achieve what he could not do before he learned.

Adjustment. From a third point of view, learning implies some form of adjustment. Ordinarily the starting point for learning is in a felt need of change, of improvement, of overcoming some obstacle, or of gaining more perfect control or understanding of a situation. Thus learning is related to the efforts of the individual to adjust to his environment by reacting to particular situations. The process takes place when the individual is confronted with a situation to which he is not able to adjust in terms of what he is or knows. Confronted

[3] W. D. Commins, **Principles of Educational Psychology** (New York: The Ronald Press Co., 1937), pp. 306, 307 (Used by permission)

with such a situation, he reacts and thus tries to adjust. As he does so, he learns and in learning he acquires patterns of behavior to meet the requirements of the situation. When the learning is in terms of mental change within experience, the result is knowledge and insight. When the change takes place in behavior, the learning shows itself in the development of skills, procedures, attitudes, etc. In either case the adjustment is made to the demands of the situation as they are felt by the learner.

Modification. From a fourth point of view, learning may be regarded as modification of experience, behavior, or conduct. Whenever learning takes place, some change is produced in the learner. After he has learned, he is something that he was not and he can do something that he could not do before. He acts, thinks, and feels as he did not act, think, and feel prior to the learning. The process of learning involves, therefore, the modification of an individual's behavior and mental processes. But learning is more than mere modification. Coal sliding down a steel chute will, in course of time, make the floor of the chute smooth. A shoestring may not stay tied until it has been tied often enough to get the necessary set. The steel chute and the shoestring undergo modification but it would not be said that either had learned. In a similar way, mere repetition of an act may bring about such a change in the organism that the act is accomplished more rapidly after practice than before. One would no more apply the term learning to this change than he would apply it to the changes in the chute and the shoestring.

Real learning takes place when, besides the mere modification of present action because of past function, the change in the individual is such that a part of an old situation will call forth the same experience or behavior as previously resulted from stimulation by the total situation. Learning may be defined, then, in terms of the progressive changes that take place in the patterns of experience and behavior toward better adjustment to the felt demands of life. Kilpatrick says, "Learning to be complete must serve a twofold function: first, it must enable the learner to grapple successfully with some present hindering difficulty, and, second, it must in consequence so modify the learner that his subsequent experience is thereby remade." This remaking, he says, will involve in varying degree three processes or activities: new insights into possibilities, new inclinations based on these new insights, and new powers of achieving. "Learning," he continues, "arises in and from experience; it is best tested by its dynamic tendency to reenter and remake subsequent experience."[4]

Change in the life. So learning, far from being knowledge gained, consists in something done to the learner. What the individual learns in terms of knowledge is of secondary importance; he himself and what happens to him is what is of major concern. Far from being a process of drilling in knowledge, teaching is a matter of discovering and directing the latent powers of the learner. The teacher seeks to know what the needs and problems of the pupil are, what state of personal experience he may be led to attain, and what method or technique may be used to help him achieve his fullest possibilities. Christian teaching is not merely a system of rote learning about Bible content; it is the bringing of the life of the pupil in line with the purpose and ideal of its aim, the man of God perfected and thoroughly furnished unto all good works.

The pupil himself is the center in Christian teaching. The Christian teacher chooses every bit of material for

---

[4] W. H. Kilpatrick, "Subject Matter and the Educative Process," **Journal of Educational Method,** February, 1923, Vol. 2, p. 233

instruction and uses this, that, or the other technique
of teaching for the one purpose of arousing within the
pupil those responses that will make subsequent experience more and more wholesome in terms of the inclusive aim. The essential thing in the life of the true
Christian is an experience of "the life of God in the
soul of man." As emphasized in a previous chapter,
the fundamental purpose of all Christian teaching is
so to guide the pupil that he will experience the life
of God in his soul. Then upon this experience as a
basis, teaching continues for the purpose of nurturing
and developing the life of God in the soul "unto a
perfect man, unto the measure of the stature of the
fulness of Christ" (Eph. 4:13).

Factors That Condition Learning

To learn consists in opening up a way of expression
for latent powers rather than in effecting entry for
knowledge coming from without. The learner himself
is the primary concern; what he learns from a book
or in any other way is of secondary importance. Learning never takes place by chance. Nothing ever "just
happens"; for every effect there is an adequate cause.
Learning takes place in accord with the laws of human
nature, and teaching, to succeed, must be carried on
in harmony with these laws. Like everything else that
happens, learning is caused by factors that precede
and accompany it. Three factors of great importance
in the learning process are: (1) original nature; (2)
environment; and (3) purpose.

1. *Original Nature*

Every child begins life with a certain capital, a stock
in trade, which constitutes the starting point for all that
he will ever become. Original nature is what one is before environment has exerted its influence. It is not what
one is at birth but the new life which is formed by the

union of two cells at the very beginning of an individual's existence. All the qualities that make any kind of a life whatsoever exist potentially in the fertilized ovum formed by the union of two cells, one from each parent.

Original nature is neither good nor bad, but it has potentialities for either good or bad. The possibilities for the lowest and the most degrading inhere in it as also do the possibilities for the highest and the most noble behavior. In the qualities of his original nature, man is not much different from the animal. In fact, he can be more savage and ruthless than the most cruel animal. He can descend in practice to depths of degredation never seen among animals. His nature teems with animal-like tendencies that often come into conflict with one another.

But while the existence of these animal characteristics in man cannot be denied, it cannot be reasonably maintained that he is merely the sum of these characteristics. Undeniably there is in original nature that which can be laid hold upon by the power of God. When this power from above takes hold of man, it so transforms the animal-like tendencies of his nature and so changes them as to make him no longer a slave to the flesh. The original nature of natural generation functions according to the law of mere animal experience; the spiritual birth by the power of God brings this original nature under the functioning of a higher law, and man lives as a child of God.

Learning depends primarily upon the inherited tendencies, or urges, of original nature rather than upon original nature itself. As indicated previously, the basis for these tendencies is to be found in the nervous system. Quite generally, these tendencies are called instincts but it is better to reserve this word for use in referring to the native mechanisms of animals. Typically, the animal inherits practically complete the necessary adjustments of nerves and muscles for performing most of the activities that it will ever need to perform. As a consequence, there is little or no need for later modification; hence the animal does not learn.

Man, on the other hand, inherits a large number of tendencies for which, unlike the instincts of animals, he has very little by way of ready-made adjustments to permit of their obtaining satisfaction. When a tendency exists, there is also an inborn desire for a particular type of activity in harmony with the tendency. Lacking the ready-made adjustments for satisfaction, man is under the necessity of finding, through experience and learning, the means of satisfying the large number of desires he has. It is in the need and the capacity for making desirable adjustments that the possibility of learning lies. An animal with equipment all ready for doing everything that instinct prompts it to do finds learning neither necessary nor possible. Man, driven by urges but without equipment for satisfying the drives, must learn. All acquired behavior rests on a basis of these drives and urges. As learning takes place, habit control and the control exerted by the other outcomes of learning gradually take the place of these tendencies in the life of the individual.

Many different lists of native tendencies have been given by various authorities. Some writers confine the list to one or two or three fundamental urges, such as self-preservation, sex, or self-assertion, while others enumerate a much larger number. To discuss the bearing on the learning process of even a few of these tendencies would take much space. An enumeration of some of the more important tendencies that function in the learning process and a few general considerations concerning what the teacher must do in respect to the drives of original nature must suffice. Some fundamental drives that are basic to learning are: physical activity and manipulation, mental activity and curiosity, rivalry and competition, self-assertion, expression and communication, love of adventure, ownership and collecting, the desire for social approval, the desire to achieve, and the drive for success.

The use of native tendencies in teaching. The task of teaching, as was pointed out in an earlier connection, is the threefold one of using, controlling, and directing these tendencies in harmony with the goal of the teaching-learning process. The teacher must remember that a normal urge will be certain to find some outlet. No impulse is bad in itself; every urge is adaptable to a wide range of activities, some acceptable and others not. To succeed, the teacher must see that the natural desires and tendencies of the pupils find expression in acceptable activities. This involves the double work of finding the right activities and the frequent substituting of desirable for undesirable forms of expression. Merely to repress unacceptable behavior is unwise, for two reasons: first, suppression means failure to use valuable possibilities of energy and activity that might well be directed toward the attainment of worthwhile results; second, since an urge is sure to find some outlet, thwarting in one line results inevitably in some form of expression even more undesirable than the original. In short, the successful teacher, far from finding the urges of original nature to be disturbing influences, so utilizes them as to make them positive opportunities for achievement in learning.

2. *Environment*

The second factor involved in learning is environment. The learner is always in an environment. From the very beginning of life, original nature is subjected to the influence of realities external to itself. Environment is, therefore, a term that includes all the factors influencing development from the moment life begins. Without an environment, there could be no growth or development, for from it come those elements which produce growth and development. A child who, at birth or at any subsequent point of time, was deprived of all contact with an environment, would cease to grow and eventually would die. A corollary to this fact is, other things being equal, the poorer or the richer environmental stimulation be along any given line, the poorer or the richer will be the quality of the life in respect to the values represented by that environment.

Three different types of environment surround each individual. There is, first of all, the physical aspect. The many things of the natural world—changes in temperature, amount of food, conditions of weather, all the objects with which the organism comes into relation, the beauty of earth, sky, and sea; in short, all the forces of physics and chemistry—make up the physical environment. The growth and learning of pupils are greatly affected by the physical conditions under which they live. Lack of proper nourishment makes good learning impossible. The kind of weather prevailing at a given time may make the difference between effective and ineffective learning. The glory of a sunset, the grandeur of a gorgeous cloud effect, or the beauty of a mountain view, may leave upon the life an indelible impression which will have no small part in the determination of future behavior.

Another phase of the environment is the psychological. It includes those objects and events that have acquired the power to call forth reactions of the mental or psychological type. For example, two books, as mere objects, are a part of the physical environment but the power to distinguish between them is a psychological function. When the person sees things as individual objects with distinctive meanings, it can be said that they have acquired for him a new status, a psychological status. This phase of environment is obviously very important in learning.

The third aspect of environment that can be distinguished is the social environment. The persons with whom one comes into contact exert a profound effect upon his life. Who can measure the influence of a mother? How far does the influence of a father extend? Other members of the family, playmates, neighbors, friends, schoolmates, teachers, companions, and competitors, as well as the cultural, the political, the economic, and the moral conditions of the society in which one lives have much to do with the determination of both the quality and the direction of his learning. Any child born and reared in a Christian home in a community where high standards of cultural life and ethical conduct prevail will, most obviously, be quite a different person than he would be if all his contacts had been with people from a home and community of the opposite sort.

"I am a part of all that I have met," is a quotation from Tennyson often cited in support of the view that environment makes a person what he is. The view is not wholly true, for one is always what he was at the beginning of his existence plus what environment did to him. In other words, original nature and environment together have made one what he is. No one inherits anything ready-made. Every trait is a product of development. All that original nature gives is the potentiality. All that environment gives is the opportunity for the potentiality to become an actuality in the life. What is produced in the development of the individual depends upon the interaction of original nature with an environment. In short, all learning and growth is the product of both the original nature of the individual and the environmental conditions of development.

Parenthetically, it may be observed that the physiological states of the pupil have much to do with his learning. As has been shown previously, there is on the surface of the body as well as internal to it a complex organization of sensory receptors that receive and record, in some mysterious way, the impressions made by stimuli. The senses are the "gateways of knowledge," for all knowledge is based on sense perception. The imperfect functioning of any sense means that learning is impoverished by so much. Effective learning is dependent on the perfection of sensory functioning and on the general tone, or condition, of the body.

In the process of learning, vision and hearing are the most important senses. Defects of vision and learning, therefore, minimize definitely against good learning. Many children are near-sighted, far-sighted, have blurred vision, or are otherwise handicapped in vision. It is estimated that ten to twenty per cent of children do not possess entirely normal hearing. Defects serious enough in nature to handicap the child greatly in his learning may exist without awareness of the fact of their existence on the part of either parents or teachers. The presence of diseased tonsils, decayed teeth, sinus trouble, adenoids, etc., may lower vitality and cause disturbances such as nervousness, irritability, and headaches, thus preventing effective learning. Malfunctioning of the glands may cause irregularities of reaction. A pupil who is fatigued, malnourished, overwrought emotionally, or the victim of any condition that causes strain is incapable of learning well. The ventilation of the room, the temperature, the time of day, the kind of chair, the physical order of the room, and a host of such factors need to be considered by the teacher who would do good work, for the pupils will most surely be influenced in their learning by any physical limitation or physical state or condition adverse to the proper functioning of the physiological mechanism.

3. *Purpose*

The third factor in learning is purpose. Man is not a mere mechanism subject to the push of original nature or the pull of environment. He is not a stick or a stone at the mercy of mere mechanical forces. Life has often been likened to plastic clay and to marble. "Like clay to receive and marble to retain," is a statement sometimes made about children because of the ease with which their lives can be moulded. But child life is like neither clay or marble, for it has within itself the power to respond to impressions. Neither of these materials has this power of inner response. Human beings are active agents moved by purpose, which is the key to learning.

Very small children give evidence of purpose, and as they grow older, their behavior becomes increasingly purposeful. Youngsters choose their games, their playthings, their activities; as they grow older, they choose their books, their friends, their vocations, and their ideals. Choices made are often adhered to with great tenacity of purpose even in opposition to the pull of insistent natural urges to opposed lines of action. Undeniably, much of the stimulus to action is within the human being; external stimulation but gives him the opportunity to make the response he wants to make. "Conduct originates in the organism itself and not in the environment in the form of a stimulus-response. We should analyze it as the expression of cravings that originate in the organism and find particular modes of satisfaction in the stimuli that happen to be available."[5]

[5] L. L. Thurstone, **Psychological Review**, 1923, Vol. xxx, p. 368

If, as some psychologists say, man is only a mechanism for receiving impressions from the outside world,
learning is nothing more than a mechanistic process and
is very simple. But learning is more than a matter of
single response to stimulation. Man is not at the mercy
of his environment. He chooses elements from his environment and responds to them. By power resident
within himself, he creates elements of experience and
adds them to his environment. He gives expression to
some of his native impulses and denies expression to
others. He sees that impulses find outlets in ways that
are desirable in terms of his purpose. By purpose he
directs original nature. By purpose he unifies life,
bringing conflicting tendencies into harmony with one
another.

In essence, man is a soul. The soul has no material
form or substance; it is spiritual in nature. Purpose is
a power of the soul, the spiritual part of man. The
aim of Christian teaching is to blend all purposes into
one life purpose centering in the abundant life in Christ.
For the Christian teacher, the pupil is not merely an
organism composed of physical elements but an immortal soul with power of choice and will, which determine his destiny for time and for eternity. This soul
is not fully complete at any stage; it is capable of learning and growth unto a perfect man. The business of
the Christian teacher is to promote the growth of the
soul. His concern is that the souls of his pupils may
prosper.

Christian education, then, is not a substitute for a
genuinely spiritual experience, not something to be
learned from a book, but the bringing about of a living
experience of God through Christ. Its central principle
is that of the personal spiritual experience of the individual. The soul's relation with God is registered within
the consciousness, and, by the witness of the Spirit, testi-

mony is borne to the spirit of man as to whether or not
he is in saving relation with God.

The existence in man of the native urges and tendencies cannot be denied, but man is more than the mere
sum of these very animal-like characteristics. There is
in man this higher power which, entering into his bio-
logical experience, puts him on a plane far above the
level of animal existence. When the Spirit of the eternal
God lays hold on these native tendencies, He so transforms and sublimates them as to release the life from
the tyranny of the flesh and bring it into freedom and
mastery. The opportunity of the Christian teacher is
to give the careful and positive spiritual nurture which
will lay the life open to the power of the working of
the Spirit so that He may change that life, be it by
gradual or by sudden transformation, into the character
of the true child of the living God.

*Learning a result of the interaction of the three fac-
tors.* All learning takes place, then through the interaction of these three factors—original nature, environment, and purpose. The individual, possessing an
original nature within which are many urges and tendencies, comes into contact with an environment.
Through the medium of a very sensitive nervous system,
stimuli from this environment produce reactions. The
individual responds, not in mere mechanical terms, but
in terms of his own God-given powers. Every response
produces change and makes easier a response to the
same stimulus in the same way. This means the beginning of the formation of a habit of acting.

A human being is always an active, never a passive,
agent in the learning process. However, purposeful
activity is less characteristic of earlier than of later
years. At the same time, childhood is the period of
greatest plasticity and, therefore, the most important
period for forming good habits. Every day, by every

phase of both physical and social surroundings, the child is constantly being influenced. Every day his disposition is being formed and something is being contributed to his life. The old adage, "Let the child run until he is seven and you never catch him," shows how important is the effect of the habits of early childhood.

What is the bearing of this upon the teaching process? The teacher must provide the environment. Admittedly, no teacher can determine the total environment of his pupils, for they are subject to all the influences of a much wider environment than any teacher can control. But while the teacher cannot do anything about many of the influences that have constant bearing on the pupils, he can control the environment of the teaching period. The teacher himself is the chief factor in that period, and it is his main business so to determine the stimuli of the period as to bring about the desired spiritual responses in his pupils. Furthermore, it is the business of the teacher to help pupils see what is involved in the situations in which they are, to see meanings in the activities, and to exercise the power of right choice. Every response made, every insight gained, every choice determined upon, results in change which, if in proper direction, means the attainment of an immediate goal and a step toward the attainment of the inclusive goal of Christian teaching.

In short, this is the way pupils learn. While the manner in which sensory impressions become a part of mental and spiritual life is very mysterious, there is no magic, or trick, about learning itself. The normal person, with normal tendencies and normal sensory life, in an environment that is made properly meaningful to him, can be led to react to it in desirable ways, and whenever he reacts, his original nature undergoes modification. In this way Christian teaching can be a medium through which the Spirit of God may find entrance into the heart and life of pupils in order to work His transforming power and influence.

Questions and Problems

1. Why is it important that the teacher understand the learning process?
2. Show why there can be no teaching without method.
3. Emphasize the inadequacy of knowledge.
4. What is the physical basis of all learning?
5. Name the three levels of reaction and indicate what teaching has to do with each one.
6. In what sense, or senses, is the functioning of the nervous system a very complex matter?
7. Explain the meaning of the statement, Knowledge exists only in the mind.
8. How would you endeavor to give correct understanding to a person who believes that knowledge enters the mind?
9. What can the teacher do in connection with the operation of the mind?
10. What is the task of teaching in relation to the unlearned tendencies of human nature?
11. Consider learning in the four views presented, showing the aspects in which each is important.
12. What is your definition of learning?
13. Can you name factors that condition learning in addition to the three treated in this chapter?
14. What are the native tendencies that count for most in the work of learning and teaching?
15. Should no native urge ever be suppressed? Justify your answer.
16. Show the importance for learning and teaching of each of the three phases of environment discussed in this chapter.
17. Can it be said that any one of these three phases influences learning more than the other two do?
18. Illustrate the existence of purpose in children, in young people, and in adults.
19. How is the work of the Holy Spirit related to the three factors in learning?
20. Show how all learning is a result of the interaction of these three factors.

154 *Principles of Teaching for Christian Teachers*

References

Baker, E. D., **Kindergarten Method in the Church School** (New York: The Abingdon Press, 1925)

Betts, G. H., and Hawthorne, M. O., **Method in Teaching Religion** (New York: The Abingdon Press, 1925)

Carrier, Blanche, **How Shall I Learn to Teach Religion?** (New York: Harper and Brothers, 1930)

Commins, W. D., **Principles of Educational Psychology** (New York: The Ronald Press Company, 1937)

Corzine, J. L., **Looking at Learning** (Nashville: The Sunday School Board of the Southern Baptist Convention, 1934)

Douglas, O. B., and Holland, B. F., **Fundamentals of Educational Psychology** (New York: The Macmillan Company, 1938)

Dunlap, Knight, **Elements of Psychology** (St. Louis: The C. V. Mosby Company, 1936)

Eakin, M. M., **Teaching Junior Boys and Girls** (Chicago: The Methodist Book Concern, 1934)

Gregory, J. M., **The Seven Laws of Teaching** (New York: The Pilgrim Press, 1886)

Griffith, C. R., **Psychology Applied to Learning and Teaching** (New York: Farrar and Rinehart, Inc., 1939)

Hickman, F. B., **Can Religion Be Taught?** (Nashville: Cokesbury Press, 1929)

McLester, F. C., **Our Pupils and How They Learn** (Nashville: Cokesbury Press, 1930)

Myers, A. J. W., **Teaching Religion Creatively** (New York: Fleming H. Revell Co., 1932)

Powell, M. C., **Junior Method in the Church School** (New York: The Abingdon Press, 1931)

Price, J. M., **Introduction to Religious Education** (New York: The Macmillan Co., 1932)

Roberts, S. L., **Teaching in the Church School** (Philadelphia: The Judson Press, 1930)

Squires, W. A., **Psychological Foundations of Religious Education** (Philadelphia: Westminster Press, 1926)

Suter, J. W., **Creative Teaching** (New York: The Macmillan Co., 1924)

Trumbull, H. C., **Teaching and Teachers** (Philadelphia, John D. Wattles & Co., 1897)

Woodworth, R. S., **Psychology** (New York: Henry Holt & Co., 1934)

CHAPTER VII

THE PUPIL DOES THE LEARNING

THE preceding chapter represented an attempt to show how learning takes place in terms of the organism of the learner. From what has been said, it seems logical to conclude that teaching is guiding and stimulating the learner and creating an environment in which learning will take place most adequately and effectively. This being true, teaching must be more than merely imparting information. To teach means to set up desirable learning situations to be met by the pupil, to stimulate the learner to react appropriately, and to see that his experiences are reorganized on a broader basis so that more elements are taken into account. All this is done with a view to enabling the learner to direct his future experiences more intelligently. In short, teaching is a means of directing activities so that desirable learning will be more likely as an actual achievement.

As suggested earlier, one's conception of the nature of learning will greatly influence what he does as a teacher. Learning is very frequently regarded as mere mastery of facts but the term has much broader meaning than this. Various conceptions of learning were considered in the previous chapter where the fact that learning is modification of life and behavior was stressed. When a pupil learns, something is done to him; he is not the same after he has learned as he was before. In consequence, his behavior is different. "Learning is the acquisition of new responses or the modification of old ones. Learning is indicated by a change in the behavior or conduct of the learner."[1]

THE NATURE OF BEHAVIOR AND TEACHING IMPLICATIONS

This point is dwelt upon because learning is so frequently thought of as mere acquisition of knowledge that many persons experience difficulty when the meaning, "modification of behavior," is given the term. The primary reason for such difficulty is that the word "behavior" is taken to stand only for acts which can be seen by someone. Behavior, however, includes much more than this because man, in addition to being able to do, can also think and feel. In other words, behavior may be mental, emotional, or physical. Hence, the definition, "learning is modification of behavior," refers to changes that take place in the pupil's methods of feeling or thinking or doing. Modification, therefore, may be modification of physical behavior or of mental behavior or of emotional behavior.

More accurately, it may be said that learning means modification of feeling, thinking, and doing because what anyone does is usually the direct outcome of what he feels and thinks. Until ideas and facts are translated into emotion, interest, and action, there is no learning. The pupil who has merely memorized facts has not learned. It cannot be said that a fact is learned until it has become so woven into the being of the learner as to make a change in his thinking and feeling. What the teacher needs, therefore, to place in the forefront of his thinking and at the center of his teaching purpose,

[1] W. H. Burton, The Nature and Direction of Learning (New York: D. Appleton Co., 1929), p. 14

is the thought that his teaching is to produce such change in the learner's feeling and thinking as will result in his becoming a person who will act properly.

The value of the mastery of facts. Somewhat parenthetically, it may be asked if mastery of facts is without value. To this question a very emphatic negative answer must be given. In the first place, the memorizing of facts causes some slight change in behavior because anyone who learns to recite facts that he could not recite before gives evidence of change. But it is most obvious that all changes in behavior do not have the same significance. Some forms of behavior are of the greatest importance while other forms are quite useless. The mere learning of facts belongs to the class of least significant kind of changes in behavior.

In the second place, facts need to be mastered for the sake of giving feeling and thought something to work upon. A person can no more think without facts than a builder can build a house without wood, brick, stone, or other building material. The mind needs a content just as truly as the builder needs materials. Mastery of facts is essential, but facts should never be mastered for the sake of the facts. Only as they become materials for thought and feeling to work upon do they have any value. Mastery must not be a mere verbal mastery, but a mastery that is functional; the facts mastered must be so worked into the learner's very being as to become an integral part of his existence.

The singular number is used designedly in this connection; facts should have meaning to the individual learner. Not all facts have the same significance to all learners. The importance of any fact to any particular pupil depends most definitely on the meaning that fact has to him and the changes the meaning bring about in his personal experience. The kind of mastery that the effective teacher seeks is, consequently, that which results in the fact's becoming so meaningful in the experience of the individual learner as to make it such an integral part of his feeling and thinking as will result in its being translated into actual experience. Facts, though worthless in themselves. have tremendous value as a means to an end.

The question faced, then, by anyone who would teach effectively is not, "What are the facts to be taught?" but, "How can teaching be a means for bringing about changes in pupils so that they will become what they should be?" To ascertain the measure of success attained in teaching, one must find the true answer, not to the question, "How well have these facts been learned?" but "What have the pupils been helped to become?" and, "To what extent have these pupils learned to live more effectively?" The great concern of all teaching is how to guide the pupil in living.

Teaching deals with present behavior. That living with which true teaching is primarily concerned is living in the present. The pupil has a very real existence here and now as a boy or a girl; he does not exist merely for the sake of the man or the woman that is to be in time to come. The express aim of Christian teaching is not "that the man of God *might* be throughly furnished unto all good works," a future reference, but "that the man of God *may* be throughly furnished unto all good works," a present reference.

To a certain extent, teaching is concerned with preparation for the adult life to come. Christian teaching looks toward the preparation of boys and girls for Christian living when they are men and women, and one of its avowed objectives is preparation of all who are subjected to its influence for an eternal existence in the ages to come. However, Christian teaching, as is the case with all true teaching, is concerned with much more than preparation for life. It deals with the child in the present as an individual in action who has a real life to live, that when he reaches maturity he may be the more able to live as a man of God. The Christian teacher teaches the child today in order that he may live to the fullest today. Living thus today, the individual is then prepared for the life of the future. The boy or girl who is best prepared for living in the future is the one who is best prepared for living in the present.

LEARNING ALWAYS A MATTER OF SELF-ACTIVITY

To be alive means to be active. Wherever there is life, there is action. In a very real sense, life is an inner principle of which activity is the expression. As stated in an earlier paragraph, the activity may be expressed in a physical, a mental, or in an emotional way, but it is an expression of activity whatever be the form in which it is expressed. Teaching can be no more than the guiding of the activity of the pupil. It is impossible for a teacher to transfer knowledge from a book, or from any other source, to the learner's mind. No one can communicate facts, ideas, principles, skills, attitudes, or ideals to another person. A teacher can give a pupil nothing; the pupil must take whatever he gets. The learner is not a vessel to receive what is poured into it nor is he an inert mass of something to be moulded by the application of external pressure. Instead, he is a living being whose growth is to be directed by the teacher. All learning comes through self-activity; the task of teaching is the task of stimulating, guiding, and directing the activity of the learner.

The teacher stimulates, encourages, and directs; the learner must do the learning through his own efforts. He who best understands the learner's normal activities in adjusting himself to new situations and who can appropriately stimulate and direct those activities does the best teaching. Only as the individual reacts can he learn; the goal of effective teaching is adequate stimulation and the wise guidance of pupil activity. The teacher can no more learn for the pupil than he can breathe or eat for him. Just as one must inhale air to supply the oxygen needed by the body or masticate and swallow food to make necessary energy, so must one learn for himself; no other can do the latter for him any more than he could do the former.

Right here lies the cause of a great deal of ineffective teaching. Unless a teacher sees this fundamental principle of learning through self-activity as essential in every concrete learning situation, he will exaggerate his part in the process of learning. To reiterate what has been said, the success of teaching must be judged by the results in the life of the learner, not by the amount of teacher-activity. No amount of teacher-activity avails except as it is a means of bringing about in the learner the desired understandings, insights, skills, attitudes, and ideals so that he becomes what the teaching is designed to make him. With a view to helping teachers and prospective teachers make this principle their own by giving it adequate application, there are given in the following paragraphs some typical teaching situations in which the principle of learning through self-activity is often overlooked.

Telling is not teaching. One of the easiest things in the world to do is to tell a person something. One of the commonest mistakes of teachers is to suppose that telling a pupil something is teaching that thing to the pupil. Telling may be a very important part of the process of teaching, but a pupil may be taught without being told anything at all. Usually, in any extended process of teaching, the teacher does do some talking, but most teachers talk too much. Frequently the much talking of the teacher constitutes a hindrance to the pupil in his learning. It is possible also that the telling may interest or impress even when it fails to instruct. But whatever telling may do by way of interesting, impressing, or instructing pupils, it cannot be too emphatically stated that telling, in and of itself, never is and never can be teaching.

A few very obvious situations demonstrate the truth of this assertion. For instance, all would readily agree that a deaf pupil who had no aid from any sense other than hearing could learn nothing from the words of a teacher however good the content expressed or however effective the manner of telling might be. Again, a pupil who is thinking so intently on what he did the preceding hour, or about what he is going to do after the class is dismissed that he does not hear what the teacher is saying will learn nothing from the teacher's talk. The teacher, who waxed enthusiastic while she talked because she judged by his attitude of rapt attention that a certain pupil was deeply interested in what she was saying but who learned later that this pupil was puzzling over the problem of why only her lower jaw moved when she talked, became quite conscious of the fact that telling is not teaching. It is sometimes said that a great deal of what is taught goes in one ear and out the other, but it might more accurately be said that a great deal of what is taught never enters the ear of the pupil.

If telling were teaching, all who hear would learn. Teaching would be a very simple matter, requiring comparatively little exertion. No one who teaches a person wholly ignorant of how to drive an automobile would care to entrust his life into the keeping of that person as a driver if the latter had been only told how to drive. The fact that he had been told about the steering wheel, the gears, the clutch, and all the other things that he needs to know in order to be able to drive would hardly qualify him as a safe driver. One who

162 Principles of Teaching for Christian Teachers

is told how to swim, what movements to make, how to make the strokes, etc., can never learn to swim so long as he stays out of the water. An artist might tell one how to paint a picture, but no one will ever paint a picture merely as a result of being told how to do it. In all these cases and in all other cases, learning to do something involves the doing of the thing instead of merely being told how to do it. The telling, if it is effectively done, will be an aid in learning how to do, but it will never, in and of itself, result in learning.

The teacher talks; the pupils listen. They will learn from the talking as they listen only if they hear, and understand, and react to what is said. Contrary to the popular idea, learning will not result merely from listening. If learning is to occur, every word will have to awaken a response in the form of an idea and cause the recall of the experiences that made the connected word and idea real and meaningful. Furthermore, each pupil must be led to integrate into a larger whole the new that he comprehends and the old that has been revived. Only after this has been done can he be said to have learned. As a result of learning thus, he will undergo changes in his feeling, thinking, and doing such as will cause him to act as he could never have acted without the learning.

When the words used by the teacher, however clear and simple they seem, cause the pupil, due to inadequate or distorted experiences, to respond along lines quite different from the thought of the teacher, learning, if it occurs at all, will not be what the teacher intended it to be. The alert teacher will be on the watch constantly for signs of the direction the mental responses of the pupil are taking. Study of changes in facial expression is one way of checking on inner responses to the words spoken. Calling on a pupil to answer a question, to make an application, or to illustrate an idea, are other means the skilful teacher may use to get an understanding of what is going on in his mind. Having the class engage in discussion is also a valuable aid. Often a graphic illustration can be used by the teacher to direct the mental activity of pupils into the right path when evidence indicates that such redirection is needed.

Ability to recite no evidence of learning. Another common mistake of teachers is to suppose that a pupil's ability to recite something from memory indicates that he has learned. Like telling, reciting may be of help to the pupil in learning but, as in the case of telling, reciting is not learning. A phonograph record can give off very accurately the results of impressions made upon it, but no one would say that the record had learned. Pupils can fasten in memory words, phrases, and sentences that have no more meaning to them than the words of the phonograph have to the record, and the children can repeat these words most glibly with no idea whatever of their meaning. Can one say that learning has occurred any more in the one case than in the other?

A writer in psychology tells of an illiterate woman who, under the influence of an anaesthetic, recited long passages in Hebrew. Hearers marveled, knowing that she could never have studied that language. Investigation of her past showed that this ability had its origin in the early life experience of the woman, who, while a servant in the home of a cultured minister, often heard him recite selections in Hebrew while he was preparing his sermons. This woman had no understanding of Hebrew, though she could recite these passages. Recitation never gave her understanding of Hebrew, and mere recitation by pupils of words they do not understand will never produce learning.

The receiving of ideas is a matter quite different from

the fastening of mere words in the memory. While the two processes may or may not occur simultaneously, they are never identical. Learning always extends and remakes experience; reciting is no more than repeating something previously learned and, if no ideas were gained at the time of learning, none will be produced by the mere recitation. One may be able to recite much content, Biblical or what not, and see no connections, relationships, and meanings—in other words, have no ideas—among the words memorized.

It is most certain that memorizing has value; much gain may come from storing words in the memory. At best, however, memorizing is only the gathering of materials for the mind to use. Without memory, little of value could be accomplished in a mental way, for it is necessary to remember many things in order to be able to act. But no teacher should ever make the mistake of supposing that mere memorizing produces learning. The learning that recitation is often supposed to represent could be attained without memorizing for recitation.

Far from placing undue emphasis on recitation, the effective teacher will strive for understanding reaction on the part of his pupils to that which they remember. Such a teacher, while he will not do away with memorizing, will be careful to see that pupils have as much insight as possible into the meaning of that which they memorize. He will realize that this meaning can come to them only in terms of their past experiences and that as these experiences are brought to bear upon new material, a unification of the new with the old must be made by the pupils as a basis for memorization. Then he will make moderate and reasonable use of recitation, recognizing that it may be desirable and important at times. No enlightened teacher will ever think that he is teaching when he is hearing pupils recite.

The proper use of objective materials. Still another common mistake in teaching is made in connection with the use of object lessons and concrete illustrative material. Because words so often fail to stimulate the learning activity of pupils, teachers frequently use various concrete materials that seem to furnish opportunities for experiences of more direct nature. Among the activities and devices that may be used to give vivid personal experiences are objects and models, drawings, diagrams, maps, still pictures, motion pictures, dramatic representations, and excursions.

While the use of such materials and activities may furnish a good basis for the right kind of mental activity, the successful teacher bears in mind always that the mere presence of objective material does not guarantee desirable learning. Mere observation of any object, half-hearted participation in any activity, or concentrated attention on some irrelevant feature of the total situation—none of these will accomplish the purpose intended. Presentation of a model or a picture of a house of Jesus' day will mean little to a child if he sees it only as an object or a picture. The making of such a house from cardboard will result in scarcely any more meaning if he regards the activity only as something to be done or if his attention during the process is centered upon the manipulation of the materials used. The learning gained by the pupils from objective materials is determined entirely by their own activity and responses to the thing done or observed.

To accomplish the real purpose of the lesson, then, it is necessary that the presentation of illustrative materials be most carefully planned and very skilfully directed. Aimless, unorganized use of these will never secure profitable pupil activity or result in pupil experiences that will function as a fruitful basis for later learning. The boy who learned much about working in wood but little about spiritual types as the outcome of building a model of the tabernacle had little background from this activity for an understanding of the great truths of the New Testament. On the other hand, the boys whose teacher planned very definitely the building of such a model with a view to guiding them into an understanding of the great spiritual truths typified and who directed their thought and understanding along these lines during the process of construction, carried away from the activity impressions and truths that meant much to them in terms of real learning.

From consideration of these common mistakes in teaching, it should be more evident that the pupil learns through his own responses or reactions. Only to the extent that the teacher's actions get each pupil to make the desired response is teacher-activity effective in bringing about learning. Very definitely, it is what the pupil does that educates him; the teacher is a factor in the learning process only as he induces learning activity of the right kind on the part of the pupil. "The teacher who teaches most is the one who teaches least" is a statement that expresses an important truth, viz., teaching consists in stimulating and directing pupil-activity and responses, not in giving manifest evidence of fulness of knowledge, of great ability to perform, or of much depth of feeling.

SELF-ACTIVITY IN THE LEARNING OF IDEALS AND ATTITUDES

The term "learning" has broad meaning in spite of the fact that it is often used in the very narrow sense, suggesting mere memorization of facts. Accurately speaking, learning refers to any change that takes place in a pupil's methods of thinking or feeling or doing. In everyday usage we speak of learning to swim, to drive an automobile, to tell the truth, to be obedient, to dislike literature, to enjoy poetry, to hate dish-washing, and so on. Hence learning, as stated before, may be motor, mental, or emotional, and the activity involved in learning may be physical, or doing; mental, or thinking; emotional, or feeling.

Of these three fields, it is probable that the necessity for proper self-activity as a basis for true learning needs most emphasis in the last. It is quite evident that a pupil cannot catch skill from someone else; common, every day observation proves that people learn to do things by trial and practice even when good examples serve to guide efforts. In respect to mental learning, such as learning how to study, how to form correct judgments, or how to reason, no great amount of argument is needed to convince anyone that the pupil learns as he acts. It is rather obvious that each learns his own best way to study and that he will never learn to form judg-ments or to reason except as he exercises along these lines, though intelligent guidance, skilfully applied, may be of great assistance. But since it is not so evident that the learner's own activity determines the nature of his emotional learning, the place of self-activity in this type of learning needs more thorough consideration.

In secular education. The outcomes of emotional learning are the result of learning activities in which the feeling side of the response predominates. Some of the many terms that are used to describe these out-comes are ideals, attitudes, dispositions, interests, tastes, prejudices, and sentiments. The importance of these in life is apparent to everyone. Secular education, which recognizes character building as a phase of the responsi-bility of the school, realizes that there can be no char-acter building without the forming of these in the life of the pupil. A writer in this field says, "Our young people must build such dynamic outlook, insight, habits, and attitudes as will enable them to hold their course amid change." [2]

Another writer emphasizes their importance in these words: "Everyone develops a large number of more or less generalized attitudes which condition and, to a large extent, determine all future responses."[3] In all that has to do with morality, an appreciation of the value of good conduct and a proper attitude toward ethical obligations are necessary. Unless these general patterns exist and function in his life, no individual will have a basis in habit for right moral conduct.

In religious education. Religious education which takes as one of its objectives "to foster in growing persons a progressive and continuous development of Christlike character" emphasizes religion as something that must have a vital place in every phase of living. Religious educators maintain that they are dealing with the whole child, whose education can never be complete except as he is educated religiously. Religious education "regards the child, not simply as having a mind, nor alone as a potential citizen, housekeeper, and wage earner; it regards him as possessed of Godlike qualities, as destined to larger life in a society which holds in one life God and all mankind. To religious education he is more than an intelligence to be developed; he is a person to come to the fulness of life in a universe explicable only on the basis of the supremacy of personality."[4]

For religious education, then, the child is a personality with a character which, under proper nurture, grows and develops from within. The task of religious

[2] W. H. Kilpatrick, **Education for a Changing Civilization** (New York, The Macmillan Company, 1926), p. 85

[3] T. H. Briggs, **Curriculum Problems** (New York, The Macmillan Company, 1926), p. 33

[4] H. F. Cope, **Religious Education in the Church** (New York, Charles Scribner's Sons, 1918), p. 42

education becomes, therefore, the task of promoting
growth in spiritual character by guiding the pupil according to discoverable laws of growth as he participates
in the life of the Christian group. The inner life that
is to be cultivated has to do with growth, which "means
finer discrimination between relative values, and between ends and means, and corresponding change in
fineness and breadth of appreciation, which is the beginning of fine and broad social conduct." [5]

In Christian teaching. Christian education has as its
aim "the man of God throughly furnished unto all
good works." However, the Christian educator recognizes that the first step toward the attainment of this
ultimate aim is regeneration by the Spirit of God of
the soul of man. To begin with, man is a sinner. Except as teaching is a means for bringing the pupil into
contact with God, it can do nothing Christian for him.
"The fact of sin is painfully real in human life. Christianity is a religion of redemption. . . . Religious education which omits an understanding of the fact and
meaning of sin, and of the means of recovery from sin
actually committed, is untrue to the Christian gospel."[6]
The basic task of Christian teaching is, therefore, to
guide pupils to such insight and discrimination as will
make them able and willing to recognize sin when it
exists and to accept Jesus Christ as Savior.

To do this, the Christian teacher must have a very
clear understanding of what sin is. Too often, the term
is used to refer to the outbroken forms of sin that find
expression in the lives of those whom society is quite
willing to designate as sinners. The original meaning
of the word is "missing the mark." There is a vast

[5] G. A. Coe, A Social Theory of Religious Education (New
York, Charles Scribner's Sons, 1917), pp. 72, 73
[6] P. H. Vieth, Objectives in Religious Education (New York,
Harper & Brothers, 1930), p. 157   (Used by permission)

difference between "knowing about sin" and being conscious of the fact that "I am a sinner." Somehow or other, under the guidance of the Spirit of God and with dependence on the Spirit to do His work of conviction, it is necessary for effective Christian teaching that the meaning of sin be brought into the present experience of every unregenerated pupil. When this is done and when Christ has been so presented as to lead the pupil to believe in Him as the one and only remedy for sin. Christian teaching has begun its work acceptably and is ready to continue to function in the guidance of a living person that he may grow and develop in spiritual experience.

The experience of conversion is the work of the Holy Spirit. Much teaching usually precedes the new birth even if it is sudden, and much teaching is necessary thereafter for the nurture of the new life. And this later teaching is ever concerned with knowledge and insight, ideals and attitudes, and habits and skills. While there is danger of overemphasis on knowledge, there is also danger of underemphasis. Knowledge is necessary. The Apostle Peter exhorts believers thus, "As newborn babes, desire the sincere milk of the word that ye may grow thereby" (I Peter 2:2). The teacher must guide the pupil in the acquisition of knowledge, but teaching for Christian conduct involves much more than giving the pupil an understanding of what Christian conduct is. Unless this understanding is given dynamic force by the presence of appreciation, attitude, and ideal, the issue in living will not be habits of Christian conduct.

All learning is by doing. From this digression, made for the purpose of seeing the place in Christian teaching of the emotional outcomes of learning, return is now made to the more direct consideration of the necessity for self-activity in the learning of ideals and attitudes.

A pupil always learns by doing. To learn to walk, he must walk; to learn to think, he must think; to learn to feel, he must feel. No more in the last than in the first two cases do results just happen. The learner's activity itself is the moulding influence that determines the nature of his ideals and attitudes. Emotional reactions produce learning outcomes, as do other types of reactions. Only as the learner acts in some way does he experience enjoyment or other emotional reaction to stimulation and, as a consequence, build up his attitude or ideal toward the object or thing that caused the reaction. The expression of appreciation, attitude, or ideal by the teacher may stimulate or encourage this self-activity, but it cannot do more. Ideals and attitudes are acquired only through the learner's own activity.

THE TEACHER RECOGNIZING THE PRINCIPLE OF SELF-ACTIVITY

The starting point for emotional learning, as for all other learning, is found in the nature of the child. His native emotional life with its great variety of likes and dislikes, satisfactions and annoyances, waits, as it were, the guidance of the teacher to become what it should be. The problem of teaching is the problem of guiding the emotional life of the child into desirable channels of expression so that he will experience proper satisfactions and appreciations and, consequently, build the right attitudes and ideals. In other words, the teacher must decide just what activity the pupil needs to perform as a means for getting him to feel as he should feel.

Point of contact necessary. In every type of learning, there must be a point of contact in the experience of the learner between the new and the old. Therefore, a necessary prerequisite for developing appreciation is an intellectual understanding of the material used. The pupil must actually live through, either in direct personal experience or in indirect imaginative experience, the emotional activities; consequently, the elements of the situation cannot be something without meaning in terms of past contacts. How, for example, could a pupil manifest reverence for a God of whom he knew nothing? Or how could he be truthful if he knew nothing about truth and falsehood? Unless he has knowledge and insight, the pupil has no foundation upon which to build appreciation.

Developing proper mental set. It is most important that readiness be developed as a basis for the teaching of appreciation. Mind set must be carefully established because deep feeling is not easy to control. Anyone knows how much a person's state of feeling, or mood, colors his responses to a situation. The careful teacher will use much thoughtful effort to find associations that will arouse pupil interest in the material to be presented, to cause the pupils to be eager and desirous for it, and to get them in a mood favorable for reception of the desired emotional response. This is the most important step in teaching for appreciation. To neglect it means failure in the early stages of the work. On the other hand, when the pupils, out of their previous emotional experiences, have created a mental set emotionally inclined in the direction of the feeling response desired, the rest of the teacher's work will be so easy that it will almost take care of itself.

Presentation with appreciation. With a content that is meaningful and with a sympathetic mental attitude on the part of the pupils, there must be an appreciative presentation. Unless the teacher himself has the affective experiences which it is desired that pupils experience, it is practically impossible for him to express the proper appreciation in presenting the materials. Sometimes it is better that a pupil or a visitor rather than the teacher make the presentation. Whoever does it must enter into the experience in his own emotional life. During the presentation, there must be active response on the part of the pupil such as will enable him to participate imaginatively in the activity and to realize satisfaction and enjoyment from so doing.

Pupil expression. Finally, pupil expression is necessary. Once the feeling is aroused, it is important that there be some further line of activity through which it may find expression with added satisfaction and a consequent reinforcement of the response. Far from dragging this response from the pupils, the effective teacher will so manage the situation that expression will be free and spontaneous. The teacher's own attitude of enthusiasm, enjoyment, and expectation with her manifest approval of pupil efforts at expression will cause the pupils to respond in a natural way. It needs to be emphasized again at this point that not all expression is in the form of overt activity such as talking, singing, or other forms of quite manifest muscular movement. Frequently, the facial expression and rapt attention are most indicative of very definite expression of pupil appreciation.

SELF-ACTIVITY IN RELATION TO OTHER PHASES OF LEARNING

It remains yet in this discussion of the principle of pupil activity to consider several other phases of the learning process that have vital relation to it. Little beyond mere enumeration of these will be attempted here, for some need only be mentioned and others will be given more complete treatment in succeeding chapters.

Unification of effort in the direction of the teaching purpose. Effective learning results when the combined forces of the individual are unified for the purpose of definite accomplishment. Behavior is an affair of the organism as a whole, not of certain segments that function independently each of the other. Within each pupil, there is an inner demand for activity prompting him to be constantly busy about something: physical movement, mental exploration, enjoyment of something. Good teaching consists in directing the total energy of pupils into channels of expression in harmony with the purpose of teaching. No situation is simple. At every moment the individual finds himself bombarded by a host of stimuli. Many and varied sensory stimuli or cues to action, a multitude of temporal and spatial arrangements, similarities, differences, attributes, and a great variety of meanings from previous experience clamor for attention and interest. In addition, the situation itself may vary in many particulars from moment to moment while remaining in general the same kind of situation. Only as the total activity of the pupil is converged toward definite accomplishment can it be prevented from finding outlets that will defeat the purpose of the teacher.

The goal-seeking nature of pupil activity. The learner is seeking always to attain some goal. Activity is never purposeless; the child does not act only for the sake of doing something but in order to reach some end. Good teaching consists, then, in recognizing a need for learning when it exists or in creating this need and so directing activity that the need may be met adequately. The most alert activity of pupils is that which is the outcome of tasks assumed by themselves rather than those imposed upon them by others. This subject will receive further treatment in the next chapter.

Varied effort. Again, the learner's activity is characterized by changes in the way of doing. In the first place, the goal set determines the nature of the effort; it is necessary to secure activity that will lead to the

particular learning desired. Just any activity will not
do. To gain information about the life of the people
of Israel, a pupil must engage in reading and listening
that will give him familiarity with this topic. To develop the attitude of loyalty, a pupil must have experiences of the appreciation and worth of loyalty. A
central problem of teaching is that of guiding the learner
in the choice of lines of effort that are relevant to the
kinds of learning desired. In the second place, behavior productive of learning is not stereotyped behavior. As the learner engages in repeated effort to
attain a specific goal, his behavior is variable within
rather wide limits. He tries one way, then another way,
and still another, consistently in terms of his desire
to attain the goal, until final success crowns his efforts.
Mere repetition does not result in learning; continual
change in the activity repeated is necessary.

However, repetition of an action is ordinarily necessary for most effective learning. Usually, the attainment of a goal one time does not carry learning to the
point desired. Acquisition of much knowledge, development of high degrees of skill, and the formation of
persistent attitudes are invariably the result of oft-
repeated action. Learning is a matter of laying "precept upon precept, precept upon precept; line upon
line, line upon line; here a little, and there a little"
(Isa. 28:10). The good teacher has a thing done again
and again whether it be repeating a verse, the singing
of a song, or the right treatment of fellow men. But
always, in harmony with what was said in the preceding
paragraph, such a teacher will see that the repetition
takes place under conditions which make for variation
in the activity so that it is not the same old thing done
in the same old way.

*Solving of present concrete problems makes for best
learning.* Pupils learn best when they engage in activity

directed toward the solution of an actual problem. Children, especially, think in terms of the present and of concrete reality. Few people, children or adults, learn by having general truths taught them with a view to applying these later in life. Though they may know the words of the Golden Rule, it is quite likely to exist in their thought as a meaningless statement unless it has received significance through the summing up of specific learnings in various concrete situations.

Past experience determines present learning. The learning of any particular thing is influenced by the total past experience of the learner. Not only does the individual initiate his activity but he also makes those modifications of behavior that constitute learning. At a particular moment one is the total of all his past, and what one is at any moment has very definite bearing on present learning. The total results of all past influences reflected in the development of the child's personality are actively gathered together to constitute the mental set, disposition, and attitude with which he meets a new situation. Thus the learner's action is guided by these past influences, causing his learning to be a matter of personal achievement instead of a passive process of receiving impressions. The place of mental set in learning will receive more detailed consideration in a succeeding chapter.

Pupils learn what they experience. The pupil should learn things in the way that he should use them. Since the individual can learn only through his own activity, it follows as a corollary that he learns what he experiences. An individual who can do no more than recite "Thou shalt love thy neighbor as thyself," when he is given the reference or asked a question calling for such recitation, cannot be said to have learned, in any true sense of the word. Far more worthwhile would it be for him to be able to use the truth of the command in various situations as he meets them in daily living. In the first case, he has learned a fact by dint of memorization and drill. In the second instance, he will have learned the truth as he should use it in life and when he meets varying life situations he can respond correctly in terms of their demands. In the first case, he experienced memorization and drill, and he learned these; in the second case, he experienced loving his fellow man, and he learned love for fellow man.

Pupils learn only that to which they react. Finally, pupils learn only those things to which they react. Every situation met by an individual has so many stimuli that it is literally impossible for him to react to all of them. Each pupil responds to those items in the total situation which past experience, mental set, and the present purpose bring into the center of his interest. If one pupil reacts to the content of what the teacher says, another to the tone of voice in which it is said, and a third to some mannerism of the teacher, three things instead of one will be learned. In all class instruction, it is, therefore, most necessary that there should be one common purpose and goal to give direction and destination to the learning activity. Only if these be present will class attention and effort be directed to the important phases of the work. When teacher and pupils have one common guiding purpose, interest and effort will be centered along lines closely related to the goal of the activity, and pupils will learn the essential elements because they will be reacting to these as individuals.

TEACHER-ACTIVITY AND ITS FUNCTION

So all learning is the result of self-activity. The pupil learns through his own responses, reactions, or behavior; he cannot learn by having someone else think or feel or do for him. Only as he thinks for himself can he learn to think; only as he maintains mastery of himself again and again does he learn to exercise self-control; and only as he experiences repeated feelings of reverence does he build an attitude of reverence.

The teacher's activity is effective only to the degree that it causes each pupil to make the desired response. So far as pupil-activity is concerned, the teacher is merely one element in the total situation, and teacher-activity is merely one form of stimulation among many. Room, furniture, books, and fellow-pupils are other sources of stimulation. Frequently a child learns much more from other pupils than he does from the teacher. That which induces most responses in a pupil produces most learning. Writing notes, drawing pictures, stimulating activity in other pupils, reading books, and general mind-wandering, are activities that may be much more productive of learning responses than is any activity of the teacher. Thus pupils may learn much in spite of the teacher.

Teachers often talk so much that pupils are given too little opportunity to respond. Or they may use many long questions that require only brief answers from the pupils. Teachers who become impatient when pupils are trying to think out an answer to a question or a solution to a problem sometimes give the child no opportunity for adequate self-activity. Skilled teaching may be characterized by frequent rather lengthy periods of silence while pupils are recalling past ideas, organizing the old and the new, and getting solutions of their own. Actual thinking done by pupils is far more worthwhile in terms of learning than is any kind of objective result which it is so natural for the teacher to desire strongly.

Throughout this chapter, constant emphasis has been placed upon the fact that self-activity may be physical, mental, or emotional. It needs to be emphasized further that self-inhibition and self-restraint are often very desirable forms of self-activity. Thorndike says, "Activity may as well result in the inhibition as in the production of ideas and feelings and movements. . . . It must not be forgotten that *not* to think the foolish irrelevant thought is an essential of reasoning; that *not* to follow the wrong impulse is the essential of character; that *not* to make the aimless and crude movement is the essential of skill. Success is in great measure not making failures. What a man does depends upon what impulses are neglected or overcome. We are what we are by reason of what we are not—what we do not permit ourselves to become. Activity is inhibitory as well as impulsive." As the learner thinks, does, and feels for himself, he finds that his first efforts may be quite crude but that these can be improved upon through further experimentation. The teacher needs, therefore, to exercise patience and restraint while the pupil is working into his experience the content at hand, for what the learner does not do in terms of visible activity is sometimes most really an activity.

Teacher guidance of pupil activity is relatively easy where the product thereof is objective. For example, if a pupil says that Beersheba is a person, states that righteous indignation prompts him to administer a punch to a fellow-pupil, or prays that calamity may befall some incorrigible playmate, the teacher has objective evidence of wrong self-activity as a basis for bringing about changes in learning. However, it is not always easy, even in such cases, to give guidance that will result in correct response on the part of the pupil. Much more is it difficult to determine if each pupil has made the correct response when that response is subjective instead of objective. "The tyranny of words" is such that the statements of the child may greatly belie his thoughts. Frequently, children and adults also use very glibly words, the meaning of which they do not at all understand. In the development of ideals and attitudes, it is particularly difficult to ascertain if the activity is of the right kind.

To be skilled, the teacher needs, therefore, to cultivate understanding of children's ways of thinking, feeling, and doing. "She must be able to infer skilfully from a pupil's words and outer attitude what are the inside facts. Having inferred his mental condition, she must know just what cue to give, what question to ask, what information to add, what praise or criticism to bestow, in order to start the pupil's mental responses in the desired direction. In order to do this, she must understand the conditions which determine a pupil's response to any situation."

QUESTIONS AND PROBLEMS

1. In what way does one's conception of the nature of learning influence his work of teaching?
2. Explain the meaning of behavior and give illustrations of its various forms.
3. What is the difference between behavior and conduct?
4. What is the ultimate purpose of the learning-teaching process?
5. Of what value is the mastery of facts?
6. Illustrate how facts have different significance for different people.
7. Why must teaching be concerned primarily with present behavior?
8. Is it true that life means action?
9. Can a teacher give a pupil anything?
10. Show that telling is not teaching.
11. What place may telling rightfully have in the teaching process?
12. From your observation and experience, would you say that most teachers talk too much? Give concrete illustrations to show how more effective teaching would have resulted from less talking on the part of the teacher.

13. Prove that ability to recite is no evidence of learning.
14. Does it follow that pupils should not be required to memorize? Why or why not?
15. Show how objects may be used effectively in bringing about learning.
16. Is anything ever taught by a teacher if there has been no learning by a pupil?
17. From the standpoint of self-activity which kind of learning, physical, mental, or emotional, stands most in need of care? Why?
18. Show the need, from the standpoint of Christian teaching, of a proper emphasis on self-activity.
19. Can one learn if he does not do?
20. Trace the steps in teacher recognition of the principle of self-activity. Which seems to be most important?
21. Emphasize the importance of unified effort.
22. Does anyone ever do anything without purpose?
23. Indicate by way of exposition and illustration how past experience determines present learning.
24. What is the function of teacher-activity?
25. When is activity not activity? Is such ever the case?
26. Show how the teacher may guide pupil activity.

REFERENCES

Baldwin, J. L., Worship Training for Juniors (Chicago: Methodist Book Concern, 1927)
Betts, G. H., and Hawthorne, M. O., Method in Teaching Religion (New York: The Abingdon Press, 1925)
Carrier, Blanche, How Shall I Learn to Teach Religion? (New York: The Abingdon Press, 1925)
Coe, G. A., A Social Theory of Religious Education (New York: Charles Scribner's Sons, 1918)
Commins, W. D., Principles of Educational Psychology (New York: The Ronald Press Company, 1937)
Corzine, J. L., Looking at Learning (Nashville: The Sunday School Board of the Southern Baptist Convention, 1934)
Crawford, C. C., How to Teach (Los Angeles: Southern California School Book Depository, 1938)
Garrison, N. L., The Technique and Administration of Teaching (New York: The American Book Co., 1933)
Horne, H. H., This New Education (New York: The Abingdon Press, 1931)
McLester, F. C., Our Pupils and How They Learn (Nashville: Cokesbury Press, 1930)
Moore, M. A., Senior Method in the Church School (New York: The Abingdon Press, 1929)

Munkres, Alberta, **Primary Method in the Church School** (New York: The Abingdon Press, 1930)

Myers, A. J. W., **Teaching Religion Creatively** (New York: Fleming H. Revell Co., 1932)

Powell, M. C., **Junior Method in the Church School** (New York: The Abingdon Press, 1931)

Reagan, G. W., Fundamentals of Teaching (Chicago: Scott, Foresman & Co., 1932)

Richardson, N. E., **The Christ of the Classroom** (New York: The Macmillan Co., 1931)

Roberts, S. L., **Teaching in the Church School** (Philadelphia: The Judson Press, 1930)

Squires, W. A., **The Pedagogy of Jesus in the Twilight of Today** (New York: George H. Doran Co., 1927)

Thomas, F. W., **Principles and Technique of Teaching** (Boston: Houghton Mifflin Co., 1927)

Vieth, P. H., **How to Teach in the Church School** (Philadelphia: The Westminster Press, 1935)

CHAPTER VIII

MOTIVATION AND LEARNING

ALL activity has a cause. No more in human life
than in the physical world does anything "just happen."
For every effect there is a cause. "Nothing walks with
aimless feet." Every movement a human being makes,
every act he performs, every feeling he experiences is
caused. In many instances the cause cannot be traced,
but it is there. Because a human being's action and
conduct seem so unpredictable, it is very easy to take
things for granted and trust in fortuitous circumstances
or in God to bring things to pass in this realm. The
first never produces anything except in terms of cause
and effect; "naturally good" or "naturally bad" conduct never just happens to come on the scene. As for
the second, Christian teaching places its firm trust in
God, knowing that change can be wrought in human
nature only by God.

But the trust of the Christian teacher is not a blind
faith that deliberately ignores understanding of God's
way of working. On the contrary, he seeks to work
intelligently and harmoniously with God as He does
His work. One of the greatest Christian teachers said,
"We are laborers together with God: ye are God's hus-
bandry, ye are God's building." (I Cor. 3:9). Just as
a gardener is dependent upon God to grow a plant, so

the teacher is dependent upon God to grow a life. But just as the good gardener seeks to care for his plant in terms of the laws that govern its growth, so does the intelligent teacher endeavor to direct and nurture the growth of a life in terms of the laws established by God. "Inexorable law governs in the making of a life quite as much as in the making of a plant."

Since all learning results from the activity of the learner and since all activity has a cause, the teacher needs an understanding of the forces that act upon life to produce activity. The question in this connection becomes: Why do people do what they do? Or, what are the basic sources of human motivation? And since the learner must take an active, purposeful part in the learning situation, the teacher has the responsibility for guiding the development of new purposes. Practical questions that confront the teacher, therefore, are: What can be done to provide adequate motive? How guide the activity of the learner in terms of the motive? And how can he be led into such understanding of the relationship between his activity and its results as to provide adequate basis for continuous modification of both his motive and his activity?

The pupil is interested and engages in effort only as he has a purpose or motive; consequently adequate and proper motivation is the key to effective learning. The obtaining of this is perhaps the teacher's most difficult problem and, it naturally follows, the teacher's greatest opportunity. Before any child comes to the teacher, he has developed purposes in many of his activities, and these developed purposes can be used effectively by the teacher in promoting learning. But since the directing of learning involves continuous development of new purposes, knowledge of the manner in which purposes are first formed gives the teacher a basis for some understanding of the procedure that needs to be followed. Accordingly, consideration is given first to the nature of motivation and then to the basic urges and drives of the human organism.

THE NATURE OF MOTIVATION

The starting point of all learning is a sense of need. The individual, feeling some lack, stress, or need of adjustment, puts forth effort to deal with a disturbed state of affairs and in so doing he learns. True it is, the disturbance may be minor in nature; in very young children, especially, it may never become conscious. Quite frequently the pupil does not appreciate the importance of his need. In older pupils, there may be keen and intelligent consciousness of the existence of need. But whether or not there is recognition of its existence or appreciation of its importance, the sense of need continues until it is satisfied. It is always present where learning occurs.

No learning without a feeling of need. Learning is the result of activities engaged in for the sake of satisfying need. The feeling of a need causes the pupil to develop purposes relative to such need and its satisfaction. Purposes cause him to put forth effort, or in other words, to engage in activity. The activities involved in meeting the sense of need or reestablishing a balance when difficulties are met may become highly conscious and intelligent but not necessarily so. The initial thing for the teacher to do as the one who guides learning, is to arouse in the pupil the feeling of need because only as he feels need will he develop purposes and become active in terms of meaningful experience.

Teacher must understand pupil's needs. To bring pupils to awareness of need, the teacher must know their needs. Without such knowledge, he cannot assist the learner to become aware of the situations he faces nor can he guide the activities of the group along purposeful lines. A child's expressed wish, want, or problem may be quite different from his actual and real need. A superficial teacher may see as fundamental some external, apparent need where the real need is not at all apparent. All attempts to teach the pupil so long as this inner need is untouched will avail nothing in terms of the real solution of his problem, for they will tend to deepen need, not to meet it. But the teacher who understands the child's needs brings them to the surface of awareness in the child's consciousness. Then he leads the child to engage in activities acceptable to him in terms of those needs and the interests developed relative to them, thus laying a solid foundation for most effective teaching.

Need leads to interest and attention. Books on teaching used to place a great deal of stress on getting and holding the attention of pupils. Attention is essential to learning, but the best way to get attention is to capture the interest of the pupil. No effective activity is put forth except as the individual feels the value of that activity to satisfy some need. This feeling of the value, or worth of something, constitutes interest. When human beings are interested, they will give attention and put forth effort. Other things being equal, the deeper the interest the more attentive the pupil will be and the greater will be his effort. Interest supplies the motive power of self-activity. If the teacher sets the situation so that the pupil's interest in any activity is secured and provides a suitable opportunity for satisfying that interest, the pupil will give all the attention and do all the work necessary for a successful learning outcome, provided, of course, that the interest is maintained.

Two kinds of interest. There are two kinds of interest, the positive and the negative. The first is the kind that prompts willing activity on the part of the learner.

He acts for the purpose of getting something that has value in itself; he does what he wants to do because he wants to do it. Negative interest is characterized by desire to avoid some unpleasant outcome. The learner acts for the purpose of evading instead of obtaining; he does what he does not want to do because he wants to escape something worse. The secret of best teaching lies in the ability of the teacher to stimulate positive interest. While learning will take place under the influence of negative interest, it is not the kind that results in concentrated attention or whole-hearted effort. The form of motivation productive of best learning is a desire on the part of the individual to do the task in hand without any pressure from the outside. If a pupil is eager to do a thing, he will bend every effort toward its accomplishment.

Needs and purposes in relation to interest. Best learning results, then, from interest based upon inner purposes growing out of needs felt. In general, the activity of pupils at any given time is such as seems to them to be directly concerned with the realization of purposes that they will have already adopted. Before they are old enough to come under the influence of a teacher, children have developed certain general purposes and interests. In motivating or controlling learning activity, the wise teacher will make use of the interests already valued by the pupil. He will connect these with the work to be done in such a way that more valuable purposes grow out of them. Control of motivation, in the final analysis, is always an individual matter, for any stimulating situation will have varying effects depending upon the individuality of the particular pupil. However, human nature is always the same in its fundamental characteristics; so the point of departure for motivating pupils is an understanding of the primary urges and desires of human beings, which are the basic sources of purpose and interest.

PRIMARY DESIRES BASED ON TISSUE NEEDS

Understanding of how interests are acquired and how purposes develop within individuals demands recognition of the fact that bodily appetites begin to function in early life and exert an influence upon the individual throughout his entire existence. Though man is a being who in essence is spirit, not body, he yet has his temporal existence in bodily form and though his experience transcends the limits of temporal and bodily existence, he is in this life subject fundamentally to the working of the physiological appetites which, in the economy of God, play a part in determining what he will do and be. The acts of daily life, the character, and the personality of any individual, have their beginning in drives or urges which come to him from original nature or what he is because he is a human being.

These drives are so compelling as to make the infant seem almost like a self-generating agent. The newborn child is moved to action almost entirely by things that are happening within its own body. No one would say that the behavior of an infant or even of a very young child gave evidence of the presence of intentions, attitudes, ideals, or conscious purposes. The only explanation possible to give is that there are inherent in the very nature of the body certain demands that are as fundamental as life itself and that the young child's activity is the result of responses stimulated by these demands. The primary drives persist throughout life, constituting the beginnings of motivated, or purposeful, behavior. Through experience and learning they become organized into complex motives in the form of vital interests, ideals, attitudes, and compelling purposes, which motivate behavior on its higher levels.

A desire is called primary if it is innate, if it is a part of what one is originally because he is a human being. Such a desire, or urge, is simple, not combined with other drives to form a complex of motives, such as are found in attitudes and ideals. The responses caused by primary desires are those made because the individual is what he is, apart from experience and learning. Among the most basic of all the primary desires are those urges to action that have their origin in tissue needs.

An inner drive of great power is hunger. While desire for food is induced by contractions in the walls of the stomach, it involves every cell in the body, and, if hunger is intense, the entire organism becomes restless as it seeks satisfaction. Thirst is a tissue need almost, if not entirely, as insistent as hunger. The desire for continuous supplies of oxygen and the desire to get rid of waste products are also very potent basic urges to action. One of the most insistent of all the tissue urges is the sex desire. It plays a very large part in the interests and the activities of human beings, especially from the age of puberty onward. The demand of the organism for rest and the relief of fatigue is another tissue need that accounts for a considerable amount of activity. Pain and the desire to escape it also prompts much action. Extremes of temperature which, of course, are a matter of external stimulation, cause tissue conditions that take the form of a drive.

Another bodily condition that seems to be equivalent to the tissue needs just described is the desire for activity. Where life is, there is energy, and where energy is, there is the desire to be active. No normal human being ever remains for a long period of time in an inactive state. From the very beginning of life, activity is in evidence. The very young infant squirms, wriggles, pulls up and pushes out its feet,

and waves its arms. Quite evidently, external stimulation, the amount of energy already expended, the kind
and quality of food, and the equilibrium of the various
systems of energy, are all factors in this desire for
activity, but the desire apparently has its basis in conditions in the tissues that make movement inevitable.
On the physical side, this desire finds expression in
random activity and in manipulation; on the mental
side it is expressed in curiosity and in interest in
discovery of the new.

OTHER PRIMARY DESIRES

In addition to these general bodily conditions, there
are other desires that seem to be just as elementary and
equally as, if not more, important for the teacher to
take into consideration when attempting to capture the
interest of pupils. It is probable that early development is concerned with learning how to respond effectively to stimuli coming from the body. By the time the
child comes under the influence of a teacher, he has
worked out many habitual ways of dealing with most of
the stimuli that have their origin in tissue needs. While
these needs cannot be ignored at any period of life by
one who would understand and guide human behavior,
the purposes of pupils with which the teacher is most
concerned are only indirectly related to these fundamental physiological desires. Other desires that apparently are just as primary demand the more direct
attention of the teacher. Since this is true, these will be
treated in somewhat more detail than those already
considered.

The desire to be active. One tissue need that perhaps
constitutes greatest exception to the statements made in
the previous paragraph is the last one treated in the
preceding section, i.e., the desire to be active. This
desire must always be of direct concern to the effective

teacher. Since the normal person of whatever age likes to be doing things, teaching must always take this tendency into consideration as a motivating influence. Instead of requiring the pupil to sit with folded hands, the intelligent teacher gives him things to do. Far from being unpleasant, work is a pleasurable activity to the child unspoiled by the attitude adults take toward work. Children are not born lazy; they are continually doing things, finding pleasure in activity itself. Successful teaching will always make adequate use of this fundamental urge of human nature.

The desire for new experience. Closely related to the desire to be active is the urge to new experience. Like the Athenians of Paul's day, human beings are constantly seeking "some new thing." Human nature dislikes monotony and demands new and changing experiences. The very young child manifests this urge in the continual investigation, exploration, and experimentation that he carries on with his world. To him, as to life at all ages, there is possible danger in following the urge; injury, wrong acts, and wrong conduct may result. The great opportunity of the teacher is to open up the way to new experience and at the same time to see that there are reasonable safeguards against its dangers.

Desire to achieve. Another desire that has close connection with the desire to be active is the desire to achieve. No one is satisfied with mere activity; any individual likes to succeed in what he does. The pupil needs to realize that he is making progress, getting certain things right, and eliminating some of his errors. He experiences a thrill when anticipated results are an outcome of his activity. To use this desire aright, the teacher must be careful to maintain goals within the limit of the pupil's attainment. Early successes need to be minor in nature, the result of tasks which the pupil can perform easily. Gradual progress can then be made to more difficult tasks. If he be required to advance so rapidly as to be incapable of successful performance, discouragement and a sense of failure with consequent crippling of effort will be the result. The pupil must be satisfied with what he is trying to do.

Desire to express one's self. A very strong human desire is the desire to tell things. The normal individual likes to be the first to tell something unusual. This tendency is the basis for a great deal of idle talking and even malicious gossip. One sees the desire in constant manifestation in a group of very small children. To use it profitably in the classroom, the teacher must provide the individual who has something to communicate with an appreciative hearing. This will not be the result when all the pupils have done the same work and are, consequently, equally familiar with the content studied. Effective teaching demands that there be opportunity for each pupil to contribute, from his own individual study and investigation, something that will be of interest to the whole group.

Desire for approval. The desire to have the approval of others is one of the strongest motivating factors in human beings at all ages. Early in life it is the approval of a parent or a teacher that is most sought but, as the child grows older, he seeks more and more the favor of his social group. The teacher of younger children, by giving or withholding commendation, can stimulate or inhibit activity, correct where needed, and equalize effort quite effectively. Pupils of any age are much influenced by their desire for commendation or fear of censure when the relationship between teacher and pupil is characterized by the degree of respect naturally felt by pupils for a teacher.

It is most easy for a teacher to overwork the desire for approval. Many teachers, because of their own desire for power and preeminence, face the very real danger of making their pupils too dependent on them. Teaching is done for the sake of developing independence and power in the learner; to make him sufficient unto himself is the ultimate purpose so far as his relationship to the teacher is concerned. In other words, the constant purpose of the true teacher is to make himself useless. Such an one seeks ever to bring the learner in his development to levels of self-sufficiency where he will no longer have need of help which the teacher can give. When a teacher dominates pupils to such a degree, therefore, that they seek to do things only for the sake of getting his approval, the pupils are made dependent and weak. The wise teacher will make direct appeal to the desire for teacher approval very seldom, striving instead to have the learner's interest established on a basis more intrinsically and more permanently valuable.

As life develops, there is need of getting to higher and higher ideals in respect to the seeking of approval. At first the baby wants the approval of his father and mother. Later, as he makes wider social contacts, the group is the source from which he seeks approval. The teacher should use group approval as a basis for interest in constantly greater degree as development moves forward. But pupils should never be carried so far that they simply follow the crowd without any opinions of their own. They should be led to think for themselves and to take a stand for the right even if this would mean loss of group approval. No one should ever follow a crowd simply because of fear of what the group might say about him. The Christian teacher will endeavor to lead his pupils to desire above everything else the approval of God.

Desire to possess. Another desire that seems to be basic is the desire to possess. It finds expression chiefly in two forms: ownership and collecting. A child does not have to be very old to assume the attitude or to say, "This is mine." He wants to own things, just as the rest of us do. Though he may have few things that he can call his own, he finds delight in possessing them. Man always wants things of his own — pets, houses, lands, gardens, cars, new clothes, or what not, according to his age or other circumstances. Very few, if any children and adults, never make collections of some kind. Stones, marbles, stamps, postcards, books, and a host of things are found in collections. The collecting tendency of groups finds expression in the bringing together of objects to form museums, libraries, and art galleries. A teacher can utilize this tendency in various phases of class work. Perhaps a part of the desire for knowledge on the part of human beings is made up of the tendency to possess information and to collect facts. Collections of various kinds that pupils have made sometimes offer possibilities for either direct or indirect use in teaching. The making of scrapbooks and other things that pupils may keep offers opportunity for fruitful learning.

Competition and rivalry. The last primary desire to which attention will be directed here is the desire to compete. This desire is not manifest in very young children, but as they become older, any activity that offers promise of competition will call forth interest and effort. Everywhere in human affairs — recreational, social, political, and industrial — there are manifestations of competition and rivalry. The teacher does well to use this tendency but must be on guard against both its misuse and its overuse. It is very easy to carry competitive exercises so far as to cause children to injure themselves by too much activity. Again, it is most easy to set competitive work on such a basis as to make it impossible for the less capable pupil to have the least chance of winning. This often leads to the development of feelings of frustration, inferiority, and social maladjustment that may work havoc in the life of the pupil who loses. Furthermore, the pupil who wins faces the danger of development of feelings of superiority, bigotry, and egotism that may be productive of just as dire results in his life.

Not only is it impossible but it is also undesirable to eliminate from class work the urge to compete. The aim of the teacher, therefore, should be to utilize it in ways productive of best results in the development of the lives of all pupils. A very good way to use the desire is to allow the pupil to compete with his own record instead of competing with other pupils. This utilizes the tendency as a basis for interest without bringing into play the many dangers that result from the practice of social rivalry. The teacher can also plan social competition so that the superior pupil competes under handicaps that make the basis for competition equal, though there is danger here of making this pupil feel that he is the victim of unfair discrimination. A third suggestion is that use may be made of competition in group undertakings rather than individual contests so that all may be drawn into the activity. Thus there will be a check against the development of individualistic and unsocial tendencies.

How primary desires should be used. This is not a complete list of all the primary desires that exist in human nature. These are only a few of the most important and will serve to show some of the forces which lie back of human action. It must be remembered by anyone who wishes to motivate human behavior that these primary drives do not act independently one of the other, that it is not now one and then another in turn which provides motivation. And there must also be recognition of the fact that human motivation is more than a simple functioning of urges either singly or in combination. All learning must start with the primary urges of human nature; they must always be taken into account no matter how elaborate the learning may become in its organization nor what method is used. But, after all, these are only the basis for motivation and learning. The motives of human beings are a much more complex matter than the functioning of any number of blind urges or drives.

MOTIVES

The teacher is dealing with far more than raw material. The child is not a mechanism to be changed as the teacher manipulates it first in one way and then in another. Child life has been likened to plastic clay, which receives readily any impression that is made upon it, and to marble, which retains permanently the impression made. But, unlike clay or marble, the child has power of responding in his own way to what is done to him. There is a self, or soul, that is something more than the physical organism. Instead of being under the bondage of mechanical necessity, the human being makes purposive choice of lines of action. The teacher has to do, therefore, with a living being who has goals and purposes.

In the section on the "Nature of Motivation," emphasis was placed on the purpose of the learner as a factor in motivation. There it was stated that best learning results from interest based upon inner purposes growing out of needs felt. In the last two sections, attention was directed to some of the basic urges and desires of human nature, and it was pointed out that these must always be taken into consideration in any attempt to motivate human behavior. To deal with the inner purposes of the learner as they find expression in motives or goals of action is the present task.

Insufficiency of primary desires. While a teacher needs understanding of the primary desires of pupils as a basis for interest, yet it cannot be expected that these alone will furnish impelling motives for all their learning. Motives have their beginning in the complex acts of living and represent the expression of inner purposes that arise from needs felt. Need supplies motive for learning. "An end which is the child's own carries him on to possess the means of its accomplishment," says Dewey, who also stresses the problem as a motive for learning and the ideal as a motive for doing. And another writer says, "There is no such thing as doing work in which one is not interested, or for which one does not have a need."

That with which the teacher is concerned, therefore, in the actual experience of motivating learning is not the relation of motive and primary desire but the organization and direction of factors so that the learner is brought to face some need, problem, or question in a vital, personal way. As he feels some practical need, meets some interesting problem, or desires to answer some question, he will put forth effort. In doing so, he will bring into play many basic urges. The direction and the energizing of pupil activity in meeting and in dealing adequately with some felt need is the fundamental problem of motivation.

Relation of motive and interest. Earlier it was said that any pupil who was interested would put forth sufficient effort, provided his interest was maintained. The pupil with a motive, i.e., inner purpose based upon felt need, will be interested. A pupil may be interested and have no motive. A motive to work is, therefore, larger than an interest in work. When a motive exists, interest is present, but there may be interest without motive. Any person's interests are many. They are also transient except as they are the outcome of impelling motive. A pupil may be interested and pay attention to the hum of passing motors, the conversation in the hall, the picture on the wall—one flitting thing after another — and, if his responses cease with mere interest, no end will be realized.

But if motive is present, activity will be directed toward the accomplishment of some end. Motivated activity is definitely purposive; it causes interest, attention, and effort to be converged toward the attainment of present aim. Effective teaching demands that the pupil meet a problem or need. He must have a motive for the work; he must see sufficient reason for what he is doing. So long as he does, his interest will be maintained in a way that will count for worth while results. The pupil is well motivated when he sees a real use in the work set for him to do, and he will be interested when the activity satisfies some need felt by him.

Motive and activity. Mere interest apart from motive, even if the interest be intense, will result in little learning. It is most important that the motive have to do both with activity and with learning. A pupil may have a motive for one and not for the other. One may have such motive for an activity as will cause him to perform it many times without resulting improvement. In class a pupil may go through the routine of work with little or no change. Conversely, there may be motive to learn without motive to perform, with the consequence that the learner never does outside of class what he learns in class. What a pupil likes to do may be performed with adequate motivation but no learning, while what he is required to do may lead to learning that is motivated without the motivation of performances.

The teacher needs to be concerned with both aspects of motivation. The pupil should not only learn but he should also develop a desire to do outside the learning situation what he has learned. A very common error is to put so much stress on learning that motivation of performance is neglected. However, emphasis on motivation of activity may be carried to an extreme. Activity for activity's sake counts for nothing; performance should be so motivated that the things learned will be used to meet the problems of life.

During early childhood, purposeful activity rather than intentional learning prevails. While learning is always an active process regardless of age, much of the young child's learning is incidental to activity done for reasons other than learning. Hence the teacher of young children is concerned with the motivation of activity, for learning is incidental to activity done for its own sake. However, interest in activity for the sake of learning should be developed as early as possible; consequently, as children become older, the effective teacher will emphasize the motives of learning more and more and constantly place less stress on the motivation of activity.

Ideals

Throughout this discussion, frequent reference has been made to inner purposes. In the preceding section. an attempt was made to show that man is a creature of purpose, not just a thing of mere mechanical reaction. In common with all animals, man has tendencies to action, comes into situations where action is necessary, and makes reactions to these situations. But man has in addition a characteristic animals do not have, a characteristic that makes him different. He can project ends by which to modify his reactions and make purposive choices in terms of these projected ends.[1] Animal behavior is a chain of three interlocking reactions: a

---

[1] W. W. Charters, **The Teaching of Ideals** (New York: The Macmillan Co., 1928), p. 20   (Used by permission)

stimulus received by a sensory organ results in a current
that travels to the brain, where it follows a preestab-
lished path from sensory center to motor center and
thence passes out along the motor fibers to produce some
particular action. As a consequence, animals are under
the domination of instinctive behavior that they are
powerless to change except within very small limits.

Man receives the stimulus, starting a current that is
carried to the central nervous structures. Here it may
cross from a sensory to a motor center by preestab-
lished paths but it does not necessarily do so. The
human being has consciousness that he is able to use in
terms of its knowledge content, its emotional attitudes,
and its volitions. In terms of these, he thinks, feels,
and formulates ideals, and then chooses the path which
the current will take as it issues in action. Man, far
from being under the domination of blind instincts that
propel him in a mechanical way, is a personality with
the power of formulating ideals as a basis for choosing
to do what he will. The pupil is a spiritual personality
with a thought life that needs knowledge, an affective
life to be directed, and a will to be developed for the
purpose of establishing right ideals of conduct.

Necessity in man for ideals. It is not the nature of
man to be satisfied with merely reacting to the stimuli
of basic urges or even with responding in terms of purposive action when need arises. He is so constituted
that he must have some single ultimate end to which
all other ends are subordinate. Through the centuries
many attempts have been made to state in a single word
or concept the ultimate end of moral conduct, for it is
recognized universally that the true end of human existence is connected somehow with character. But though
moral philosophers have sought diligently, they have
never found a statement that completely satisfies. "The
nebulous ends of action cannot be expressed in terms

of one end, such as pleasure, the greatest good to the greatest number, self-realization, observance of law and custom, or the satisfaction of conscience. The ultimate end is not, or has not yet been, amenable to exact definition. It is probably a composite of the foregoing ends and may perhaps contain elements over and beyond any or all of them." [2]

The Bible states the inclusive ideal. But the Bible, which reveals to man the will of God, the supreme Personality who governs the universe, does what all the thought of man has been unable to do; it states an ultimate end to which all other ends in the conduct of a spiritual personality are subordinate. The ultimate end is the perfect man of God, "throughly furnished unto all good works." This is an objective end, i.e., an end stated for man, not the product of the inner working of his own being. But what is thus stated objectively is what it is because the spirit of man in its activity is ever striving for the attainment of this ultimate of all goals. That is to say, God in revelation gives as an end that which man, the finite being under the dominion of sin, seeks in blindly groping activity to attain.

In the chapter on aims, it was pointed out that an inclusive aim contains within it various minor aims which, once attained, result in the attainment of the final inclusive aim. What is true of the teacher is also true of the pupil: the ultimate aim can be reached only as various subordinate ends are reached. In other words, the activity of pupils moving them in the direction of the ideal, the man of God perfected in good works, must find expression first in seeking one end and then another with a view to final attainment of the inclusive goal of perfection. Thus the final, or ultimate, ideal is made up of many composite ideals.

---

[2] W. W. Charters, op cit., p. 21 (Used by permission)

Man does not live by bread alone. He is a spiritual being who has spiritual incentives that cannot be satisfied in terms of the satisfactions of an organism. Early in the life of the child, while bodily appetites and primary desire are the prevailing motivators of behavior, the beginnings of other than selfish and mechanical motives appear. And even if these are near kin to the first, the two become more and more unlike as the character of the individual develops. The business of Christian teaching is to use these, to nurture them, and to guide them to a full and complete expression in the form of traits of godly character and Christ-like personality. The highest motives of human conduct, then, are to be found in the realm of ideals, which the individual, a spiritual personality, formulates for himself and uses as the determiners of the purposive choices that he makes.

The following statement expresses very well the substance of what it has been the attempt of this section to say: "Man craves more than a knowledge of himself, of nature, and of organized society. He hungers and he thirsts after righteousness. Knowing his own imperfections, he feels that somewhere there is perfection. The great universe calls to his spirit, and unless he ignorantly or wilfully closes his ears, he hears the voice of God. . . . The individual soul reaches out to orient itself in the universe and to find its place of labor and of rest. When this orientation takes place, life assumes poise, dignity, grandeur. Otherwise, its strivings, its struggles, its achievements seem trivial and insignificant. No greater task rests upon the school than to help its pupils to find their God. How this is to be done is the greatest of problems. We cannot solve this problem by ignoring it."

FINAL CONSIDERATIONS ON MOTIVATION

This lengthy discussion has, no doubt, brought the reader to the realization of the truth of a commonly accepted fact: i.e., all forms of human motivation are exceedingly complex. The path from the simple urges of bodily existence to the lofty ideals of Christian living is a long one and it leads through a veritable maze of inextricable impulses, habits, tendencies, desires, attitudes, motives, purposes, and ideals. Not only are motives very complex but they are also exceedingly numerous and beyond possibility of accurate analysis. Much of what any human being does is controlled by unconscious impulses and by motives that are quite indefinite. The subject has been presented in the way it has been with a view to impressing upon the mind of the reader its importance and its difficulty and with the hope that all teachers and prospective teachers who read may be led in practice to use a better basis of motivation of pupils in their teaching.

After all, the fact remains that the teacher must base motivation upon the nature of the learner. In order to do so, he must have an understanding of pupils as individuals and as human beings. "Human nature is so large, life touches life at so many points and words are so elusive." The sources of motives that have been mentioned in this chapter are only a few from a very large number; as stated previously, the sources are very numerous and motives are exceedingly complex. The motivation of learning is a task to challenge the best in any teacher. The realization of the complexity of the task should lead to unremitting effort to master the act more fully in the interests of better teaching. Each and every teaching situation affords the teacher opportunity to get better understanding of pupils as a basis for better motivation.

To learn effectively, the pupil must engage in work that is meaningful to him; it must satisfy needs that he as an individual experiences; it must gratify hunger for learning that he has felt; it must solve problems that he has met in actual life; it must answer questions that his experiences have raised in his mind; it must awake to life ideals that are inoperative; it must touch springs of action resident in a being who has within himself the power of purposive choice to reach goals set by a supreme Personality so that he may realize the end of his own existence as a spiritual personality. Motivation is accomplished when the learner sees sufficient reason for the work he is doing. As soon as he accepts and pursues an ideal, it becomes the strongest possible motive in his life, determining all the efforts he puts forth in seeking to realize it. Without motivation, there can be no definite purpose; with motive, there is impelling purpose to realize present aims.

To the Christian teacher is given the task, the privilege, and the opportunity not only of finding motives that will impel pupils to obtain worthwhile results in their work but also that of cultivating in them an appreciation for and a disposition to choose lofty, uplifting motives of the highest kind, the kind leading to activity that meets the deepest needs of human nature. Any such teacher who has the right attitude toward his work will be quite in harmony with the truth expressed in these words: "The mere merchandizing of information will never seem to him to be his main purpose; the kindling of the will, the enrichment of the emotions, the lighting up of the imagination, the making of students sensitive and eager will seem to him more important than all else."

QUESTIONS AND PROBLEMS

1. Does a person ever think, say, or do anything without a cause?
2. Show the relation between cause and the work of Christian teaching.
3. What are the chief questions that arise in one's mind when he meditates on the reasons for which people do as they do?
4. Emphasize the importance of motivation in the work of teaching.
5. Do you agree with the statement that all learning has its beginning in a feeling of need? Why or why not?
6. Why should a teacher understand the needs of pupils?
7. How are attention, interest, and need related to one another? Illustrate.
8. Consider the teaching worth of the two kinds of interest, showing which is more important and why it is so.
9. Differentiate between purpose and need.
10. Can a teacher do his work without recognition of the bodily appetites and desires of pupils?
11. Name the most important tissue needs of the organism.
12. Justify the inclusion of the desire for activity among the tissue needs.
13. Illustrate how the teacher needs to take into consideration the past learning of a child who comes to school for the first time.
14. Why is teaching more concerned with "Other Primary Desires" than with "Primary Desires Based on Tissue Needs"?
15. Show the relation of each of the primary desires mentioned to the work of the teacher, emphasizing right and wrong use thereof.
16. What other desires can you name that seem to be as primary as those given in this treatise?
17. What is a motive? Does it differ from a purpose?
18. How is motive related to interest?
19. Show the importance of coupling the motive with both activity and learning.
20. Define ideal. How are ideal and motive related?
21. Show the place of ideals in the life of a human being.
22. What is the highest ideal possible to man?

23. Do you think that animals have ideals? Give reasons for your answer.
24. Is anything more basically worthwhile in teaching than the proper motivation of pupils?
25. Summarize in a sentence or two the essentials to adequate and proper motivation of learning.

REFERENCES

Betts, G. H., **Teaching Religion Today** (New York: The Abingdon Press, 1934)

Betts, G. H., and Hawthorne, M. O., **Method in Teaching Religion** (New York: The Abingdon Press, 1925)

Boring, E. G., Langfeld, H. S., Weld, H. P., et al., **Introduction to Psychology** (New York: John Wiley and Sons, Inc., 1939)

Charters, W. W., **The Teaching of Ideals** (New York: the Macmillan Co., 1928)

Dashiell, J. F., **Fundamentals of Objective Psychology** (Boston: Houghton Mifflin Co., 1928)

McLester, F. C., **Our Pupils and How They Learn** (Nashville: Cokesbury Press, 1930)

Moore, M. O., **Senior Method in the Church School** (New York: The Abingdon Press, 1929)

Rice, W. F., **The Psychology of the Christian Life** (Chicago: Blessing Book Stores, Inc., 1937)

Roberts, S. L., **Teaching in The Church School** (Philadelphia: The Judson Press, 1930)

Schmauk, T. E., **How to Teach in Sunday School** (Philadelphia: The United Lutheran Publishing House, 1920)

Smith, R. S., **New Trails for the Christian Teacher** (Philadelphia: The Westminster Press, 1934)

Smither, E. L., **Teaching Primaries in the Church School** (Chicago: Methodist Book Concern, 1930)

Squires, W. A., **Psychological Foundations of Religious Education** (Philadelphia: Westminster Press, 1926)

Thomas, F. W., **Principles and Technique of Teaching** (Boston: Houghton Mifflin Co., 1929)

Young, P. T., **Motivation of Behavior** (New York: John Wiley and Sons, Inc., 1936)

Wilson, H. B., and Wilson, G. M., **The Motivation of School Work** (Boston: Houghton Mifflin Co., 1921)

CHAPTER IX

BUILDING ON PAST EXPERIENCE

THE preceding discussion has developed the thought that learning is a complex process dependent on personal experience gained by the learner as he reacts to situations. It has also emphasized the fact that learning occurs only when the learner is grappling purposefully with some present hindering difficulty. Learning always takes place under the conditions imposed by some situation to which the learner is adjusting with a view to attaining a goal. His adjustive behavior is not mechanical or stereotyped but variable as he endeavors to cope with the many and varied elements in the situation. Among the most important of the conditions imposed by any situation to which the learner is adjusting are those that have meaning to him in terms of his previous experience.

Twofold function of learning a basis for learning and teaching. A complete act of learning always serves a twofold function. In the first place, it meets a present need of the learner. When one learns, some felt inadequacy is removed, some question answered, some problem solved, some strain relieved, some stress eliminated, or some difficulty met successfully. To learn means that one has overcome something, arrived somewhere, and has become something that he was not before he learned.

The second function served by learning is this modification of the learner. Having experienced and met a need, he becomes something that he was not. Being something that he was not, he will meet future situations in a different way. Learning produces a change in the way in which the individual feels, thinks, and acts. One who has learned can feel something, think something, do something that he could not feel, think, or do before the learning took place.

No effective teaching can be done, therefore, without building on the past experience of the pupil, for his past experience influences his present response. All teaching is done in a situation. Obviously, the most manifest elements of a teaching situation are a teacher, a pupil, or pupils, and the materials used or studied. The initial task of the teacher in such a situation is that of so arousing interest as to call forth activity. However, just any activity will not do. The teacher faces the delicate problem of getting aroused the activity that makes for response of the right kind.

The most careful and complete control of the elements of the situation alone will not give the teacher control of pupil responses. Each individual pupil responds to these elements in terms of his previous experiences and the responses that are in his consciousness at the present moment. In a particular situation, the number of possible responses that any pupil may make is very great. Given a hundred pupils in a situation, the elements of which are precisely the same for all, and it is probable that every one of them will respond differently.

Success in teaching depends upon getting the pupil to make responses that are desirable in terms of the objectives of teaching. The teacher must make sure that each pupil interprets words, objects, events, and other elements of the situation in proper ways. To do this, the teacher must understand clearly the past experiences of the pupil and build upon them securely. If the pupil has had the necessary experience, the teacher must connect the new teaching with it. If his experience has not been such as to arouse the proper ideas or feelings, the teacher must provide experiences as a basis for the new teaching.

The teacher must see that the pupil is prepared to use his experience. Not only must the pupil have had real experiences, but he must be prepared to use these. To connect the new teaching with past experience necessitates on the part of the teacher definite and intelligent preparation of the mind of the pupil so that he can bring his past experiences to bear upon the new. It is not sufficient to trust that his readiness may be as good as could be expected under the circumstances. If he has insufficient understanding of the matter at hand, a misunderstanding of it, or an indifference or aversion toward it, his grasp of the new material will be incomplete. The sole means for the interpretation of new experience is the experiences of the past; yet few pupils have so thoroughly made their past experiences a part of themselves as to furnish them with a correct basis for digestion and assimilation of the new. Therefore, the careful teacher will have pupils call up such elements of their past experiences as are suitable in terms of the present demands, subject these to examination, and, when necessary, correct them before leading the pupils into the new learning activity.

Mental set in activities other than teaching. This is a procedure that is understood and used by people in activities other than teaching. What sensible salesman would walk up to a prospective customer and say, "Won't you let me sell you an automobile?" Instead, he is careful to find out all he can about his prospect, his interests and attitudes, his hobbies and his needs, especially his need, real or imaginary, for the product to be sold. Then he provides this item of information, makes that observation, and stresses the other fact which will suggest the feelings and ideas appropriate to arousal of the desired response. The skilful salesman knows that he must make use of the principle of readiness, or set, in getting the individual to want to buy. He knows also that there is not the least doubt but that he will fail to make a sale unless he succeeds in getting a favorable hearing, which is impossible except as the prospective customer is led to respond in terms of his past experiences.

This principle of mind set is constantly recognized in the practical experiences of every-day life. The sensible parent does not take a child to task when he is overwrought emotionally. To give needed guidance and correction, he either waits until the child is in a suitable frame of mind or induces such a frame of mind by suggestion in terms that the child can understand. Even the comparatively young child knows that his parents are much more likely to respond as he wishes to requests and desires if these are presented when the parents are in a good humor. And little children are often quite adept in helping their parents recall previous experiences that will incline them to a more favorable response. Everybody knows that there are times when and circumstances under which it is wholly inexpedient to approach even his most intimate friends about matters unrelated to their present mental set.

The teacher should set all tasks in light of background of pupils. Yet teachers are most prone to ask pupils to engage in activity without considering whether or not they are ready. If children read the Twenty-third Psalm without interpreting it through old and familiar thoughts, they will do so with no enthusiasm for learning because they will not understand it. If pupils full of the zest and hilarity of a play period are required to settle down immediately to the study of the story of the Prodigal Son, they will find it impossible to do so. When pupils are eagerly interested in planning for some social activity, the requirement to memorize Bible verses constitutes an imposition they will resent. A child who is rankling with feelings of unjust treatment by a cruel father is not so likely to respond wholeheartedly to study about the love of God. The boy or the girl who is treated as an outcast by fellow-pupils will find it rather difficult to appreciate the meaning of the Golden Rule. Yet how often do teachers attempt to get their pupils to respond to such activities without having made the least attempt to prepare the pupils for the tasks.

A few concrete illustrations of the result of ignoring the background may serve to emphasize the necessity of adequate preparation of the individual for the reception of new truth. The oft-repeated story of the zealous barber who, while stropping his razor, bluntly asked the lathered customer, "Sir, are you prepared to die?" indicates what may happen to a teacher even though his pupils may not run down the street with soap-covered faces. The pupil in the Sunday-school class who thought that Ananias and Sapphira were cities had rather an inadequate background for understanding either the geography of the Holy Land or the biography of Bible characters. The little boy who understood "the tale of bricks" which the Hebrews were required to make under Pharaoh's oppression to mean that "bricks had tails" would have rather an unusual visual image of the buildings made from those bricks.

The little girl whose mother could not convince her that mice do not talk because her Sunday-school teacher had said that "mice do talk" evidently had not been properly prepared for what the teacher was trying to teach. The person, child or adult, who knows nothing whatever about sheep and the work of the shepherd cannot get a very complete understanding of the meaning of the fifty-third chapter of Isaiah, the twenty-third Psalm, or the tenth chapter of the Gospel of John. The very small child who, when the teacher was trying to convey the ideal of a kind heavenly Father, volunteered the information that "my father often beats my mother," could not very well understand the kindness of a father. The boy or girl who resents going to Sunday school, who dislikes the teacher, or who hates the activities he or she is required to participate in, is not in a frame of mind conducive to learning.

The teacher, like anyone else who wants to get a person to respond in some desired way, must set in motion, as it were, an inner drive based upon the purpose of the pupil in meeting his needs and interests in the work to be done. Neglect of this step is most likely to result in disaster so far as desired learning is concerned. Learning activity can be started only by beginning where the individual is in experience and by getting him ready or set for the work to be done through assisting him to develop interests and purposes that he wants to realize in connection with that work. Next to stimulating activity, the greatest task in teaching is directing activity into appropriate channels of expression. The difference between right and wrong direction is the difference between good and poor teaching, between effective learning and ineffective learning, and between right and wrong individual growth and development.

ORIGIN AND PHASES OF MENTAL SET

Learning is natural and inevitable. It needs to be remembered that learning is a much broader matter than formal teaching; that is, children learn many things apart from what is ordinarily thought of as teaching. In the broadest sense, the process of learning is the process of growth, whereby an immature, undeveloped infant is changed step by step into a perfectly developed, mature adult. Like growth, learning begins with life, and it continues apace as the individual develops. Every contact that the developing individual makes with his surroundings is a factor in his progress toward maturity. Any school merely represents an attempt to organize the child's environment so that his activity may bring fullest return in growth toward the goal of maturity. The only objective that true teaching can have is to help pupils grow to be what they should be. Children will grow and learn without the aid of a teacher; with the aid of a teacher they should grow and learn better and more rapidly.

The attitude of learning does not need to be created in a child; it is there from the beginning of life. Before a teacher ever touches his life, the child learns many things. From birth onward, he lives in an ever-widening environment. During the first few months of life, he engages in few activities because he is limited to the stimuli that come to him from things within the range of his sense organs as he lies in his crib, but his learning even during this period is not insignificant. As he develops, his environment expands in ever-widening circles to include his house, the yard, the children of neighbors, the street, the playground, the community, etc. With constantly expanding environment, activities increase in number and in complexity; so the learning process is well under way when the child comes to the teacher.

Learning is inevitable; a child in possession of anything like normal power learns. Mental sets are also inevitable; they can be prevented no more than learning can. Like learning, they are built up from the multitudinous contacts the individual is making constantly in the great world of experience. The normal child reacts continually, and every learning reaction constitutes a basis for a mental set. A reaction to a situation has three phases, always present under normal conditions. Each of these affects all later reactions of the individual. First, it leaves its impression on the organism and, consequently, there is a tendency to repeat the response when a similar situation is met. Second, each reaction has affective quality, giving the learner a feeling of some kind, usually satisfaction or annoyance. Third, in the consciousness of the learner, meaning is given to the experience as he associates it with other experiences.[1]

Therefore, the child, when he comes to a teacher, has already formed mind sets in terms of his past experiences and learnings. And as he continues to learn under the guidance of the teacher as well as in other ways, he continues to form mind sets. Not only does a child learn before he comes to the teacher, but he also continues to learn many things without the aid of any teaching. Whenever he reacts he learns; whenever he reacts, the three phases of reaction are present.

Learning is at times relatively less active. To understand fully how mental sets are built, it is necessary at this point to indulge in what seems on the surface to be a sort of digression. As might be inferred from several statements in this section, there are two kinds of learning, i.e., that which the individual gains when no attempt is made at teaching him and that which may be the outcome of a definite attempt to get him to learn. That is to say, everyone learns some things he is not trying consciously to learn, and everyone learns some things by dint of conscious effort. In other words, it might be said that learning is sometimes passive and sometimes an active process.

[1] F. W. Thomas, **Principles and Technique of Teaching** (Boston: Houghton Mifflin Co., 1927), p. 37

But is not this last statement a partial denial of the principle of self-activity, which has been stressed as a characteristic of learning? Not at all, for the principle of self-activity is basic to all learning and cannot be set aside. Learning is always gained through personal experience; learning is doing. A human being is neither like a sponge, which absorbs water, nor like clay, which receives passively any impression that is made upon it. Learning is always a response.

What, then is passive learning? It is a term used to refer to the learning that results from a minimum of activity on the part of the learner. Even where appearances indicate an extreme degree of passivity, something may be learned. For instance, children who seem to let information pass in one ear and out of the other, may give evidence later of having learned. In such a case, there was learning activity, for the information actually entered one ear and was perceived; the very process of perception is really an act implying at least a readjustment of the mechanisms of hearing. Therefore, though most effective learning occurs when the learner takes an active part in the learning process, there is passive learning in the sense that the learner is more or less inattentive during the process.

Learning is always taking place. Teaching is most directly interested in the more active forms of learning, but it can never ignore passive learning and its effects. The more active part the learner takes in the learning process, the more effective is his learning. But every individual, whether he is subjected to teaching or not, is constantly learning many things in the more passive way. And, as indicated heretofore, all learning is accompanied by mind set of one kind or another which must always be taken into consideration when new teaching is begun.

Mental sets built in two ways. It should now be evident that mental sets are built in two ways: through the passive influence exerted upon the individual by the environment in which he lives, and by the active, purposeful reactions that he makes to the experiences of life. The attitude and the example of people among whom one lives exert potent influence over him. Racial attitudes, political prejudices, social customs, and religious beliefs are largely an outcome of the subtle effect of the environment of early years. Thus, one may like or dislike negroes, be Republican or Democratic in sympathy, or adhere to Baptist or Presbyterian interpretations, depending upon the moulding power of environmental forces under which he was reared. Mind sets thus determined are not a passing thing; quite to the contrary, they constitute most firmly rooted forms of adjustment in the lives of people even in their early years.

Mind sets of a more active kind are developed as a by-product of an individual's conscious and purposeful reactions. One's environment constantly impinges upon him, and the human being is so constituted that he ever seeks to deal with those aspects of it that he can subject to any kind of control. Inevitably he develops mental sets as he thus seeks control of his environment. These sets may be healthful or unwholesome, depending on the kind of reaction. Right mental sets cannot come about from wrong reacting and, just as surely, right mental set results from right reacting. Whichever mind set is developed, the fact remains that it develops in terms of definite experiences such as reading, reasoning, yielding to companions whom one admires and whose viewpoints he chooses to follow, or some other active, purposeful experience.

Herein lies the great opportunity of the teacher, viz., to nurture in learners the right kind of mind set. It is most easy to make the false assumption that the learning of assigned lessons, the performance of certain set tasks, and the mastering of a certain minimum of knowledge and skill is the measure of success in teaching. The truth is that if a teacher has succeeded in getting his pupils to do no more than this, he has not accomplished anything worthwhile. The real value of teaching consists in the type of human being that is produced. It is not enough that a pupil be able to repeat the names of the books of the Bible, that he know where Jesus was born, or that he be able to locate Palestine. These acquisitions are important, but they are not by any means all-important.

Far more important is it that the pupil learn to think properly and that he develop sound points of view, right attitudes, convictions, and ideals. The great function of teaching, along with the inculcation of knowledge and training in skill, is to ascertain what desirable attitudes and mind sets pupils should have and then so to manipulate the whole learning situation that these will not fail to become realities in their experience.

Effective teaching always deals with mental sets, old and new. But, to return to the point of digression, no teaching can be effective except as it starts with mind sets already formed and takes recognition constantly of new ones as they develop either in connection with or apart from the teaching. To repeat what was said previously, every learning reaction has three phases always present to a greater or less degree: impression with tendency to repetition of the response, an affective element of satisfaction or annoyance, and meaning arising through association of the experience with other experiences. Corresponding to these are three phases of set: motor, feeling, and mental or ideational. All three of these phases have great importance for the teacher. Neglect of any one of them may greatly affect the quality of the learning. While the discussion here takes each separately, the best teaching often merges all three as a background for beginning.

1. The Motor Phase of Preparation

It is a matter of common everyday observation that any act once performed successfully tends to be repeated when a similar situation occurs. Most habits would never come into being were it not for this tendency. Habit simply means that an act has been performed a sufficient number of times to cause its effects to become embodied in the nervous structure. An old story serves as an illustration. A practical joker, seeing a veteran carrying home his dinner, suddenly called out, "Attention!" The man instantly brought his hands down and lost his dinner in the gutter. He responded as he did because his nervous system was set for that particular response when the appropriate stimulus was given. What is true of habit in an intensified way is true of the single act to less degree because every habit begins with a single act that carries with its performance the tendency to repetition.

Everyone has observed in animals and man, motor sets that are preparatory to some specific action. The cat crouching to spring upon the mouse, the dog cocking up its ears when it hears a sound, the runner maintaining an alert posture while awaiting the signal to start, are ready for action. In each case the entire body is quite obviously set, but there must also be set in the nervous system. The environmental stimulation exerts some control over the set but it is partially dependent upon inner stimulation. The total attitude, regulated both by outer and inner stimulus conditions, helps, in turn, to regulate the course of behavior by predisposing the organism to react in a specific way.

What the teacher must always be concerned with is

a living organism. Teaching cannot be done by dealing with a mind only, nor with a body plus a mind. It has always to do with an individual who is body and mind. Behavior is constantly limited, and, to some degree, determined by the bodily structure of the individual. If children left their bodies at home when they came to be taught, the work of the teacher would be far easier but, since they cannot do this, the intelligent teacher will recognize each pupil as a single living organism that functions in physical and in mental ways. Teaching can no more ignore the physical than it can concentrate its activity upon the mental. Both aspects of behavior are constantly present in inseparable relationship. Sometimes the one and sometimes the other is in predominance but never to the exclusion of either the one or the other.

Any motor set, then, has its mental accompaniments and the skilful teacher will seek to utilize all phases together. However, there are times when it is expedient to use the motor phases of preparation in a more definite way than at other times. For example, in getting the attention of pupils, it is often helpful to have them assume the physical posture of attention. The phrase "concentrated attention" signifies a motor set relative to a particular task. An attentive pupil is definitely predisposed toward some activity while the inattentive one lacks a definite goal. Obviously, the motor set of attention does not mean that attentive activity is, or will be, an actuality, but it can be a great help in getting attention. It is very certain, on the other hand, that a teacher who sets an exercise demanding attentive activity suddenly into the midst of a group of pupils who are engaged in all kinds of physical contortions will not get their attention readily.

Again, in drill work used for the purpose of developing habits and skills, it is most necessary that the pupils have both mental and motor images before they are required to begin practice. Without clear and correct images to guide efforts, wrong ways of doing will be the inevitable result. Merely telling or showing a pupil what to do is insufficient. The teacher must see that each pupil secures the correct guiding image through his own activity and in terms of his own experience. Mental images may be visual or auditory; both play an important part in learning activities. But the motor image is another kind that is of extremely great importance in guiding correct practice. Without the muscular "feel" of the activity he is asked to undertake, a pupil can make very little progress in practice.

Success in teaching handwork, in guiding pupils in the pronunciation of words, in the memorization of Scripture, or in any other teaching for the development of habits and skills, is dependent upon the ability of the teacher to help the pupil get the necessary motor image of each process. Whatever the teacher does by way of telling, showing, and criticizing, and whatever the pupil does in practicing, will avail little if he does not have adequate motor set in terms of the initial image. On the other hand, progress is made quite rapidly by the pupil who has the "feel" of some difficult activity. Of course, a pupil may find telling and showing helpful in enabling him to get the motor image, but the latter is essential as a basis for getting a start for his own motor learning. It should be noted also that, as practice proceeds, motor images tend to be lost, and attention is given more and more to the visible or the audible results of activity.

2. THE MENTAL OR IDEATIONAL PHASE OF PREPARATION

Any human being's ideas are built up through many experiences. During the first years of life, the child

sees, handles, tastes, smells, hears, and thus receives
his first impressions. Through direct contact with individual things, he begins to acquire knowledge. He also
perceives individual events and relationships from which
he receives other impressions. The senses furnish the
elements of all that can ever be in the mental life; it is
only through individual notions, or percepts, that concepts and ideas can be reached. Percepts obtained
through direct contact with things, events, and relationships do not, then, constitute the whole of knowledge,
but they are the foundation upon which knowledge
rests, or to use a better figure, they are the raw material
out of which ideas are produced.

The physical world of all children is essentially the
same, but the reactions they make to its stimuli are
different, corresponding to differences in the sense organs. Identical events do not happen to any two children, even to those of the same family. Furthermore,
because children differ one from another, they do not
perceive relationships in the same way. For these
reasons the experiences of children are not alike and,
consequently, the ideas generated from these experiences
differ greatly from individual to individual.

Furthermore, while learning by direct experience
continues throughout life, most persons are so careless
and superficial in their observations as to make this
kind of learning quite ineffective. It is the mission
of teaching to supplement such experience with a view
to more correct observation and better learning. Obviously, it is impossible for the teacher to bring into
the direct experience of pupils many objects with which
instruction must deal. Objects distant in place and in
time that need to be presented definitely to the mind
cannot, in the nature of circumstances, be presented to
the senses. The teacher does well to make use of pictures, drawings, diagrams, sketches, object lessons,

demonstrations, models, and other means of graphic representation that serve to give correct notions of individual things or events. Manifestly, however, learning that deals with objects not present to the senses makes for at least as great variety in experiences among people as does learning by direct contact with things and events.

The first cause of differences in the experiences of individuals is, therefore, found in the variations in the products of sense-perception, the original raw material of knowledge and ideas. A second and just as troublesome source is the words by means of which ideas are expressed. Words have no meaning in and of themselves; they are nothing more than arbitrary symbols of ideas. No word means the same, in an absolute sense, to any two people. Even a common word like "dog" stands for two different sets of ideas in the minds of two individuals, and the two sets may be very much unlike each other. "Any word merely reflects the results of the self-activity of the individual in the light of the experiences which have been associated with that term." For example, let the reader notice the idea or mental response aroused in his own mind by the word "bill" and then imagine the different mental interpretations that would probably be aroused by the same word in the mind of each of the following persons: a bank teller, an advertising man, a freight agent, a legislator, a householder harassed by obligations he cannot meet.

Even for the same person, a word has different meanings under different circumstances, and his choice of a particular one will depend on his mental set at the time. Consider the significance of the word "nail" in various associative connections such as manicuring, carpentering, cobbling, speech-making. So the words that an individual sees or hears may mean little or nothing to him, or they may suggest a wrong idea or one quite

unlike that intended by the speaker or writer. Of themselves they have no power for recalling past experiences
or conveying new knowledge. Quite to the contrary,
they may most definitely hinder new learning. A certain writer has used an expression, "the tyranny of
words," to express the thought of what they may or
may not do.

The most troublesome matter connected with the
use of words in teaching is not misinterpretations tha
are markedly unsuitable, for these can very readily be
corrected. If, for example, a pupil pronounces the name
of the place where our Savior was crucified, "Cavalry,"
the teacher can readily detect the cause and correct the
misinterpretation. But often less manifest errors of
interpretation go undetected and uncorrected to prepare
in turn for more fundamental misconceptions later.
Only as the teacher by much foresight and care guides
the pupil into clear understanding of terms and into a
mental set conducive to a correct interpretation can the
foundation for effective learning be laid.

To comprehend any new knowledge, the pupil must
have ideas that are closely related thereto. This means
that he must have had experiences of similar nature,
for whatever ideas anyone has have been built up from
experience. The country child in the city or the city
child in the country, at a loss to understand much that
he sees for the first time, makes incorrect interpretations thereof because he sees in terms of his past experiences. The average American child reading or hearing for the first time about Oriental people going out
on the house-top will wonder why they do not fall off
because he has had experience only with houses that
have inclined roofs. A pupil who thinks that modern
electric fixtures are the only source of artificial light
will be unable to understand the Parable of the Ten

Virgins. Without a certain class of experiences, no one can interpret ideas belonging to that class.

The fact that pupils remember words they have learned from the teacher or from books and can repeat them glibly is no proof of knowledge. Many teachers are deceived, believing that their pupils have acquired knowledge when, in fact, it is only the symbols for ideas and not the ideas themselves that the pupils have mastered. As previously iterated, words are wholly without power except as they have meaning in terms of experiences; a word is nothing more than a symbol by which experiences are called to mind.

The first step in bringing new knowledge to a pupil is, then, to ascertain if he has ideas in terms of past experiences closely enough related to the new to enable him to understand it. In short, there must be a point of contact between the new and the old. The mind is so constituted that it cannot take in the new except as this is related to past experiences; only as there are in the mind ideas built up from experience can anything new be received and comprehended. Things begin to carry meaning as soon as they begin to come within the range of the knowledge and interests of the pupil. It must be remembered, however, that if new knowledge is to be comprehended at all fully, the relationship between the new and the old needs to be very close.

To direct learning aright, the teacher must not only see that the pupil has an adequate basis in terms of related experiences and ideas but he must also make sure that he is fully conscious of the close connection between the old and the new. If the pupil does not know that such relationship exists, it is to him as if it did not exist even though the connection be close and real. Instead of being passive, the mind is very active and, when something new is presented, active effort is made to test that thing in terms of past experience

Whatever seems foreign is ignored while whatever appears closely related is received. Hence, it is essential that the teacher direct attention to the relationship between the old and the new, for only as the pupil becomes fully conscious that there is a close connection will he welcome that which is offered and learn from the presentation.

3. The Feeling Phase of Preparation

Mental set and preparation have to do as much with feeling as with the motor and the mental. In fact, since feeling is deep and strong in all that any human being does and thinks, the feeling phase exerts even greater influence than these two upon the character of the responses made to situations. In all learning, purposeful activity on the part of the learner is the prime essential. Purposeful activity is always performed with a view to the achievement of some chosen end or goal. As the pupil seeks purposefully to attain his goal, he finds it necessary to make repeated efforts with the feeling that the particular object or thing sought possesses value justifying the effort required for its attainment or performance. Without the feeling that there is something to gain, the individual will not long engage in effective activity.

To prepare the pupil for learning, the teacher must, therefore, so set the situation that definite purpose is felt. If a pupil approaches new material with indifference or aversion, he will develop an attitude of mind unappreciative of, or even hostile to, the material. On the other hand, if he meets the new material with a strong purpose to attain some definite goal, he will have a mental set most favorable to appreciation and effective learning because he will devote active attention to elements meaningful to him in terms of his objective. For example, the pupil who memorizes the

Beatitudes because he wants to have available at any moment a summary of the characteristics of the people whom God favors will accomplish his task much better than will the pupil who memorizes the Beatitudes as a set task that he detests. Furthermore, the first pupil will have some appreciation of the meaning of the content memorized while the latter will, in all probability, be quite void of such appreciation.

Purpose to learn is the key to the interest and effort of the pupil and the effectiveness of what he learns. Anyone who visits a class and sees the pupils conversing with each other in whispers, idly gazing around, or attending with stiff, strained attention under compulsion while the teacher vainly tries to get them to manifest active interest in lessons from the Bible knows at once that these lessons are not connected with the purpose of the pupils. So long as what the teacher is trying to teach is without significance and value to the pupil in terms of some one or more of his fundamental interests, no amount of pressure by the teacher will make for deep and permanent learning results.

On the other hand, a teacher who gives such skilful preliminary guidance as will lead to discovery on the part of the pupil that there is a real and vital connection between the materials of learning and his own fundamental interest or interests lays a foundation for meaning and an appealing aim. A visitor to a class taught by this kind of teacher will find the pupils listening eagerly, discussing, working, and searching for elements to help them realize their purpose. Because they are responsive toward and attentive to the task, their learning will be effective and permanent, for there is a real connection between their interests and the material of the recitation. Without this connection, there can be no purpose and, without purpose, there can be no effective learning.

From a more general point of view also, the teacher does well to consider the background of feeling. Any person's mood is an important factor in determining the direction of his interest and activity at a particular moment. The child recognizes this in dealing with his parents; he will refrain from asking favors that he thinks might not be granted until he judges the parent to be in a proper mood or, before making the request, he will endeavor to arouse the mood he believes to be the most favorable. The business man appreciates these moods; he knows that it is not wise to take up an important matter until his customer is in a mood that will predispose him to respond in the manner desired. Surely the teacher does well to take note of the affective predisposition of pupils which, though it may not always be pronounced, is a phase of mind set that plays some part in the determination of the response to every situation. The coloring it gives the response definitely helps or hinders in the building of desirable appreciations and attitudes.

Therefore, to prepare the pupil for learning, the teacher must induce the right feeling tone before engaging in the learning activity. No one can interpret and appreciate new feelings except in terms of old feelings. The mind goes from the known to the unknown here just as it does in the realm of ideas. True teaching necessitates constant planning to provide for the most favorable mind set preparatory to any contemplated learning activity. The right mood must either be caught or induced before the pupil is required to react to the new situation and material. The pupil's sympathy with content taught is absolutely essential to success in teaching.

A fairly good understanding of what is taught avails little if the pupil does not also have a feeling of appreciation for what he learns. Too frequently, teachers

seem to assume that possession and appreciation of
knowledge are one and the same. Pupils may know
much Bible and be quite irreligious. The possession of
few or many Bible facts, even very complete understanding of the Bible, counts for little or nothing if
such facts and understanding are obtained under conditions that cause the pupil to feel indifferent toward or
aversion for the Bible. To make truth most truly effective in the lives of their pupils, teachers of the Bible
need to induce in their pupils the attitude and the appreciation of the Psalmist, which prompted him to utter
the words, "O how love I thy law!" (Ps. 119:97).

PRACTICAL APPLICATIONS

Since building on the past experience of pupils is
of extremely great importance in teaching, it may be
well to refer in conclusion to a few considerations
of a definitely practical nature. Though these are quite
obvious, they are very frequently ignored in the actual
work of teaching.

First of all, teaching must be carried on in terms of
the understanding of the pupil. The instruction given
must be on the level of the learner. The teacher needs
to use language the pupil can understand and must deal
with content comprehensible to the pupil in terms of
his first-hand experiences. One of the most frequent
faults of teachers is that of "talking over the heads"
of their pupils. It is most easy for a teacher to become
so absorbed in his own thoughts and their formulation
in terms satisfactory to himself that he becomes quite
obvious as to whether or not the pupils are following
understandingly. It is of far greater consequence that
the activity be carried out on the level of the pupil's
understanding than that it should proceed in terms of
teacher-activity. Unless it is, the teaching will be fruitless because not comprehended and, what may be of

even greater consequence, perplexity and indifference on the part of the pupils will be the result.

Very much teaching of the Bible is a matter of handing over experiences of someone else, which means nothing to pupils, because there is no background for it in their own experience. Many of the experiences of Bible characters are so unrelated to those of pupils that they are without reality except as they are brought within the range of pupil experience. Only as the teacher follows the needs of the pupil and discovers in Bible stories spiritual values like pupil experiences will these stories take on meaning comprehensible to the pupil and useful to him.

For the accomplishment of its inclusive aim, Christian teaching must ever make use of this principle of utilization of past experience as a foundation for the building of new experience. The man of God perfected and thoroughly furnished for all good works is the outcome, first, of a sinner's being brought in his own experience to a realization of the need of a Savior who, when presented and accepted, meets that need. Then as teaching and learning about God and His ways continue, this regenerated soul is built up in Christ on the basis of the initial experience of having received Him as well as of succeeding levels of onward moving experiences from each of which further learning and growth result. The teacher who is guiding this growth and learning needs to exercise care to present that which can be digested and assimilated by the growing soul. To give strong meat to one who is able to bear milk only will not, to say the least, produce desirable results, and it may have most undesirable consequences. (I Cor. 3:2; Heb. 5:14.)

Another consideration of importance is that of the necessity of making instruction just as concrete and graphic as possible. The ability to think abstractly is a very difficult accomplishment. Children and youth, lacking the mastery of language and the fulness of imagery given by experience, are especially handicapped in understanding abstract ideas. Most of the thinking of human beings is carried on with the aid of mental imagery to give meaning and color to the idea. As a general rule, good teaching is characterized by the use of much illustrative material rather than by dependence on words as a means of relating the new to the known. There are two main forms of aid to the clarification of thought. The first includes materials that the pupil may see, feel, and manipulate; such things as sand-tables, objects, demonstrations, projects, activities, pictures, maps, charts, and diagrams, constitute very concrete materials or activities.

A second type of illustrative material is that of word symbolism. Stories, anecdotes, descriptions, and word pictures that introduce the learner to first-hand experiences may serve to provide the mental imagery necessary to understanding of the abstract idea. He who would teach successfully does well to make constant use of illustrative material. By means of it, he can attract attention, make experience living and real, facilitate understanding, stimulate imagination, and incite to action. The wise teacher will always be on the lookout for examples and illustrations and will be prepared at each point to choose from several as the occasion may justify for the purpose of building on the past experience of pupils in the most effective manner.[2]

---

[2] The Christian teacher will find excellent suggestions for the use of the illustration in teaching in the following treatise: Mathewson, L. B., **The Illustration**, New York, Fleming H. Revell Co., 1936.

QUESTIONS AND PROBLEMS

1. What is a situation? A learning situation?
2. How is the twofold function that learning serves related to the subject of this chapter?
3. Show how teacher control of the elements of a learning situation may not avail in getting proper response on the part of a pupil.
4. Does it follow that a pupil who has had the necessary background in experience will learn? Why or why not?
5. Give further illustrations from practical life of the importance of mental set.
6. Illustrate from your own experience and observation how necessary proper mental set is for effective teaching.
7. Show that learning is natural.
8. Illustrate how a child learns apart from all teaching.
9. Do you think that mental growth and learning are one and the same thing?
10. Prove that a normal person cannot live without learning.
11. Illustrate mental set in children who have never yet been subjected to the influence of a school.
12. Is learning ever a passive matter? Explain.
13. Which of the two kinds of mind set do you think is most potent in a person's life?
14. Is it possible to teach without any thought of the mental set of pupils?
15. Show how the motor phase of mental set may be used to advantage in the work of teaching.
16. Why do people in the same environment not respond in the same way?
17. Why is it that people learn so little from ordinary everyday experience?
18. Show how words may hinder learning activity.
19. What is meant by "a point of contact"?
20. Emphasize the essential importance of the teacher's recognizing the feeling phase of preparation.
21. How would you undertake the task of preparing pupils in their feeling for the teaching of a lesson?
22. In the light of the content of this chapter, explain the meaning of the statement, "There is no new thing."
23. How can Bible facts and Bible truths be brought within the range of the experience of children?

24. Indicate the value of making instruction as concrete and as graphic as possible.
25. Show how Jesus in His teaching built on the past experience of those whom He taught.

REFERENCES

Adams, John, Exposition and Illustration in Teaching (New York: The Macmillan Co., 1910)

Garrison, N. L., The Technique and Administration of Teaching (New York: American Book Co., 1933)

Horne, H. H., Jesus—The Master Teacher (New York: The Association Press, 1920)

Kuist, H. T., The Pedagogy of St. Paul (New York: George H. Doran Co., 1925)

Mathewson, L. B., The Illustration (New York: Fleming H. Revell Co., 1936)

McCallum, E. B., Guiding Nursery Children in Home and Church (St. Louis: The Bethany Press, 1934)

McCoy, C. F., The Art of Jesus as a Teacher (Philadelphia: The Judson Press, 1930)

McLester, F. C., Our Pupils and How They Learn (Nashville: Cokesbury Press, 1930)

Myers, A. J. W., Teaching Religion Creatively (New York: Fleming H. Revell Co., 1932)

Reagan, G. W., Fundamentals of Teaching (Chicago: Scott, Foresman and Co., 1932)

Richardson, N. E., The Christ of the Classroom (New York: The Macmillan Co., 1931)

Roberts, S. L., Teaching in The Church School (Philadelphia: The Judson Press, 1930)

Shields, E. M., Guiding Kindergarten Children in the Church School (Richmond: The Onward Press, 1939)

Smith, R. S., New Trails for the Christian Teacher (Philadelphia: The Westminster Press, 1934)

Smither, E. L., The Use of the Bible with Children (Chicago: Methodist Book Concern, 1937)

Squires, W. A., The Pedagogy of Jesus in the Twilight of Today (New York: George H. Doran Co., 1927)

Thomas, F. W., Principles and Technique of Teaching (Boston: Houghton Mifflin Co., 1927)

Vieth, P. H., Teaching for Christian Living (St. Louis: The Bethany Press, 1929)

CHAPTER X

METHOD IN TEACHING

TEACHING is a very complex undertaking. Someone
has said that it is "the most complex, intricate, and
subtle of human enterprises." While this is true of all
teaching, it applies with even greater force to the teaching of Christian truth than it does to any other teaching
because the Christian teacher has immeasurably finer
and more lasting work to do than has any other teacher.
His work is that of so directing and guiding the experience of pupils that the grace of God may operate
in their lives to bring them from death to life, to build
them up in Christ, and to send them out as workers for
God. The teaching of Christian truth cannot, then, be
done according to any rigid set of rules.

Notwithstanding, Christian teaching must follow very
definite principles. The laws of mind are as fixed as
any other laws are, and the child, in his spiritual growth
and development, uses and is dependent basically upon
the same mental processes that apply to education in
other lines. Though this be true, the teaching of Christian truth does not imply the substitution of natural
law and educational devices for the working of God in
the life. God exists as a reality; no amount of teaching
avails apart from the operation of the Holy Spirit in
the heart and life of the one taught. But the teaching of

Christian truth, like all other teaching, must be based on the same definite principles and laws as are operative in all the mental processes of human beings. Christian teaching, far from undertaking to eliminate God, is so dependent upon Him as to realize that it has no potency whatever except as He works. It seeks always to be so in harmony with the natural laws that He has made as to make it possible for Him to work as He will. Its major concern is the effective presentation of the truth of the Word so that the Spirit may be able to work.

The purpose of this treatise up to this point has been to present clearly the leading principles of learning and teaching. Thus, attention has been called to the importance of clear perception of aims, the necessity for an understanding of pupils, their needs, their interests, their way of learning, their motivation, the necessity for building on their past experience, etc. But after the teacher has understanding of these matters, he must decide just how he will proceed. In an actual teaching-learning situation, some course of procedure must be followed in order to realize the aims perceived and to capitalize on the understanding attained in order to bring about the desired results. What medium will best serve his purpose? Clearly, choice must be made among some specific methods.

THE PROBLEM OF METHOD

Teaching is an art based on very definite principles. As is often emphasized, teaching presupposes three basic factors: the pupil, an immature, undeveloped being; the subject matter or content taught, a body of potential, new experience by means of which this being may be brought from his original state to one of full and mature development; and the teacher, who will stimulate and guide the pupil in his experiences as he appropriates and utilizes the subject-matter during his passage from the one state to the other. Whatever may exist by way of school plant, equipment and supplies, courses of study, and programs of activity, has its justification only as it serves to bring pupils, materials, and teacher into such relations as will make effective development of the pupil an actuality. In the final analysis, it is only as the art of teaching is perfected in terms of the principles inherent in the development of life that teaching accomplishes anything worth while.

To the efficient teacher, desirable changes in the lives of the pupils are the goals. The art of good teaching consists in using all available means and tools effectively and not becoming enslaved by the tools themselves. One who observes a teacher at work sees that there are numerous things to do while teaching. Skill in doing each thing is important, but the power most needed in teaching is the ability to see quickly the elements of each learning situation and to decide properly and accurately what ought to be done in each connection. This necessitates thinking. Effective teaching is never a mere mechanical matter; it involves ability to solve problems quickly and yet with due consideration of all the facts. For such thinking, a background of knowledge of the various methods of teaching is necessary.

Good teaching is characterized by the use of the method that is best for the attainment of the specific goal in mind. There can be no teaching without some kind of method. The method used may be the wrong one, but it is a method nevertheless. The better the method used, the better the teaching will be. Since no two teaching situations are ever identical, and since it is impossible to forecast exactly what will happen in any true teaching process, there are a variety of methods based upon the definite principles that underlie the learning process. Teaching is a matter of bringing pupils and subject matter together, of making a connection between new experience awaiting the learner and the pupil who is to do the learning. Teaching is effective to the degree that proper connection is made, and the choice of method is a most important factor in determining the kind of connection. The method used, like the subject matter, is a means to an end, never an end in itself.

It follows, then, that method is not merely a device to be employed by teachers in making the subject-matter or content of teaching the content of the child's mind. The child is a self-acting being who, in order to learn, must be in a stimulating and guiding environment that meets the needs of his self-activity. Method is without meaning or value except as it serves as a means for accomplishing the purpose for which it is called into use. Good method in teaching implies the use of material in an orderly and effective way to produce certain desired growth and development in the life of the pupil as a consequence of his being stimulated and guided in the making of proper responses. In teaching, as in everything else, he who accomplishes the best results in the best way is he who uses the best method. But always the product rather than the method by which it is produced is the thing of greatest importance.

"Method is a utilization of activity and materials, and not something set up separate and distinct from them, all of these being utilized so that the pupil's experience may develop toward Christian ends. It is, in other words, arranging opportunities for learning."[1] Method always has double reference: to the learner on the one hand and to the materials on the other hand. It is but a way in which the teacher uses materials to accomplish a

---

[1] The International Curriculum Guide, Book One: Principles and Objections of Christian Education (Chicago: The International Council of Religious Education, 1935), p. 21

desired purpose in the life of the pupil; it is determined, on the one hand, by the requirements of the learner, and, on the other hand, by the requirements of the materials. The teacher who sees clearly the purpose of his work will never allow method to assume a place of first importance, for he will see it only as a servant to that purpose. Such an one will never be tempted to substitute clever devices for that which is of vital importance.

"Method consists in bringing about those conditions under which enrichment and control of experience can best take place."[2] The constant question of the efficient teacher is: How can this particular material best be used to accomplish its purpose with this particular pupil or class? This teacher's concern is not about any specific method as such but with the arrangement of opportunities and conditions that make for growth. That which the teacher should have as a consuming ideal is the growth and development of his pupils in spiritual life and power. When he has this, method will take its proper place in thought and practice. The one great test of best method is in the answer to the question: Does this way of using materials make for conditions under which the life of God in the soul grows more and more? Since teaching is so complex and so variable from one situation to another, no one method is best in all cases. There is, however, a best way of arranging opportunities for learning under the conditions present at the time the teaching is done. The really efficient teacher selects this best way and uses it skilfully.

FACTORS TO BE CONSIDERED IN SELECTING METHOD

From the preceding discussion, it is evident that method is the use the teacher makes of materials to

---

[2] The International Curriculum Guide, *op. cit.*, p. 21

arouse the pupil to activity and to give him guidance as he works with these materials so that learning, with consequent growth and development, may take place. The operation of any method depends on the total situation in which it functions. The teacher, the pupil, the subject matter, the method, and the total situation form one unitary whole. The method is far from tangible. Any particular method, such as a story, a lecture, or a discussion, will have different outcomes in different total learning situations. The story may be effective or ineffective, depending on the nature of the aim and the attitude of the pupils. The lecture method may be good or bad, depending on the teacher's presentation and on the nature of the content given. An excursion may succeed or fail, depending on the interests of the pupils and the management of the teacher. The value of any method depends on the extent to which it is adapted to the requirements of the total situation.

All methods are not equally good for all situations. There is no "best" method for all settings. It is impossible to say that any particular method is always superior to any other. Any good teacher will probably use several methods during the course of a class period, changing from one to another and using them in various combinations as the demands of the total situation change from moment to moment. The teacher will likely do this without consciousness of the fact that he is using any particular method because his interest and attention will be centered upon the realization of his objectives. However, the conscious and intelligent selection, use, and adaptation of tested methods is a means for increasing the effectiveness of teaching. While no one can always be certain concerning what method to use, the following are some factors that will serve to guide the teacher in the conscious selection and use of the best method.

1. *The nature of the aim.* If the aim is to develop skill, the method of practice must be used, for skill comes through practice. If the teacher's aim is to increase the knowledge of pupils, the method of problem-solving should be chosen. The teacher should never aim at mere impartation but at such mastery of knowledge as will develop ability to use and apply this knowledge in appropriate situations. Mere telling and fact-learning provide only for the first of these while the problem-solving technique makes for mastery. A thought-provoking question asked by the teacher is a good form of problem-solving as may also be a good, lively discussion by the class. If the aim is to develop appreciations and attitudes, then methods of setting before pupils the emotional experiences leading to the desired outcomes must be used. Story, picture, music, drama, or worship may serve as a medium for the appeal of the beautiful or the good or the true. An aim that is so closely related to the pupils' present life and activity that they are eager to learn will demand a different procedure in teaching from that necessary if the pupils see no purpose in the learning. Method must be selected in terms of the final inclusive goal as well as in terms of the more immediate goals, though the latter have most bearing on the choice of specific methods. The teacher should ever be checking up on what has already been accomplished and adapting method and procedure with a clear perception of the objectives that still lie ahead.

2. *The maturity of the pupils.* Obviously the story method is the most suitable method to use in teaching small children, while with young people the discussion method may be most effective. Commonly used methods of teaching adults are the lecture method, the research method, question-and-answer, discussion, and the project method. But maturity is not a matter of age level only;

often there are varying degrees of maturity in pupils of the same age. Adaptation of method should be made in terms of the capacities and interests of the pupils and other demands of the situation. If they will ask and answer questions and join in discussion, they may well be permitted to do so. On the other hand, if they will do no more than sit and listen, it would be unwise to try to teach by use of question or discussion. "It is futile to undertake a plan of teaching, however attractive or effective, that is beyond the present development of the class, or that is foreign to their interests."[3]

3. *Attitude of pupils toward the learning.* The teacher needs to be very sensitive to pupils' attitudes and to select methods accordingly. Pupils who are bored and uninterested must be handled in quite a different manner from that which would be appropriate in a class of alert, interested pupils. A pupil who is eager to work can engage in some piece of research or carry on some project, while such a method will only result in failure when used with a pupil who has the attitude of getting by with the least possible expenditure of energy. If an attitude of antagonism toward the work prevails, something must be done to break it down before any real learning can take place. Sometimes pupils in Bible classes are hostile to all Christian truth. When such is the case, some method must be used to eliminate this hostility. If the pupil has an unfavorable attitude toward the teacher or one of antagonism toward teachers in general, this must be taken into account.

4. *Previous study in the same field.* A boy or girl, a man or woman, who has been in regular attendance at Sunday school for a number of years and who has a good grasp of Bible knowledge, needs to be taught by

[3] G. S. Dobbins, **How to Teach Young People and Adults in the Sunday School** (Nashville: Sunday School Board of the Southern Baptist Convention, 1930), p. 103

a different method from that which would bring best results when used with pupils who know little or nothing about the Bible. Pupils do not learn except as their powers are challenged in some way; so a special project of some kind, such as a research investigation, a special report, or a problem may be appropriately used in the more advanced classes. Problem-discussions may also be used to good advantage with pupils who have done much work in a particular field. Debates have possibilities for pupils who have a good background of knowledge. A particular pupil who has had exceptional advantages in some field of special interest should not be dealt with in the same manner as those pupils who have had no opportunity to do work in that field. An alert teacher will be quick to use, in some way productive of good to all members of the class, the benefits of the special study or the exceptional advantages of an individual pupil. By so doing, he will lead the pupil as well as the other members of the class to higher attainments.

5. *Nature of the material.* It is very necessary that the teacher study carefully the content to be taught before selecting the method of teaching. A method that is excellent for use with one kind of material may be quite ineffective when used with some other type. Incidents from the lives of well-known Bible characters are usually best presented in the form of a story. An unfamiliar Bible passage might well be made clear by a lecture or extended comment, while a very familiar passage may constitute a point of departure for extensive and helpful discussion. Problems may often be analyzed by means of the discussion method. Sometimes the use of assigned readings and supervised study may serve to make problems clear to learners. Some Bible passages open up debatable questions, thus lending themselves to effective presentation by means of argument.

Some Biblical materials lend themselves readily to the use of the dramatic form of presentation, while other content is not at all adaptable to this method.

6. *Physical equipment and facilities.* Christian teaching must often be done under very definite limitations in respect to buildings, separate classrooms, blackboards, supplies, etc. Obviously, these have bearing on method. For instance, in a situation where several classes must meet in the same room, general discussion might be impossible. Where there are no blackboards, chalk talks and illustrations cannot be used. Map exercises cannot be carried on if maps are not available. Little can be done along the line of supervised study if dictionaries, concordances, and other helps are lacking, though the fact that Bibles are present will make for great possibilities of varied methods. An effective teacher will be resourceful in making the best of whatever facilities are available and will, at the same time, do his utmost to secure conditions favorable to improvement in method.

7. *Time for teaching.* Not only do most Christian teachers do their work under the limitations of physical equipment and facilities but also under the limitations of time. The Bible teacher has a small part of the children for a few minutes each week, while the teacher of secular subjects has them for hours. It behooves the former, therefore, to make the very best use of the short time that he has to teach the most important of all truth. Accordingly, those methods which make for the greatest and best results in the shortest time should be selected. An activity that might be very desirable as a teaching method when unlimited time was at the disposal of the class, may have to give way to a simple type of procedure that can be carried to a conclusion in a short period. For example, an extended project should not be undertaken except as it may be possible

to work on it in instalments. It would be unwise to start handwork that pupils may be obliged to stop doing just when their interest is at its height. Methods well suited for use in short periods are the question and answer method, the story method, oral presentation, and possibly the discussion method, though time limits will have to be considered in the planning for the use of each of these or of whatever method is chosen.

8. *Skill and qualifications of the teacher.* Finally, the teacher himself is a limitation on method. Each person has his talents, his strong points, and his weaknesses. No teacher can use every method with equal success; most teachers are facile in the use of only a few; some can make most effective use of only one or two. Wise is the teacher who uses the methods he can employ with best results. Any teacher can strengthen his weak points; a good teacher will constantly be seeking to do so. Every teacher does well to use at first and predominantly those methods for which he is best adapted and not to try to use other methods until he has developed reasonable facility. Few people are brilliant lecturers, masters in story-telling, or good crayon artists. The teacher who does not have qualifications along these lines should recognize his limitations instead of trying to be what he is not. Such an one may be good at asking questions, conducting discussions, directing research, or in the use of some other method. Each does well to cultivate the abilities given him by God and not to strain his powers in trying to be something that his birthday gifts prevent him from becoming.

Before taking up the treatment of some of the chief types of method, it may be well to reemphasize the things that have been touched upon thus far in this chapter and to seek a perspective from which the problem of method may be viewed most rationally. Method has to do with that phase of the teacher's work that is concerned with preparing for and actually conducting the work of teaching. It consists of procedures planned to arouse and to guide the learning activities of the pupil. The methods of instruction cannot be profitably considered in isolation from the learner and the teacher. All methods have their weaknesses. Any method may be good or bad, depending on the factors treated in this section and many other variables. No one method is a panacea. A method that is best in one case may not be good in another. In any good class, it is likely that a variety of methods will be used during each session.

The teacher must be a constant student of method in general and of his own methods in particular. No good method is the result of some clever invention. The foundations of sound method are laid in insight into the nature of the learner and in thorough understanding of the learning process. No teacher can use correct method except as he knows how and when learning actually takes place. Any alert teacher who knows pupils, who understands how they learn, who knows his subject matter, and who understands method will be led almost intuitively to choose his method of teaching. Such a teacher will always be seeking to improve his method. As he teaches, he will consider this, that, and the other effect and be making constant adaptations and re-adaptations. In retrospective examination of the teaching session, he will put this, that, and the other procedure in the test tube of totality of teaching experience to ascertain how well it accomplished its intended purpose.

THE STORY METHOD

One of the oldest, most effective, and most used means of conveying truth is the story. The basis of the world's classics hangs on the thread of stories that have been told over and over. The story has been used by the great teachers of the world as one of their chief methods. Jesus presented the most sublime truths in the form of stories. The story was His favorite method of teaching; no other teacher of whom we have record used parables so freely and so effectively. Any teacher, whatever be the age level of his pupils, who does not make use of the story is missing one of his greatest opportunities for presenting truth.

Reasons for its effectiveness in teaching

The story presents truth in action. Truth made concrete in characters who live before the hearer is much easier to understand than if presented in any other form. The lawyer who asked Jesus the question, "Who is my neighbor?" and who was told the story of the Good Samaritan, had an answer that gave him and all others who ever hear the story a far better understanding of who one's neighbor is than any amount of abstract discussion could give. The story stirs the imagination; by its use, any particular virtue can be made to stand out in such a way as to cause its significance and beauty to be unmistakably clear or, conversely, any unlovely quality may be so portrayed that the effect is a feeling of revulsion toward it. Because it makes the abstract virtues so living, concrete, and vital, the story has no equal in its power to carry truth into action.

Carrying its own lesson and making its own application, the story sets before the pupil an opportunity to learn and apply for and to himself. In accord with the fundamental principle of self-activity, a lesson learned thus is worth many lessons handed over by the teacher with moral and application already made but not welcomed or accepted by the pupil. By means of the story, the teacher can do less teaching while the child is doing more learning. Because of its interest, a story is also more likely to be recalled, or even retold, by the pupil with the result that its lesson is repeated many times. Thus spiritual truth gets a firmer hold on the mind and moral principles become well grounded in his thinking and in his habits.

The story is one of the most effective means for capturing interest and attention and thus for motivating pupils. Let a teacher or a preacher launch into the telling of a good story and the lagging interest of class or congregation soon rises. A story arouses curiosity and awakens a desire for new experiences. The story also gives pleasure and thus makes for a mental set conducive to good reception of content taught. Not the least important of the uses of stories is that of the development of a wholesome sense of humor, which has many values in classroom situations. Furthermore, stories may be most valuable as an indirect aid to teaching because they afford relief from mental tension, emotional set, fatigue, and misunderstanding that may be hampering the child in his work. Speaking a language both can understand and feel, the story may serve as a medium of fellowship between teacher and pupils.

The story may be used as a basis for making connection between the known and the unknown. Thus much material that might otherwise be too difficult for the learner to grasp may be opened to his understanding. It can be used most effectively as a means for enlarging the growing concepts of the child and thus enriching his experiences. Frequently, stories serve as very striking illustrations of facts and truths the pupil might not be able to grasp apart from their use. Facts of nature, events of history, circumstances of human relationships, and all matters having to do with God and His dealings with man may be more satisfactorily interpreted or made more intelligible to pupils by means of the story than by the use of any other method.[4]

Structure of the story

What is a story? is a question every teacher might well ask, not for rhetorical purposes but for definite and accurate understanding. A story is not a description, neither is it an exposition or a narration—at least much narration is not story. A story has a structure of its own; to be complete structurally, it must consist of four parts: an introduction, a succession of events, a climax, and a conclusion, or ending. "Every good story must have a beginning that arouses interest, a succession of events that is orderly and complete, a climax that forms the story's point, and an end that leaves the mind at rest."

A story must have a beginning.[5] This should be very short; often a single sentence will serve as an introduction. It should introduce the hearer to the chief characters, arouse interest, provide a background for action, and stimulate curiosity about what is to follow. The introduction should be a vital part of the story, not something about the source of the story, how much enjoyment the story will give the hearers, an admonition to listen, or a question. The words should be suggestive, presenting some concrete picture to the mind. If possible, the introduction should make an appeal to the senses. Sentences should be short, clear, and concise. An effective introduction is the most important part of a story.

After the introduction comes a series of events progressing in regular order. A jumble of incidents strung together and leading nowhere is not a story; there must

[4] G. H. Betts and M. O. Hawthorne, **Method in Teaching Religion** (New York: The Abingdon Press, 1925), p. 227 ff (Used by permission)

[5] Alberta Munkres, **Primary Method in the Church School** (New York: The Abingdon Press), p. 52 ff (Used by permission)

be progression toward a climax. Though each incident
and bit of conversation should be interesting in itself,
nothing should be introduced to break the thread of
the story. Unnecessary details and more descriptive
material than is needed to make the incidents clear—
anything that interrupts action needlessly—should be
omitted. The story should move steadily and uninter-
ruptedly toward the climax.

The climax is the high point of the story. Without
the climax, or with it obscured by details of explanatory
material, the effect of the story is wholly lost. The
climax provides the thrill of the action; so it must be
clear and outstanding. Before selecting material for a
story or telling it, the climax should be found, and this
should be the peak on which the narrator keeps his eye
set every moment as he moves on his way. Every bit
of material should be subjected to rigid scrutiny and
rejected if it in any way obscures the climax or delays
unduly the action leading to it. Not the story itself but
its purpose or effect is the justification for its use, and
it will have neither purpose nor effect if the climax
is missed.

The ending of the story should be very brief. It
should dispose of the characters and put the mind at
ease. Many good stories close with the climax, but
usually a few concluding words are necessary to put
the mind at rest so that it may ponder the thought of
the story. Often the conclusion can be stated in a single
sentence. A story should end when it has been told; explanation of the meaning, pointing the moral, or sum-
marizing the incidents destroys the effect. Make sure
of a good conclusion; then let the story carry its own
message. For children especially, the story should have
a happy ending. It should close with a note of certainty so that the mind may be given over to the enjoyment of what has been heard instead of being sent on

a search for an answer to some question or a solution
to some problem.

Telling the story

The first essential for success in the use of the story
method is a deep conviction that the story is a most
useful way of teaching. The least doubt on this point,
the feeling that story-telling is mostly for entertainment
or something to fill in when there is nothing of greater
importance to do, will make the use of stories ineffective
in teaching. The second essential for success in story-
telling is thorough preparation of the right sort. A story
should always be told, never read. The teacher should
plan the story carefully, making himself thoroughly
familiar with the details but not committing it to
memory word for word. The form of a written story
may well be preserved and some few choice portions
may be memorized, but the teacher should so make it
his own that it takes on something of his character when
he tells it.

A very important part of preparation for story-telling
is the choice of the right story for the right purpose.
Stories of many different kinds are available—stories
about nature and animals, stories about heroes and great
men and women, stories of romance, stories of adventure and missionary enterprise, stories of Christian
sacrifice and service, and Bible stories. The Christian
will make predominant use of Bible stories but may,
very appropriately, use stories of many other kinds. In a
particular situation when there is need of a story for a
definite purpose, careful selection must be made. Some
suitable Bible story may be chosen, perhaps the right
one may be found in the lesson material, recourse may
be had to some book of stories, several of which the
wise teacher will have available, or the teacher may
make his own story from material furnished by other

stories, from incidents in books, magazines, or newspapers, or from his own experiences. At any rate, the story chosen should be one that will produce the feeling, mood, or action desired.

Once chosen, the story should be studied from all angles in the light of the needs of the pupils and the purpose for which it is to be used. It should be worked over thoroughly according to the principles already discussed and adapted to suit the present need. Superfluous characters and incidents will need to be eliminated. The teacher should become perfectly familiar with the events, the characters, and what they say. He should think of the effect he wishes to produce and arrange the incidents and the climax accordingly.

Having done these things, he is ready to practice telling the story. Telling it aloud is of the greatest value, helping the narrator to realize how it is going to sound and to choose his own words definitely and accurately so that there will be no need to search for words when telling it to his actual audience. Furthermore, practice in telling has the effect of making the characters live and the situations real. Characters should be made to talk, expressing their action and their feelings in words. The story should be told again and again until one is at home with the words, until every word counts, and every phrase and sentence carries its full meaning. It should be told until it becomes second nature, until one can put his whole self into it and thus be able to give to actual hearers not words merely, but a part of himself. A story thus mastered by a teacher will serve his purpose on many occasions. A good story, well-told, never loses its charm through repetition. People who heard Russell H. Conwell's story, "Acres of Diamonds," as many as forty and fifty times were always glad to hear it again.

In using the story with an audience, the teacher must

remember that its charm depends much upon the way in which it is told. A story most perfect from a structural point of view, most beautiful in its message, and very well selected to accomplish its purpose will be ineffective if not told well, while a story far less desirable in terms of these qualities may make strong appeal because of the manner in which it is related. First of all, the narrator should fix his attention on the story, for he must himself see the things that he wants others to see. At the same time, he should think of the pupils, trying to get the sense of sharing with the group what he sees. He should also enter definitely into the feeling of the characters in his story and feel with his audience as they are led into the feeling of characters and events. If preparation has been adequate, the teacher will have such thorough knowledge of the story, its characters, their circumstances, their actions, and their intentions that he can completely forget himself and become lost in mutual enjoyment with the pupil of the message the story presents. Such forgetfulness will enable the teacher to tell the story in his own way without imitation of the qualities of some other story-teller. A story should be told in a simple, natural way, with animation but with utmost sincerity.

Dangers in the use of the story method

Like all other types of method, the story has its dangers. For one thing, children may be too richly fed with stories and thus not learn to gather facts and solve problems by independent thinking. The story may serve useful purposes in teaching at every level but the receptive mental process needs to give way to a more active process of gathering and using knowledge on one's own initiative. There comes a time, therefore, when the story, as the main type of method, should be superseded by other forms. Again, the story in practice may be used for mere entertainment, not for educative values. Though the story may well be used for purposes that do not bear directly on educative values, it should never be used in teaching for mere entertainment. A third danger is that the story may be so interesting in itself as to lead the attention of pupils far afield from the matter at hand with the consequence that much energy and time may have to be spent in getting back again.

THE QUESTION AND ANSWER METHOD

The question has always been one of the chief tools of teachers. Through all the history of human life, the value of questions in education has been recognized. Socrates made the question famous as a form of teaching, but the method of questioning was used long before his day. Questions lay at the very heart of the teaching methods of Jesus; the four Gospels record more than one hundred questions asked by Him. In catechetical instruction, a system that dominated education during the Middle Ages and one that has even yet a very definite hold on certain phases of religious instruction particularly, the question was central. Today, in spite of the great multiplicity of methods of instruction, much teaching is yet done by means of the question, either as the chief method or as a component part of other methods.

Importance of the question

Though the question is so frequently used, its true significance is not always appreciated. The native impulses of wonder and curiosity are the principal incentives to learning. As soon as the child becomes capable of speech, natural curiosity expresses itself in the form of questions. With increasing age, the world becomes more and more perplexing; so questions, expressed or unexpressed, increase in number and, as they are answered, the child learns. To teach is to stimulate and direct the activity of the learner. The question touches the springs of curiosity and interest in the learner's mind and thus becomes an important instrument for directing the process of learning. "Questioning is one of the supreme methods by which a maturer mind can assist a learner's growing mentality." It both stirs to action and guides the direction of the acting.

A question presents a problem to the mind, and all thinking has its source in problem-solving. When one faces a problem, he is in a situation that demands a response of some kind. Any pupil who really faces a question will not rest until he has found a correct answer. Thus by means of the question, the teacher, instead of confining the main activity of the lesson to himself, can get the pupil's own mind to be active and turn him from a mere listener into one who sees the truth for himself. The question is also a very important factor in securing attention through the very fact that it requires a response. It interests the mind by giving it something to do and, if well asked, there is also an appeal to the mind to show its power. Furthermore, good questioning is a way of managing a class. There is no occasion for disorder in a class engaged with stimulating questions asked by an alert teacher or by members of the class who are interested in the process of doing something about the matter in hand. Management is never an end in itself, but there can be no teaching unless management be good. The best kind of management is that in which the problem of managing is lost to sight through absorbing mental activity.

Good questioning is, then, an essential to good teaching. While a good teacher does not rely on questioning alone in directing learning, any teacher who questions well cannot fail altogether in his teaching because he will stimulate mental growth. By properly directed questions, the teacher can ascertain what the pupils have already learned, guide them in further learning, correct misconceptions and imperfect understanding, help them to see the interrelationships among facts, aid them to organize their thinking, and lead them to fruitful expression of their learning. Questioning is often poorly done; yet the art of asking questions is perhaps more easily improved than any other of the teacher's arts. By thought and effort, any teacher can develop a much higher degree of perfection in the art. To do so, he needs to consider the uses of questions, the characteristics of good questions, and the technique of asking questions.

The uses of questions

It is impossible to state all the functions of questioning. While some of the most important uses are listed here, many more will come to the mind of the thoughtful reader. One important use of questions is to discover what the pupils do and do not know. The purpose may be to determine whether the pupil has mastered the essential facts in the lesson, but a better purpose is to test his understanding of these facts and his ability to use them in fruitful ways. By so doing, the teacher will be enabled to meet the real needs of pupils in a more effective manner. A second use of the question is to aid the pupil to build upon his past experience. By questioning him concerning what he knows and has done, a wise teacher will lead the pupil to draw from the old treasures of past experience to supplement and interpret the new material. Third, the question arouses curiosity and stimulates interest. A few well-directed questions can change an apathetic student into an alert, interested one who is ready to undertake almost anything. Fourth, the question may be used to cause the pupil to think. By asking questions, the teacher brings problems and difficulties to the mind of the pupil and by further questioning he can lead the pupil to develop insight, see relationships, and organize his facts for purposes of definite accomplishment in working out a solution.

A fifth use to which questioning may be put is that of directing attention to the significant elements in a situation or in materials. The immature mind lacks power to make proper discrimination between major and minor factors; well-directed questions can assist the learner in distinguishing between the two. Sixth, questions enable the teacher to secure and keep contact with the minds of the class. Understanding questions asked by the teacher and a sympathetic interest on the part of the teacher in eager questions asked by a pupil, make for good rapport between teacher and taught, something that is very important for all learning and particularly so for the learning of Christian truth. In the seventh place, good questioning gives the pupil opportunity for expression of his own thoughts in his own way, thus allowing for growth and also providing the teacher with a basis for rendering further assistance in directing growth and learning. The questions put to a pupil should take him where he is and lead him on to higher levels of attainment in mind, personality, and spirit.

Eighth, the question may be used to develop appreciation. By means of it, the teacher may draw out, for encouragement or discouragement, the likes and dislikes of pupils. By subtle suggestion in the question itself, in its form, or in the manner of asking it, pupil attitude may be influenced. Sometimes the mere fact that a certain question is asked becomes a basis for change in attitude. In the ninth place, the question has value as a means for drill and review. It stimulates

pupils to expression, thus deepening impression and
fixing facts and ideas in memory. In review work, it
may be used to help the pupil to see all the relevant
facts in an integrated way. Finally, in the tenth place,
the question may be used to examine the class to determine how well the instruction has accomplished its
purpose. Used in this way, it provides incentive for
study.

Characteristics of good questions

1. Questions should be brief. The fewer the words
used in stating them the better, provided that they are
sufficient in number to express the problem adequately.
The pupil should be able to grasp the meaning quickly
and to hold it in mind while he is formulating an
answer. Hence, all parenthetical explanations and involved clauses should be omitted. Questions should
also be simple; that is, two distinct questions should not
be asked as one because this will likely make for unclear
thinking. To ask brief, concise questions, the teacher
himself must think clearly and know exactly what he
wants to ask.

2. A good question is clear. For it to be so, the
teacher must think out his main questions before asking
them and phrase them in terms of pupil experience. A
good question asks one thing clearly and definitely. It
means just what it should and nothing else. The pupil
has no doubt at all as to what a good question means.
Clearness demands that utmost care be exercised in the
choice of words and the phrasing of sentences so that
the exact thought is conveyed.

3. A good question provokes thought. It tests the
judgment, not merely the memory. It challenges the
pupil to give evidence of understanding what he has
read or studied. It is so stated that it requires, not an
answer learned from a book, but one representing the

application of what has been learned. To answer such a question, the pupil must draw upon his new knowledge in relation to his past experience, something that he cannot do except as he has integrated the two in the terms of thoughtful mastery. Of course, there are exceptions as, for instance, when the purpose of the questioning is to drill, to review, or to bring a fact into the center of attention. However, as a general rule, questions should require thought.

4. A good question does not suggest the answer. In other words, it is not a leading question. Such a question merely asks the pupil to agree with the statement made in the question. While the leading question may induce considerable activity in the pupil, it does not force him into action; hence he tends to let the teacher do the thinking. "The question should stand upright and not lean toward either the correct or the incorrect answer."

5. A good question does not offer the pupil a choice between two possible answers contained in the question. For example, "Did Peter or Thomas deny the Lord?" illustrates the type of question that should be avoided. A better way to phrase the question would be, "Who denied the Lord?" The question calling for a "yes" or "no" answer is one of similar nature. Such questions do not compel the pupil to do much more than guess in order to offer an answer. Furthermore, they give no training in organized and connected discourse. Besides, it is difficult to frame such questions without a tendency to suggest the answer.

6. Questions should not be formulated in the words of the textbook. For one thing, the phraseology of the question may give a cue to the answer. Furthermore, the practice encourages verbatim memory of the content studied with little or no attempt at understanding thereof. The teacher should so master the content of

the lesson that he becomes wholly able to find his way about without being obliged to use the original phrasing. Thus, he will stimulate the pupil by example and by practice to independence of thought and study. One of the surest ways to kill class interest and to deaden pupil initiative in learning is for the teacher to become a slave to printed questions.

7. The question should be adapted to the knowledge and experience of the pupil. The least capable pupil should be assigned questions that he can answer satisfactorily. The most difficult questions should be put to the pupils who are most capable of answering. A question should challenge the pupil to put forth his best effort; it should not be so easy that it fails to stimulate thought nor should it be so hard that he must guess or be unable to answer. The alert teacher will adapt his questions to the level of ability and experience of his pupils.

8. A good question prepares the pupil for further study. It starts a train of associated ideas and makes for deeper interest in the materials of learning. A puzzling question arouses curiosity that may lead to a whole chain of new investigations. By use of well chosen questions, a teacher can stimulate and direct observation and lead the pupil into a search for new data. A question can give the pupil a mind set for what is to come later in the period or in the course of study.

9. Questions should be logical. Each succeeding one should be related definitely to preceding ones and to the matter at hand. Often the answer of a pupil to one question will be the best cue for the next question. A series of questions should lead to a gradual unfolding of the subject; continuity in the presentation should be so manifest that the pupil will carry away a unified impression of the whole. Near the end of a lesson, a few unifying questions may well be asked to lead pupils

to an integrated understanding of the whole truth that is being studied, thus making it easy for them to apply the truth to life.

10. A good question fulfills an essential purpose. It is not asked merely for the sake of asking; it leads somewhere. To the pupil, it has definite relationship to the purpose of the work. It calls out main points, not non-essentials. To ask questions that have meaning in terms of the purposes of the lesson, the teacher must analyze the materials carefully and judge relative values properly. Questions asked for a definite purpose encourage pupils to stress the main points and help them to get the real meaning of the lesson. Such questions tend to make pupils eager and alert, because they will feel that something worth while is being accomplished. Purposeless questioning makes lifeless pupils.

11. Good questions are often a source of real information that is new to both teacher and class members other than the one who gives it. The good teacher, as was stressed in an earlier chapter, is always a learner; so he is quite justified in asking a question to obtain knowledge new to him. Many pupils have traveled or had other experiences that may have an important bearing on the content of the lesson. Each pupil brings to the class a great deal of information and experience that can be of much worth to all the members if it is capitalized by the teacher. A wise teacher will use the question to tap these resources for the purpose of supplementing and interpreting other materials.

The technique of questioning

It is easy to ask questions but it is not easy to ask good questions. It is also easier to gain an understanding of the characteristics of good questions than it is to use good technique in questioning. There are no hard and fast rules governing the latter. All that can be offered are suggestions that should be followed or ignored as intelligent understanding of educational values in a given situation may direct.

1. Questions should keep the whole class interested. While a particular pupil may be designated to answer each question, asking and answering should not be a matter between the teacher and one pupil. The question should be addressed to the whole class and a particular person called upon to answer only after the class has heard the question. This manner of procedure secures general attention, gives each pupil an opportunity to think about an answer and serves as a means to get critical reaction to the answer given.

2. Questions should be asked conversationally. The ideal is a sort of informal conversation in which the teacher takes the lead but in which each member of the class is included, with one pupil looked to for a reply. The manner in which the question is asked should imply that the pupil is able to answer. Thus he is challenged to do the best he can and will utilize his latent powers to the limit.

3. Questions should be distributed so that all pupils have opportunity to learn as nearly equally as possible. It is very easy for a teacher to put most questions to those pupils who are alert, eager, and always ready with a correct answer and to leave out those who are timid, bored, or unable to present anything that seems to be worth while. Often it is the latter who most need the experience that classroom participation gives. However, warning need be sounded against any purely mechanical way of distributing questions. Pupils should not be designated to answer in alphabetical order, in the order of seating, or in any other very obvious order. Participation of all should be secured by effective devices that are not obvious. The practice of having questions answered by volunteers has merit, if it does not

lead to the doing of all the work by a few pupils while
the others just sit.

4. The teacher should allow the pupil sufficient time
to answer. As a rule, teachers tend to be too impatient
about delay in answering. If he is adequately prepared,
the teacher knows the question and its answer before it
is put, while the pupil must think through the question
and think an answer thereto before he can respond. Besides, the pupil may be much more immature in thinking power. Rapid placing of questions with allowance
of insufficient time to answer them distracts instead of
develops the thinking of pupils.

5. The question should be asked in such a way as
not to suggest the answer. Even if the wording does
not give a hint as to the answer, the inflection of the
voice or the setting in which the question is placed may
suggest it. Not only may wording and inflection suggest
the answer, but the facial expression of the teacher
may give the pupil a clue as to whether he is on the right
track or not.

6. A set of questions on a lesson or topic should
possess coherence and unity. Each should be based on
what has gone before and serve to reenforce other questions. The whole set ought to build up in the mind of
the pupil an integrated system of thought. Unity and
coherence in the questions make for general interest
and motivation in the class, as well as for connected
thought and unified impression.

7. As a rule, neither questions nor answers should
be repeated. Repetition of questions tends to make
pupils less attentive to the discussion. Not to repeat
implies that the question was properly asked the first
time. If the pupil was attentive and did not hear because of some defect in the way in which the question
was asked, the teacher should repeat the question. Repetition of answers tends to cause pupils to be inattentive

to the pupil who is answering. It also causes the pupil who answers to feel that he is speaking to the teacher rather than to the group and to depend upon the former to elaborate and clarify his answer, whereas he is likely to formulate his answer much more carefully if he is conscious of an audience situation.

8. When a pupil says he cannot answer a question, the teacher usually does well to assume that his statement is correct. For a teacher to prod a pupil who says that he does not know makes for wasted time and it may cause him much embarrassment. It is much more worth while to call on those who have something to say than it is to waste the time of the class on one who has nothing to offer.

9. Occasional questions may well be asked of the inattentive. As stated earlier, the question is one means of getting attention and serves as a help in the management of a class. Questions asked for this purpose should, however, have educational value.

10. The questioning of the teacher should give evidence of adaptability. The material should be so well in hand that the teacher is able to ask questions spontaneously. No good teacher will ever teach without a plan but no plan need be followed without deviation. The good teacher will, before entering the classroom, decide upon certain questions but often the best questions he asks are those that come to his mind during the course of the recitation. Questions prepared beforehand should not convey to the class strong evidence of this fact.

11. The teacher's attitude toward pupils' sincere answers should be one of kindly appreciation. The attitude of the teacher should be such as will give the pupil fullest encouragement to do his best and to participate freely. At times, corrections will have to be made, but these should be given in such a manner as

will not make the pupil feel repressed. The teacher should give sincere recognition for whatever is good in answers and supply further enlightenment, if it is needed, by explaining or by further questioning to draw out the complete and correct answer. An encouraging, interested, sympathetic, confidence-inspiring teacher will call forth the best efforts of the pupil. Elaboration and criticism of answers may well become an activity of the class instead of being left entirely to the teacher. Such participation in the evaluation of a pupil contribution makes for a greater amount of thinking and the bringing to light of more angles of the problem.

12. Beware of asking too many questions. A common fault of unskilful teachers is to use the question too freely. If the purpose of questioning be drill and review, the number of questions will need to be relatively great, but it is very easy to ask entirely too many thought questions. The teacher needs to be much more concerned with what is going on in the minds of his pupils than with his own questions and the answers he desires. The tendency of most teachers is to ask so many questions that pupils are given little or no time for thoughtful consideration of either questions or answers. Time is needed by the pupil to think through the question and to formulate a thoughtful response. Rapid-fire questioning with impatient expectation of immediate answers fosters habits of snap judging instead of careful thinking.

13. The teacher should make constant self-critical examination of his questions and his questioning. A feeling of failure should lead, not to discouragement, but to a resolute attempt to ascertain the cause of the failure so that it may be removed. One can learn to question by questioning, but reflection upon his questioning will teach him much about the act. Constant and critical examination of techniques is an essential to

success in teaching. The time to make this examination is as soon after the class session as possible, while its details are in mind.

Pupil questioning

Teaching is not a one-way process nor is it predominantly a matter of teacher activity. Learning pupils are active pupils. The good teacher welcomes worthwhile questions from pupils because they indicate that pupils have an active attitude toward learning. The teacher who can teach by answering questions will accomplish far more than he would by asking them. It is most natural for pupils to ask questions; children are very curious until native curiosity is crushed by repressive treatment. Any teacher who manifests a sympathetic willingness to answer will be asked many questions. Good teaching, then, is characterized by much questioning on the part of pupils. Every possible means should be used to encourage pupils to participate in asking questions.

However, the teacher is responsible for the proper guidance of pupils in their asking of questions. Sometimes pupils are very eager to deal with matters that are foreign to the purpose in view. Being interested in irrelevant matters, they may ask questions that carry the activity far from its proper course. Sometimes trivial questions giving evidence of no thought are asked. A pupil may ask insincere questions merely for the purpose of leading the discussion into by-paths. To detect the motive back of questions is not always easy. Unless it is obvious that the motive is wrong, the teacher does well to accept the question in good faith and give it the attention it deserves. However, he should always try to have questions significant in terms of true learning purposes.

It is also a responsibility of the teacher to stimulate

questioning. Taking a few minutes of time at the beginning of a lesson to answer questions that grew out of a previous lesson, is good practice. Asking if there are any questions may be a means of getting pupils to state their questions though this will accomplish little if the teacher does not react sympathetically when questions are asked. Encouraging pupils to note questions while they are studying is also a good means. Sometimes pupils know so little, or feel that they know so little, about the topic that they either cannot or will not ask questions. In connection with the first difficulty, the teacher must provide sufficient background of information, while in the case of the second, his task will be that of developing self-confidence in the pupil. The commendation of good questions also encourages further questioning by pupils.

On the negative side, the teacher may do some things that will definitely discourage pupils in the asking of questions. For example, the use of ridicule when a question is asked will likely result in a pupil's asking no more. Excessive formality such as requiring a pupil to raise his hand or to stand when he wishes to speak is also discouraging. Informality in the classroom is much more likely to produce questions. A teacher's refusal to deal with a question in a manner adequate to the satisfaction of the mind of the questioner tends to make him hesitate to ask another. Evidence of the teacher's ignorance of his field and consequent inability to handle questions when they are asked will cause pupils to refrain from asking him questions. If pupils feel that a teacher resents questions indicative of sincere disagreement with his position, they will be prone not to state questions that might be so interpreted. No teacher should set himself up as being so infallible that pupils must always agree with him. To do so stifles the tendency of pupils to think for themselves.

In dealing with answers to the questions of pupils, the teacher should be helpful and frank. If a question is manifestly unimportant, it may be dismissed tactfully. Any question asked in the right spirit should be dealt with in a respectful manner. If it is asked from a real desire for information, the answer should meet that desire provided the issue is one of general concern to the whole class. Of course, the interests of one individual should never be served at the expense of the welfare of the class. Therefore, if he can do so, the teacher should invariably answer a question immediately and fully as soon as it is asked. Should a question deal with an important issue but one at present irrevelant or if it serves the interests of the questioner alone, the wise course to pursue may be that of delay. In the latter case, the teacher may well volunteer to take up the matter with the individual at some mutually convenient time.

Obviously, pupils may ask questions the teacher cannot answer. Far better is it for him, in such a case, to admit frankly that he does not know. To attempt to deal with a question he does not know how to answer by bluffing does not fool pupils; it only causes them to lose respect for their teacher. No person can know everything; so a frank admission of ignorance is not necessarily reprehensible. If the teacher could know or should know and does not, he needs to learn so that he will not be under obligation to say that he does not know. Either of two courses of action may be taken when a question which he cannot answer is asked. The teacher can simply say he does not know the answer but that he will get the information and give an answer at the next meeting of the class. Having said this, he will be careful to fulfil his promise.

The other thing that he may do is to set a pupil or the class to work on the solution of the problem. The teacher's duty in this connection is to give suggestions as to sources of data, methods of attack, and organization of effort lest pupil energy be wasted to no purpose. Frequently pupils receive greater benefit from the investigation of questions proposed by themselves than they do from those asked by the teacher. Any assignment for further investigation needs to be made on the basis of a genuine and sincere desire on the part of the teacher to direct learning activity. No teacher worthy of the name Christian will use such a course of procedure as a subterfuge for escaping work or under the pretext of getting the pupils to do something that will be good for them.

Limitations of the question method

The question method, no more than any other method, is a panacea. "Any fool can ask questions." Merely asking questions is not teaching. The use of this method will not make an able teacher of a person who does not know his material thoroughly. The teacher who uses the method of questioning successfully must not only master the content of teaching but he must also plan his questions well in advance. Such preparation will itself improve the quality of any spontaneous questions that he may use. Much poor teaching results from the use of questions that lack the essential qualities of good questions as well as from poor technique in questioning. Perhaps one of the greatest limitations of the method is the deeply implanted idea that the question should be used primarily for the recall of facts rather than as a means of assembling new data and provoking thought.

A direct question cannot secure from a pupil who does not know, any fact that lies beyond his experience. Questions cannot impart knowledge but, if properly used, they can serve to develop new lines of thought.

All learning is a matter of gaining new experiences. Except as the question makes for a point of contact between the unknown and the known, the pupil cannot be led into an understanding of the former. Both Socrates, who gave great value to the question, and Jesus, who used it so freely in His teaching, based their questions on concrete data, on illustrations drawn from the daily lives of the people whom they taught.

It may be noted that none of these limitations is the fault of the method but rather of a wrong use of the method. In fact, the method rarely, or never, serves as a self-sufficient method to be used apart from other methods of teaching. On the other hand, it is most valuable as a supplement to almost every other method, for seldom is a lesson taught by any method in which the question has no place. While the method is often misused, there can be no doubt but that every effective teacher is expert in its use.

QUESTIONS AND PROBLEMS

1. Why is Christian teaching less subject to rigidity of rule than other teaching?
2. Why can the Christian teacher not ignore the natural laws of mental life?
3. Explain the interrelationship of the work of God and the work of Christian teaching.
4. Which is more to be desired, a fine building or good teachers? Why?
5. What is method?
6. How is method related to other factors in the teaching-learning process?
7. Which method is the best to use in a given teaching situation? Explain your answer.
8. For what reasons is teaching never a purely mechanical matter?
9. Explain the double reference of method.
10. What determines the choice of method that the efficient teacher uses?

11. Illustrate how various methods may be used during a class period.
12. Enumerate the factors that may be used to guide a teacher in the choice and use of the best method and show how each may guide such choice.
13. Why is the story so effective as a method of teaching? Is it effective with pupils of all ages?
14. Give the structural parts of a story and comment briefly on each part.
15. Outline the procedure for the telling of a story.
16. What dangers are there in the use of the story method?
17. Can you name a more effective tool for the use of teachers than the question is?
18. Do you accept as true the statement, Good questioning is good teaching? Why or why not?
19. Comment on the uses of questions. Can you suggest additional uses?
20. Formulate several questions, or take some that you have heard teachers use, and judge them in the light of the characteristics of good questions.
21. Is it easy to ask good questions?
22. Do you think that teachers in general ask too many or too few questions?
23. Do pupils usually ask enough questions? Why do they not ask more?
24. Is anything wrong with the question-and-answer method of teaching?

CHAPTER XI

METHOD IN TEACHING
(Continued)

THE LECTURE METHOD

The place of the lecture

THAT which is to be treated under this topic might perhaps go better under the heading, "Oral Presentation by the Teacher," for it includes the whole range of the teacher's presenting to the pupil a ready-made content. This presentation takes a variety of forms, stretching from the one extreme of brief and impromptu statements made by the teacher in a class discussion or by way of rounding out pupils' answers to his questions, to the opposite extreme of the very formal lecture which may be written out with great care and read to the class.[1] Of course, it is recognized that telling and lecturing differ each from the other; yet the two are so alike in nature and use that they may well be considered together. The lecture method, then, is the procedure that includes all oral presentation by the teacher whether it be by way of an extended formal exposition or by way of remarks made to clarify issues, to elaborate upon pupils' answers to questions, to supplement data

---

[1] G. W. Reagan, **Fundamentals of Teaching** (Chicago: Scott, Foresman & Company, 1932) p. 262

already at hand, or to indicate how something is to be done.

It is a matter of common knowledge that oral presentation is practiced to a great extent at all levels of instruction. The formal lecture is more generally used in dealing with mature minds, but even teachers of quite small children spend a considerable part of the teaching period in the oral presentation of material to their pupils. It is often said that most teachers talk too much, giving pupils too little opportunity for expressing their own ideas. While this is not the place to consider the effectiveness of this procedure, it may not be thought irrelevant to observe that, as there are extremes in the form of oral presentation, so there are variations in its effectiveness. Sometimes the teacher's presentation serves a good purpose and results in real learning. At other times, however, it fails to bring about the desired changes in pupils and even produces undesirable results. Between these extremes, there are various degrees of effectiveness. However, it stands to reason, in the light of what the nature of learning is, that most of the talking done by a teacher fails to produce best results in learning.

It may be said that it is perhaps more difficult to get good learning by use of the lecture method than by the use of any other method. If the work of teaching is centered in the teacher, and the pupil is considered an empty vessel into which age and experience pours its wisdom, the lecture meets all the requirements of being an excellent method of teaching. However, when the learner is looked upon neither as a vessel to receive nor as a passive absorber but instead as a seeking, interested being who can learn only when he acts, the value of the lecture decreases. Learning, for this latter conception, becomes much more than a matter of mere passive receiving of knowledge, and teaching must do more than pour knowledge into the empty mind of a waiting pupil. It becomes, instead, a matter of effectively stimulating and properly guiding a responding being in his activities. This can be done by use of the lecture method, but it is not easy to do. As iterated in previous connections in this treatise, mere telling is never teaching; no amount of oral presentation in and of itself can produce learning.

But it is impossible to carry on the work of teaching without oral presentation. Instruction needs to include telling. There are times, whatever the method in use may be, when recourse must be had to presenting some ideas to the minds of the pupils in an oral manner. It is often the most advantageous way and sometimes the only way to establish mind sets, to arouse adequate emotional tone, to make necessary explanations, or to present a needed bit of information. Any teacher who has a sense of responsibility for the quality of his work will, therefore, wish to master the technique of effective oral presentation that has to be made with the same care for details in the short period of a few minutes as it does in the more formal lecture. It is impossible to eliminate oral presentation from teaching.

Advantages of the lecture method

Some of the advantages of the lecture method when it is used with a reasonable degree of skill are:

1. The lecture makes possible the effect of the spoken word. Words spoken have, on the whole, better value as an effective means of communication than the printed page can ever have. The spoken word has color and vitality lacking in the printed page. The less proficient pupils are in reading ability, the more do they stand in need of being told. Despite the large amount of reading that is done, most people are vitally influenced by what they hear. The language used in oral pre-

sentation is likely to be simpler and therefore more easily and correctly understood. Besides, the possibility of inflection and emphasis afforded in oral presentation makes the spoken word a better means of communicating thought. The spoken word has power to impress.

2. The lecture makes possible a more effectual operation of the influence of the personality of the teacher. A lecturer puts his whole self into his speaking as can be done in no other method of teaching. He becomes the focal center of interest while he is speaking and whatever he is in personality leaves its impress. Because all lines of attention are converged upon one who is speaking, the impact of his personality becomes greater. The measure of the influence of a dynamic personality in the classroom is the degree to which it is permitted to express itself.

3. The lecture arouses interest and motivates pupils. It makes possible a more effective appeal to emotion; it gives the teacher opportunity to use imagination; it enables him to bring in an incident, a story, or some item of information that may serve to create the mental set necessary for most effective learning. The spoken word has dynamic quality which draws pupils, causing them to follow in the direction of its emphasis.

4. The lecture saves time. More ground can be covered in a short period by means of the lecture than by the use of any other method. The teacher can say in ten minutes what it would take the number of pupils multiplied by ten to read. Furthermore, the teacher can thus supply information that the pupils might have to spend long minutes or even hours to find. Also, the teacher can tell a number of pupils something with little more effort than he would expend in telling one or two pupils that thing.

5. The lecture serves to introduce and summarize material. By it, a new topic can be opened up, made

to seem important, and placed in proper perspective. Rarely do teachers try to introduce a new topic or unit without using oral presentation of some kind. It may serve also as a means for bringing together in summary the results of a study just completed, enabling the teacher to organize the products of learning so that they may be more effectively integrated and applied by the pupil.

6. The lecture provides opportunity for the use of supplementary material. There are things that cannot be made available to the pupils by any other means. Reference sources are often limited. Frequently, written materials present only one point of view. The teacher with his wider experience, greater intellectual resources, and more advanced learning is able to bring pupils facts, ideas, views, illustrations, and examples impossible for them to get in any other way. By means of the lecture, the teacher can not only supply materials that pupils could get through collateral reading, were it possible for them to do it, but he can also present and organize these more effectively for use.

7. The lecture provides a means of giving the pupil proper perspective. Immature minds experience difficulty in making proper evaluations, in seeing relationships, and in discriminating between what is important and what is not. The lecture constitutes a valuable means of showing them the way, helping them to see the peaks, and leading them to higher heights where they can distinguish all things clearly.

8. The lecture affords opportunity for imparting information. The teacher can be certain of the correctness of what he gives in a lecture whereas he cannot be certain about what pupils obtain from other sources. He can also make sure that the data are correctly interpreted and properly organized in terms of the use to be made of them.

9. The lecture may provoke and guide thinking. A skilful speaker can say things in a way that makes pupils sit up and take notice. By the dynamic power of his words, he can make them think his thoughts after him. He can play upon their imagination with this, that, or the other appeal, varying his technique as they follow him and taking them where he wants them to go.

The technique of lecturing

As is the case with every teaching method, most careful preparation should be made for lecturing or talking. The effectiveness of a lecture or a talk depends upon two things: what is said and how it is said. Planning is very important in connection with each. In the first place, the content should be selected and arranged in the light of the objectives the teacher wishes to attain. The problem should be kept obvious to the pupils during the whole course of the lecture. Second, it is most important that the lecture be clearly outlined. Third, all illustrations should be selected with the utmost care; the wise teacher will not trust to the inspiration of the moment to find the exact illustration needed to clear a point.

In the fourth place, preparation should be made to establish at the very beginning of the presentation the proper apperceptive background. The known interests of the class, the level of the pupils' experience, their degree of familiarity with the content, and their mind sets are some things that need to be considered. It is important also that the teacher keep the apperceptive basis of pupils clearly in mind throughout the period of presentation. The ideas expressed and the language used should be adapted to the background of the pupils. Fifth, a problematic attitude on the part of the pupils should be aroused whenever possible. Nothing holds attention like a problem or a question for which the mind is seeking a solution or an answer. As much as possible, the class should be kept in a problematic or expectant attitude during the presentation. Sixth, concrete materials such as objects, pictures, diagrams, maps, familiar illustrations and examples, etc., are an aid in presentation. Seventh, simplicity and clarity should characterize the content, the organization, and the presentation. The psychological approach is more important than the logical though the latter cannot be ignored.

In the actual telling or lecturing, proficiency is dependent on a number of factors. Success in the use of the lecture method is determined much more than is the case with any other by factors resident in the teacher himself, such as magnetism of personality, quality of voice, and command of language. Obviously, these cannot be called into service at a moment's notice simply by force of will. However, most teachers who are willing to pay the price may, over a period of time, improve themselves along these lines. Some general factors, more amenable to control by the attention of the moment, are:

1. Give attention to voice and bearing during the presentation. Speak distinctly but with animation. Enunciate clearly. Smile while speaking. Give evidence of interest and enthusiasm. Avoid any appearance of self-consciousness.

2. Observe a proper rate of presentation. Most speakers talk too fast. Some talk too slowly and make many painful pauses. Be careful not only of the rate of speaking but also of the rate of thought movement. It is easy to have this proceed too rapidly. Time should be allowed pupils to think and assimilate ideas. Adjust rate to difficulties of the material, proceeding more slowly with and enlarging more upon, the difficult parts.

3. Use the conversational tone. Stilted, artificial, or

oratorical manner is out of place in the classroom. Talk not to the class but to the pupils, looking into their faces. The gaze should not rest upon one or a few exclusively but should move to include all in succession. Observe pupils closely and note their responses.

4. Check up on the audience occasionally to see whether it is following. Pauses for questions and discussion will make for better attention and also enable the teacher to ascertain if pupils have understood what he has said. He himself may well ask questions to see if what has been said is clear.

5. Give evidence of a sense of humor. Phrase remarks in an attractive way. Avoid frequent use of funny stories, especially the time-worn ones.

6. Avoid digressions. It may be well at times to clarify related issues, but going off on a tangent, however interesting it may be to the teacher, serves as a distraction to pupils.

7. Hold pupils responsible for the content given. Note-taking may or may not be advisable but pupils should realize that they will be asked to give evidence of having learned. Questions, quizzes, requests for application of truths, and reviews are means for giving incentive to listen carefully.

Disadvantages of the lecture method

1. The lecture demands a minimum of that participation which is so essential to all learning. Pupils naturally like activity and change which listening to a lecture restrain to a great degree. The teacher is the one who is active in the presentation and, unless he presents his material forcefully and attractively, there is little incentive for the pupil to engage in learning activity. In general, the lecture method fails to stimulate activity of a desirable kind where pupils are lacking in sense

of responsibility or in desire to learn. It puts the burden of thinking on the teacher rather than on the pupils.

2. The lecture affords pupils only one contact with the material. With books in hand, they have the material in permanent form, which permits of its being referred to and used when they desire, whereas what is said in a lecture is heard and likely forgotten. Even if pupils take notes, they are not likely to have more than a mere outline of the main points with no details in memory to support these.

3. The lecture is not economical of the pupils' time. If the teacher gives merely what the pupils can get from a text just as well, the time given to lecturing is wasted. And too frequently this is done. However, this is a weakness not of the method but of the use of the method. The lecture rightly used to bring to the pupils what they cannot get, to summarize and clarify what has been studied, and to reorganize material for better apprehension does not prove wasteful of the pupils' time.

4. The lecture makes no provision for individual differences among pupils. Obviously, the presentation is the same for all members of the class regardless of what they may be as individuals. Adaptation in choice and arrangement of materials and manner of presentation must be made largely in terms of the group as a whole, with the consequence that the individual's needs may not be met.

5. The lecture requires ability in public speaking possessed, or possible of acquisition, by few teachers. Comparatively few people can develop exceptional ability in public speaking though all may improve themselves in oral communication. However, some teachers can use the lecture method more effectively than they can use any other.

6. Teachers are prone to use the lecture over much.

This also is a fault of the use of the method, not of the method itself. However, it is a very real one, for teachers somehow seem to find great enjoyment in hearing themselves talk. An alert teacher will be on the lookout to see that methods productive of best results get the place of prominence in his practice.

7. The lecture gives the pupil a content that he is unable to analyze and summarize. Too little opportunity is afforded for understanding and assimilating the content presented. Not being able to refer to anything more than a skeleton outline and not being able to remember what he heard, the pupil is unable to work it over in his thinking.

8. The lecture is a difficult method to maintain on a high level. Few teachers can be at their best constantly. Demands on time, energy, and vitality made by the things around us and the experiences of life, work against an even level of excellent teaching by use of this method.

9. The lecture tends to become a monotonous, mediocre method, if not well done. More than any other method, the lecture calls for the best in the teacher and, if he lets himself slip, the effectiveness of his teaching suffers.

The Discussion Method

Men have carried on discussion ever since they had an existence. Everywhere in life—in the home, on the street, in the store, at the shop, in the informal social gathering, at the banquet—wherever they assemble in groups, people engage in discussion. These discussions assume many forms, ranging all the way from that which is little above gossip to forums and conferences where the weightiest matters of human concern are considered in a careful, deliberate manner. As there are variations in forms of discussion, so variations in aim prevail all the way from what is closely akin to aimlessness to intense purpose to find a satisfactory solution of the most important problems of existence.

Nature of the Method

As a procedure in Christian teaching, the discussion method consists in "directed but free conversation on some well selected question or problem which arises in the individual or social experience of class members, with the definite purpose that a satisfactory solution is sincerely sought. It is a practical attempt to lift up life situations where Christian truth can positively function in offering the best way out." The basic essential is a problem to be solved by the group. It must be a problem that affects the lives of members in some way. Free opportunity for sharing experience and knowledge, spontaneous interchange of thinking and opinion on the part of all the members of the class, the presentation of contrasting statements of the elements of the problem, genuine group thinking in which the thinking of each member is stimulated by the clash of other minds and the consideration of opposed points of view, and a leader who functions to guide the discussion toward a conclusion the whole group can share, are other essentials.

A discussion is not idle talk without a purpose. It is not a going round and round in circles without finding a conclusion. It differs from an argument or a debate, which is characterized by an attempt on the part of one member of the group to win his point in the face of opposition. In discussion, every member coöperates with a view to helping the thinking of the group as a whole. The discussion represents a search for truth, and every member contributes the best that he can from knowledge, experience, opinion, and thought to find a better conclusion than he alone could have found.

Values of the discussion method

Some of the valuable characteristics of this method, which also goes under other names such as "Problem Method," "Problem-Discussion Method," are:

1. It creates vital interest from the very beginning through the appeal that it makes to the natural desire for self-expression.

2. It tends to eliminate the stiffness of formal recitation, for each member of the group can participate without the feeling of timidity or constraint that is likely to be experienced when one person becomes the center of attraction as is the case with various other methods.

3. It stimulates thought because it calls everybody in the class to do some clear thinking. Clash of opinion, challenge of statements, and mental competition cause thinking before speaking and lead, not only to quickening of thought but also to clarification of ideas.

4. It teaches tolerance of the viewpoint and opinions of others and a willingness to compromise personal views for the sake of reaching a group opinion.

5. It puts everybody on an equal basis, because each person's contribution is received for its worth and his opinion is regarded as having value. Thus it leads to feelings of respect for the worth of one's own personality.

6. It makes for a broadening of thought because it tends to extend horizons far beyond the limits of one's own living. As all sides of vital questions are presented, the whole extent of personal vision is widened with the result that a broader foundation is laid for making judgments and formulating conclusions.

7. It forces clear-cut reasoning and trains in skill in putting thought into comprehensible and convincing speech.

8. It makes for right attitudes toward materials and their use as a means to an end. So often pupils feel

that a lesson is to be learned for its own sake and that it has no value apart from the present situation. The discussion method places quite a different emphasis on subject-matter because the end in view is the solution of a problem, and lesson material becomes something that can be used in solving the problem.

9. It provides opportunity for making a very real and natural connection between the course and the practical needs of the pupils in their daily living. Bringing the content close to the interests and problems of pupils as it does, discussion helps them to see and apply truth to themselves without the necessity of the teacher's telling them to do so.

Structure of the discussion

Like all other procedures, a discussion may be good or bad, depending on the way in which it is carried on. A good discussion proceeds along well-defined lines. Four rather clear phases of structure are manifest.

1. The setting up of the problem. There must be a significant problem, one that is so clearly and sharply defined that every pupil sees what it is. Every member of the group should feel that it is a problem that concerns him and one to which a solution would be welcome. The more natural and unforced the problem, the better. If possible, the statement should come from the group.

2. Analyzing the problem. Group discussion will get nowhere so long as all do not understand the problem alike. If one feels that this is the important issue and another feels that something else should be stressed, there can be no common meeting ground. The issues of the problem itself and every word and term connected therewith should be made so plain that even the dullest pupil will understand clearly all the implications. Proper analysis will lead to the conservation of

one or two principles and the dropping of things minor
in importance.

3. Suggesting solutions. Once the problem is really
understood by all the members of the group and clear
in all its issues, the class is ready to seek possible solutions. As each makes his contribution, expressing his
ideas and views, getting help from experts, books, and
other available sources of information, new lines of
thought that add to the idea develop. Out of the discussion, as values are weighed, opinions criticized,
suggestions accepted or rejected, and criticisms received,
there will gradually develop some line of reasoning
moving toward a group solution.

4. The solution. When a group finally arrives at a
solution, it should be a better one than any member of
the group alone could have reached. A solution may be
such in nature as to need to be tried out before it is
accepted. Also, it may have to be studied more before
its full meaning is clear. Acceptance should not be
regarded as so final that a change could not be made
if and when new experience indicated the desirability
of changing. On some questions, it may not be possible
for the group to agree on a decision; it may be necessary
to agree to disagree except as the discussion may have
been about something the group must do. In this event
compromise will be necessary on the plan supported
by the majority.

The technique of discussion

The success or the failure of the discussion method
depends upon the teacher. Tactful, resourceful leadership is essential. His work is that of a guide who is
always fair, tolerant, and well-poised—one who does
not dominate and repress, on the one hand, or who does
not, on the other hand, permit the group to saunter along
so lazily that it gets nowhere. To lead a discussion suc-

cessfully, a teacher must know the field of knowledge and action to which the problem belongs, the problem in hand, and the issues raised. He must also know the members of the class, their general preparation for the work, their personal traits, their interests and needs, and their general characteristics.

One very important phase of technique is ability to help pupils discover problems. A good teacher will often teach pupils to become conscious of difficulties they do not know they have, merely raising a difficulty to the level of felt difficulty so that pupils can take hold of it. A good teacher will also plan for the discussion well in advance so that materials, sources of data, and everything necessary will be available for use. Thorough preparation and thoughtful planning are essential for worth while results even more than is true in the case of other teaching methods.

In the actual discussion, the teacher must guide with sympathy and understanding, showing utmost respect for the personality of each pupil. Out of his fuller knowledge, he will by interpretation, by suggestion, and by skilful questions guide the group from one situation to another nearer the goal. It will be his to see that tangents are not followed, to remind the group of the points at issue, and to keep the discussion on these points. He will see that the facts given are accurate and authentic, that adequate research into relevant issues is made, and that talk is not substituted for thought. At appropriate times he will gather from the total mass of expressed ideas and opinions those contributing to the solution of the problem and present these in summary to the group so that pupils may feel that progress is being made. In all of his work, the discussion leader must realize that he is a leader; the responsibility for the discussion must rest upon the group, not upon the teacher. If the teacher is not willing to let the class

work out a satisfactory solution to the problem, he
cannot have a discussion group and he might better use
some other method of teaching.

Dangers of the discussion method

This method, like every good thing, has its dangers.
An outstanding one is that the problem may not be
clear to all members of the class with the consequence
that all will not be talking about the same thing. Or
there is the ever-present danger that the problem chosen
may not be one of vital concern to all pupils. Again,
the discussion may degenerate into mere talk. Aimless,
uninformed talk and mere expression of doubts or hazy
opinions accomplish nothing. "Everyone may talk about
everything without knowing very much about anything."
Another danger is that discussion may drift into acri-
monious debate. Or it may easily wander off into unimportant or irrelevant lines if the teacher is not an alert
guide. Or the discussion may be monopolized by a few
individuals instead of affording each and every member
of the group opportunity to voice his opinions and views.

A very real danger is that discussion may result in
no increase of knowledge. Mere discussion as such has
no value. If it simply goes round in circles, if knowledge of facts be lacking, if facts at hand are not organized aright to give proper perspective, or if interest
is in mere presentation instead of reading, study, research, and thought, the outcome of a discussion will
not be worth the time and energy it entails. Likewise,
a discussion may lead to conclusions far from the truth
even though such be accepted by the group as a whole;
the group opinion of a number of people or a mere
pooling of prejudices does not make truth. A final
danger, related definitely to various of the preceding,
is that the teacher may not be a teacher while he is
using this method. As a leader of a discussion group,

the teacher is much more than a presiding chairman. His is the responsibility for intellectual and spiritual leadership, for stimulating, encouraging, and directing the activity of pupils so that they learn, grow, and develop in Christian life and stature.

THE PROJECT METHOD

The project method is nothing new, for what goes under its name has probably been used ever since there has been any teaching. Almost every teacher has used projects even if they have not been so named. However, the term came into education within the present century in connection with teaching in such fields as the manual arts and agriculture. Thence it spread rapidly to other fields until today it has a recognized place among methods of teaching in almost every kind of human learning. Its existence is but one result of the attempt to make learning a natural process of acquiring information not for its own sake but for the purpose of use in meeting the practical needs of everyday living. Many teachers know nothing about the method while some have recognized its value almost to the extent of making it a fad.

What the project method is

In reality, the project method is not so much a separate method as it is a principle of method that may be used in connection with all other methods to give them vitality and effectiveness. Since learning is doing, it follows that best learning takes place when the pupils are doing something very worthwhile in terms of their purposes and interests. Interests and purposes of the best kind are those that arise when the thing done constitutes a vital part of normal experience. A true project, then, is something done by the pupil in a real situation recognized by the pupil as natural and worthwhile, which he does because he wants to do it, and which he carries to completion in order to accomplish some purpose of his own.

Many divergent views concerning the nature of the project have been expressed. The definition of Stevenson is one of the most helpful definitions: "A project is a problematic act carried to completion in its natural setting." Betts and Hawthorne state that the method consists in setting "the child at work upon some real project, problem, or enterprise suited to his interest and related to his experience," and expecting "him to gather information, discover facts and relationships, work out solutions, and finally carry the enterprise through to completion."[2] The essence of the method, as indicated by these and similar statements about the project, would seem to be comprehended under these four points: First, some problem is involved; second, the setting is of practical nature, that is, the problem is natural, not artificial; third, the pupil, accepting the responsibility for planning and executing, engages in activity for the purpose of solving the problem. The activity may be physical, mental, aesthetic, social, moral, or spiritual. Fourth, the project is carried to completion, not just discussed or considered or thought about. A definite objective is in view and activity continues until it is attained.

Projects differ widely from one another. Some are simple and are quickly completed with a minimum of activity while others are complex, involving long periods of time and a maximum of activity. Some depend on physical activity; others necessitate intellectual, moral, or other kind of action. Several kinds of projects the Christian teacher may well use are: (1) those in which objective expression is given to an idea or purpose

---

[2] G. H. Betts and M. O. Hawthorne, **Method in Teaching Religion** (New York: The Abingdon Press, 1925), p. 215 (Used by permission)

through some form of physical or social activity; (2) those in which the purpose is to create some subjective experiences in the pupil; (3) those calling for the mastery of intellectual difficulties; (4) those making for enrichment of experience by providing fuller information and broadening the outlook; and (5) those the purpose of which is to develop skill of some kind.[3]

Using the project

The project method does not mean merely doing something nor does it refer to the practical activities a class may be doing. As stated above, the essence of a project is a problem to be solved by purposing pupils. Almost every class comes across things that can well be put into the form of a project upon which the class may work for a longer or a shorter period of time. Teachers may take advantage of these occasions to launch the new method, being careful not to undertake too complex an activity until some skill is developed. The teacher must understand the interests and abilities of his pupils in order to suggest things that they can undertake. He should guide them in choosing the best in terms of their powers to achieve.

The problem of the project must be the pupils' problem. In cases where the project originates with the pupil, genuine purposing is achieved because the problem is his own and he has a definite urge to carry it out to completion. The good teacher will never superimpose a project upon his class but he will be obliged to exercise very definite guidance in their choices. Left to their own initiative, pupils will often select projects without educative value, or those that may be of no benefit to them because of the placement of the projects. With his larger perspective and knowledge and with his ability to lead, it is the task of the teacher to guide

[3] *Op. cit.*, pp. 218, 219

pupils in selecting projects that best meet their needs. He must also secure wholehearted enlistment of the pupils in carrying out selected ones. Without such purposeful guidance, the project method has very little value.

Having so guided that the project has been wholeheartedly accepted, the teacher should help pupils to develop their plans. This should be their responsibility. No pupil can learn good planning as a result of having someone else plan; only as he plans and fails, plans again and again and succeeds, will he learn wisdom in planning. However, it is the teacher's responsibility to guard him against errors of too serious a nature, though minor ones may well be experienced for the sake of the pupil's learning to be alert and critical at each step. Planning is a most important step in the project method, and it should be done very carefully.

Plans, once made, need to be carried out; they will not execute themselves. Executing demands action and results. Something has been achieved. What is its lost in the things he is doing and forget entirely the original purpose of the activity. The teacher must see that attention and energy are converged toward definite accomplishment. To guide execution does not mean that the teacher should do the work. Pupils may be exceedingly slow and awkward, taking much longer to do a thing poorly that the teacher could do better in shorter time, but the teacher needs to refrain from doing things for the pupils. It is not the speed with which the work is done nor the good quality of the product that counts. What is worthwhile is the results of the activity in the training and the development of the pupil.

The final stage in project activity is criticism of results. However, it is easy for the pupil to become worth? Here again, the teacher may be tempted to do too much. He who has created should judge for him-

self. Of course, the teacher must equip the pupil with
needed standards for sound evaluation and guide him
in the use of them. Only when pupil judgment proves
quite inadequate should the teacher become the judge.
A very large part of the value of the project method
lies in the training in self-criticism it gives. So the
wise teacher will help the pupil to see the whole process
of the activity in perspective: the problem with which
it started, the plan by which the project was carried
out, the way in which the plan was executed, and, finally,
the extent to which the whole process succeeded or failed.

Values of the project method

The advantages of this method are so manifest as to
need only enumeration.

1. It makes learning more natural and interesting
through the definite, tangible motivation that it provides.

2. It results in a wholesome attitude on the part of
pupils since they do their work because they wish to do
it, not under compulsion and coercion.

3. It trains the pupil in initiative, responsibility, perseverance, foresight, alertness, judgment, and evaluation.

4. Group projects develop in pupils a spirit of co-
operation.

5. It connects learning and experience, thus giving
good training for the solving of problems in practical
life.

6. It develops tolerance for the actions and opinions
of others.

7. It emphasizes learning for use rather than as an
accomplishment.

8. It makes learning a unified process, bringing interests, ideals, character traits, and attitudes together in
functioning relations.

9. It fixes the materials learned more securely in memory.

Limitations of project teaching

While the method has outstanding advantages such as have been given, it has also certain dangers and difficulties. Some of these are:

1. It requires, for successful use, a versatile teacher of superior skill. Only a teacher who is adept at detecting worthwhile purposes in pupils, skilful in encouraging these purposes, and able tactfully to discourage unsuitable purposes can succeed in getting the right kind of projects started. And skill is needed in the directing of planning, executing, and judging. No teacher should adopt this method unless he is capable of using it to accomplish better results than he can obtain by the use of the more common methods.

2. It requires much more preparation than the average teacher makes for his work. No project will run itself. Successful use of this method necessitates an immense amount of work on the part of the teacher.

3. There is danger of overemphasis on physical activities.

4. Any kind of activity, be it physical, mental, or spiritual, tends to become an end in itself instead of a means of learning.

5. It takes much more time than is ordinarily allowed for the lesson period. To use the method predominantly would mean that much less content could be taught.

6. The average class does not possess the seriousness of purpose requisite for successful completion of a project.

7. Projects undertaken sometimes have little educative value. It is easier to be active than it is to be fruitfully active.

8. Adequate classroom space and suitable equipment are often lacking.

9. Without supplementation by other forms of instruction, much of the knowledge gained and many of the principles learned may fail to be integrated into the total mass of the pupil's experience.

10. In group project teaching, there is a danger of forgetting the individual and his particular needs.

THE DRAMATIZATION METHOD

The drama has, through the ages, been much used as a method of presenting the truths of Christianity. At different periods and in various circles it has been subjected to a great amount of criticism. However, it must be recognized that dramatic representation is a natural activity of people and that it constitutes a good method of teaching and learning when it is rightly used. The sad fact is that the natural activity has been so perverted and debased in the theater that even those who recognize its great teaching power must hesitate to give dramatization sanction as a method of teaching lest in so doing they become the innocent means of lending support indirectly to an institution and to practices so degenerate as to be one of the festering sores of society. It would not seem to the present writer that a treatise on teaching method should ignore the dramatization method; yet he would have it distinctly understood that treatment here does not in the least sanction any of the subtle and serious evils that are an outcome of the natural tendency of man to act a part.

The basis of the dramatic method

Quite small children act out a goodly part of what they see and hear. They have an inherent tendency to imitate, to play a part, and to use imagination in making real the experiences they cannot have in actual life.

Along with these urges, there exists also an innate tendency to desire social approval and to give vent to feelings in emotional or physical activity. As children grow older and come into the period of adolescence, these different urges, with such others as the desire to express ideas and ideals in concrete forms, desire for companionship, and the desire to create, are manifest. Thus a considerable number of basic urges combine to constitute the dramatic impulse that expresses itself differently at various stages of development.

The tendency to imitate is a matter of reflex action at the beginning of life. To a very large degree, then, imitation is a product of the social environment of the child. What a child imitates and what he becomes because he imitates is a matter of habit. Therefore it becomes highly important that he be guided in his choice of models and that he be trained to discern the consequences of right and wrong choices. By means of the dramatic method, the teacher can set before the pupils life situations depicting moral and spiritual values and thus provide models and lessons for appropriation and learning.

The use of the dramatic method

As a teaching method, drama has to do, not with presentation of pageants, tableaux, and plays, but with the values pupils may realize from engaging in the activity. Through participation, the pupil is given opportunity for coöperation in purposing, planning, judging, and carrying out enterprises that have value apart from any public performance. Some principles to be observed in using the method are: (1) the drama is a means, not an end; the purpose is to develop the pupils, not to put on plays; (2) the teacher is a guide or coach. The pupils must be free at each step in the process to take initiative and shoulder responsibility; (3) the dramatic production provides a natural, lifelike situation where various characteristics, good and bad, are called forth. Opportunity is given for learning, for interpreting situations, for entering into the experiences of others, and for identification of the self with the highest and best in emotional experiencing.

Advantages of the dramatic method

First, it enables the pupil to express himself without feelings of self-consciousness. Second, it makes use of a natural tendency, directing it in the acquisition of Christian truth. Third, it so appeals to interest as to make possible a very deep impression of facts, events, and truths on memory. Fourth, it helps the pupil to put himself in the place of another, thus calling for an understanding of the character and the situations he meets. The reflex influence on his life may be great. Fifth, it develops traits of personality such as initiative, self-reliance, originality, and self-expression. Sixth, it trains the pupil in ability to make right responses to situations.

Dangers of dramatization

Some of the leading dangers have been touched upon, at least by inference, in the preceding discussion. Mere mention at this point should suffice. A great danger is that pupils may become more interested in dramatics than they are in learning the truth. Attention may be so much on performance that the teaching value is lost sight of wholly or in part. Again, the method may be overdone, especially in respect to the use of certain pupils who act well. All pupils should be permitted to take parts at times. Furthermore, it is easy to select and present performances that are not of the best type from the standpoint of content. Finally, it is not easy to keep the material itself and the spirit in which a performance is rendered such as will enrich and deepen the spiritual life.

HANDWORK

In recent times, there has been a considerable amount of emphasis upon handwork in the schools. The church school felt the effect of this emphasis and, for a while, carried handwork activities pretty much to an extreme. Though there have been many abuses of this line of activity and though it had better not be used at all than to be practiced as it sometimes is, handwork can be a most valuable aid to learning. For a long time, the public school, and later the church school, stressed "busy work"—merely something for pupils to do. The public school no longer does any "busy work" and not even handwork except in minimum amounts as an aid to other forms of learning, but too often church schools even yet use "busy work." In its rightful place, handwork activity has justification only as it contributes to learning. Therefore, it does not so much constitute a separate method as it does a means possible of use in connection with other forms of teaching for the purpose of making learning more effective than it would otherwise be.

A great number of things of varied nature are comprehended under the name of handwork. Paper work of many different kinds, pen work of various sorts, the keeping of notebooks, the constructing of models, the making of posters, map-making of several kinds, the use of plasticene, clay, raffia, and many types of material, the use of pictures in a multitude of ways, filling a box or making something for a missionary, the use of the sand table—all these and many more are included in handwork. In fact, anything that pupils may do that will enable them better to master and comprehend Christian truth may well be used for construction work in Christian teaching.

Values of handwork

The great fundamental value of handwork lies in the fact that doing with the hand is an aid to learning. As has already been emphasized, there is no learning without doing. A pupil is *doing* when he reads a book, participates in a discussion, or answers a question. Doing with the hand is only one form of self-activity, but it is a valuable form. Subsidiary to this value are others such as the following: handwork provides profitable occupation for small children who have a large amount of abounding energy; it gives training in the judging and handling of materials; it cultivates power of concentrated attention; it develops power of creative thought; it trains in unselfish coöperation with others; it develops self-control and perseverance through the holding of oneself to the accomplishment of a given piece of work; it has utilitarian value, especially with older pupils, who can make things of worth for use in the classroom; it trains in appreciation of the beautiful; it increases self-respect and confidence; it affords opportunity for self-expression; it makes for variety and a consequent release of tension during the class period; and it makes facts and truths more concrete and vivid.

The technique of handwork

Inasmuch as handwork should not be used merely to keep pupils busy or to interest them in attending the school, it follows that it should be used only when it contributes to learning. The question, therefore, which is always an accurate test of its worth is: Does the activity teach something of value that could be taught in no more effective way? The handwork activity should be interspersed with mental activities to make the learning project a part of a total learning situation. It should always be a necessary and component part of the most effective teaching, not something merely tacked on to the lesson period. The fact or the truth of the lesson should become much more real and vivid as a result of its use and it should accomplish this in a more economical manner than could be done by the use of any other technique.

The pupil should see the value in the work and know the connection between it and the total purpose of the classwork. He should have the feeling that the objectives of the lesson are being attained in part through the use of the handwork activity. He should also be genuinely interested in the work as a means to the attainment of this end. This work, as all other, should be within the range of his ability to accomplish, but it should not be so simple as to make him feel lack of respect for the activity. The result of his activity should be good handwork. Since the primary purpose is to aid learning, quality of product should never take precedence over teaching value; yet the pupil should think well enough of what he is doing to desire to finish it in a manner worthy of its importance. As in learning of all other kinds, the teacher is a guide; so it is his to make adequate and careful preparation, to see that the work goes along well in terms of its purposes, and to maintain a proper balance between pupil initiative and teacher contribution and help.

Dangers in handwork

The following are some of the outstanding things against which the teacher should set a guard:

1. The tendency to make handwork activity an end in itself.

2. Separation between handwork and the total work of the class.

3. Carrying on handwork with materials, supplies, and equipment inadequate in amount for doing it well.

4. The teacher's undertaking to guide pupils in doing that which he does not know how to do and which he himself could not do properly.

5. Asking the pupils to do something that is too difficult for the amount of skill they possess.

6. Overemphasis on perfection in quality of finished product to the exclusion of the realization of the teaching and learning value of the activity.

7. Failure to keep clear the spiritual values that should be realized.

FINAL CONSIDERATIONS ON METHOD

For the sake of emphasis, though at the risk of repeating some thoughts expressed at the beginning of Chapter X, it seems best to conclude this discussion of method with a few considerations on the use of method in general. For effective teaching, it is most necessary that the teacher be constantly on the alert, first, in the choice of the best method to use; second, in observation of the effect of the method used; and, third, in retrospective study of the results obtained from the use of a particular method. Teaching has no meaning except in respect to the learning of pupils and their development as an outcome of having learned.

It follows, therefore, that the best method to use in teaching is the method that will bring best results in terms of the objectives of the teaching. Every single pupil in a class is an individual and what may work very well in the case of one pupil may not produce best results when employed with a second. Each pupil comes to class with many habits, skills, and attitudes that have been developed through the course of the whole of his preceding life. It is essential that the teacher use a method adapted to the peculiar make-up of the individual and one utilizing to the fullest degree all previous learning. In other words, the choice of right method must be made in the light of what the pupil is and of his past experiences. Other factors to be considered when determining the method to use were discussed in the beginning of the preceding chapter.

Finally, the teacher who would do his best must be impressed with the fact that the best way to teach is in a number of ways. Constant variation in method should be made as the teaching situation changes in its particular elements. Jesus not only used many different varieties of approach to those to whom He wished to impart spiritual truth but He also made adaptations as the one to whom He was talking changed in his attitude or in his degree of comprehension. Any Christian teacher who wishes his message to evidence the quality and freshness that will lead to acceptance and understanding on the part of pupils will need to make use of ways of presentation such as will predispose them toward full, easy, and complete acceptance.

QUESTIONS AND PROBLEMS

1. Consider the various forms of oral presentation.
2. Show what place oral presentation has in the work of teaching.
3. Do you think that the lecture method constitutes the least effective method of directing pupils in their learning? Why, or why not?
4. State the chief advantages of the lecture method. Can you name some that are not listed in this chapter?
5. What do you consider to be the chief elements in the technique of oral presentation?
6. To what degree do you think that the average teacher might improve his technique?
7. In terms of your experience and observation, what would you say are the chief weaknesses in the talking of teachers?
8. Do you think that any of the disadvantages of the lecture method listed in this chapter are not such? Give reasons for your answer.

9. When did you last engage in a discussion? Criticize it in the light of the nature of the method as a teaching means.

10. Which do you consider to be the three or four chief values of the discussion method? Why do you choose these?

11. Enumerate the phases of structure of a discussion and comment briefly on each one.

12. What are the qualities of personality that a teacher should possess in order to use discussion effectively?

13. Do you think that a lazy teacher should use this method? What method could such a teacher use to good advantage?

14. State what you consider to be the chief dangers in the use of the discussion method.

15. Just what is the project method? Do you think that it should be used in Christian teaching?

16. What kind of a teacher can put it to best use; that is, what characteristics should he possess?

17. What is the essence of the project method?

18. Explain what is meant when it is said that "The activity may be physical, mental, aesthetic, social, moral, or spiritual."

19. Give the primary essentials of the use of the project.

20. State the chief values of the project method. Are there some that are not given in this chapter?

21. How would you criticize the enumeration of limitations given?

22. Does the dramatization method have a basis in human nature? How?

23. Can the method be used by a teacher who does not put on plays, pageants, tableaux, etc.? Explain.

24. State the chief values of the method.

25. What dangers would you add to the list given?

26. Should pupils in a Bible school ever be given handwork to do? Explain.

27. What could be the only justification for its use in any school?

28. State the essentials of technique for handwork.

29. Give illustrations to show the dangers that inhere in it.

30. State in a sentence or two your final conclusions on the subject of the use of method in teaching.

REFERENCES

Baker, E. D., **Kindergarten Method in the Church School** (New York: The Abingdon Press, 1925)

Betts, G. H., and Hawthorne, M. O., **Method in Teaching Religion** (New York: The Abingdon Press, 1925)

Bryant, S. C., **How to Tell Stories to Children** (Boston: Houghton Mifflin Co., 1905)

Crawford, C. C., **How to Teach** (Los Angeles: Southern California School Book Depository, 1938)

Dobbins, G. S., **How to Teach Young People and Adults in the Sunday School** (Nashville: Sunday School Board of the Southern Baptist Convention, 1930)

Eggleston, M. W., **Use of the Story in Religious Education** (New York: Harper & Bros., 1936)

Horne, H. H., **Jesus—the Master Teacher** (New York: The Association Press, 1920)
   Story-Telling, Questioning, and Studying (New York: The Macmillan Co., 1916)

McCoy, C. F., **The Art of Jesus as a Teacher** (Philadelphia: The Judson Press, 1930)

Miller, E. E., **Dramatization of Bible Stories** (Chicago: The University of Chicago Press, 1918)

Munkres, Alberta, **Primary Method in the Church School** (New York: The Abingdon Press, 1930)

Powell, M. C., **Junior Method in the Church School** (New York: The Abingdon Press, 1931)

Reagan, G. W., **Fundamentals of Teaching** (Chicago: Scott, Foresman and Co., 1932)

Retan, G. A., **Management and Teaching Technique in the Elementary School** (New York: Prentice-Hall, Inc., 1936)

Roberts, S. L., **Teaching in the Church School** (Philadelphia: The Judson Press, 1930)

St. John, E. P., **Stories and Story-Telling** (Boston: The Pilgrim Press, 1910)

Shaver, E. L., **The Project Principle in Religious Education** (Chicago: University of Chicago Press, 1924)

Smith, R. S., **New Trails for the Christian Teacher** (Philadelphia: The Westminster Press, 1934)

Stevenson, J. A., **The Project Method of Teaching** (New York: The Macmillan Co., 1921)

Vieth, P. H., **How to Teach in the Church School** (Philadelphia: The Westminster Press, 1935)

Wardle, A. C., **Handwork in Religious Education** (Chicago: The University of Chicago Press, 1916)

Chapter XII

PLANNING TO TEACH THE LESSON

At least three types of planning must be done by anyone who would teach well. The first of these concerns matters that should be considered before any teaching at all is done. It has to do with things other than the content to be taught but related thereto. For example, thought must be given to the conditions under which the teaching is to be done and the things that will be needed during the process of instruction. Proper teaching facilities, suitable tools, the right kind of materials of instruction, and adequate supplies need to be provided. The second type of planning is concerned with the totality of the content to be taught; that is, with the entire course of study. This is a very necessary type of planning but one that will not be treated here except to say that the planning of a course of study should be made in the light of the needs and development of the learner and should be definitely related at every point to his life and experience. The third type of planning has to do with the organization of the lesson for presentation to the pupils during the class hour. This is the kind of planning that will be treated in the present chapter.

The Importance of Lesson Planning

While lesson plans may not be very important, planned lessons are supremely so. Anything that is not planned is planless, and anything that is planless will likely fail to accomplish its purpose. No teacher, however experienced, can do his best work unless he gives careful consideration before entering the class room to possible ways of proceeding in the teaching. Every good teacher has in mind a certain inclusive aim that is to be attained as a result of his teaching. For each lesson, he chooses objectives to be attained through the teaching of that lesson. If attained, these objectives contribute to the realization of the inclusive aim of all teaching. Then from the large mass of available material, the various activities possible, and the many problems and questions before the pupils, the teacher must be able to select, or guide the pupils in selecting, that which will best contribute to the attainment of the objectives of the lesson.

Some form of lesson planning is essential to effective teaching. Just as any intelligent person demands detailed plans, specifications, and estimates of cost before proceeding to the building of a house, so teaching needs to be planned before it is carried into practice. No amount of experience in teaching, no degree of proficiency attained, no perfection in mastery of subject-matter, or no number of times a particular lesson has been taught can eliminate the need of specific planning for the teaching of each lesson. Every lesson and the activities of every class hour must be fitted directly to the needs and interests of a particular class. The very best manuals for teachers, such as are supplied with most of the lesson series, cannot be substituted for specific planning by the teacher himself for the particular class. As the carpenter cannot build without a plan, so the teacher must have a definitely worked out plan. And as the carpenter on the job must modify his plans to suit the nature of the materials and the working conditions as they develop, so must the teacher adapt and modify his plans to fit the situations as they arise in the course of the class work.

As a general rule, Christian teachers should do more actual planning than most of them are accustomed to do. Quite commonly, a series of lesson helps with teachers' manuals is used and it is very easy to place the greater burden of responsibility upon the writer of these, unmindful of the fact that they are "helps." However good the lesson series may be, it cannot take the place of the teacher or do his work for him. While a good lesson series may be well adapted to the age level and the general needs of the pupils with whom it is being used, it cannot meet their individual and specific needs. Accordingly, the teacher desirous of accomplishing best results will not slavishly or unthinkingly use the writer's material. On the contrary, he will work out his own plan, using that material if and when it is helpful and drawing on material from a variety of other sources as well. Furthermore, the lesson plan of the efficient teacher will be a statement, not only of the things he proposes to do during the class period, but also of the activities to be engaged in by pupils during the period for the purpose of realizing the objectives set for the teaching of the lesson. In other words, a good lesson plan suggests activity for the pupils, not for the teacher only; it puts the emphasis on pupil effort rather than on teacher activity.

Some of the values of lesson planning are:

1. It makes more likely the attainment of the inclusive aim of teaching.
2. A lesson plan helps to clarify objectives and to make them definite.
3. It provides for suitable transition from previous experiences to contemplated ones.
4. It makes for better selection and organization of content, material, procedures, and activities.

5. It tends to use of better methods of teaching.
6. Lesson planning gives confidence to inexperienced teachers and develops in them ability to improve more rapidly.
7. It serves as an incentive to the teacher to make adequate preparation.
8. It enables the teacher to teach with greater freedom.
9. It makes possible better planning for individual differences and special situations that need to be met.
10. It leads to elimination of many difficulties by anticipating them and by planning how to avoid or minimize them.
11: Reflective thinking done beforehand, makes for better unity in lesson development than is possible from spontaneous planning done on the spur of the moment.
12. It tends to insure availability of materials needed for classroom use.
13. It stimulates the teacher to have ready pivotal questions and appropriate illustrations.
14. Lesson planning provides for adequate summaries of the lesson.
15. A lesson plan gives a definite basis for an adequate checking of the outcomes of instruction.

KINDS OF LESSON PLANNING

Any teacher who is at all worthy of the office makes some preparation in advance, for he realizes that he cannot teach what he does not know. And any conscientious teacher makes not merely general preparation but also gives some thought to the teaching of the particular lesson, no matter how many times he may have taught that lesson. Such an one knows that teaching by spontaneous planning done under the spur of the moment cannot make for good teaching. Obviously, lessons should be planned. One very important question is: What kind of plan should be made? An earnest teacher, who sincerely desires to fulfil his obligations and who makes careful preparation may hit upon a method of lesson planning that is faulty and inadequate. Attempt is made here at examination of various kinds of plans

with a view to giving understanding of the better type
of lesson planning.

1. *The haphazard plan*

This is the kind of plan that results, quite typically,
from the planning of the lesson in the classroom while it
is being taught. In other words, the teacher goes before
the class with no plan at all, wanders from point to
point and back again, and gets nowhere. It is the kind
of planning the preacher does who takes the Bible for
his text and goes everywhere preaching the gospel. Co-
ordination and purpose in such teaching are conspicuous
by their absence; the result is time wasted, or worse
than wasted, in asking or answering questions without
point, in irrelevant discussion, and in aimless impartation of facts that never come to mean much to pupils
because of the lack of certainty, connection, and integration.

The haphazard plan may result not only from failure
to prepare but also from taking too little time to prepare
adequately. Too much planning is done at the last
minute—the night before or the morning before the
lesson is to be taught. No good teacher intends to neglect
preparation but many things crowd in upon his time
and, though he may undertake preparation heroically,
he cannot accomplish much by last-minute preparation.
Concern as to whether he will get plans made may dis-
tract attention. Unforeseen interruptions may even prevent the making of any plan at all. The making of adequate lesson plans demands an ample amount of time.
To teach successfully, the teacher must begin to plan
days, weeks, or even months in advance of the time for
teaching the lesson. Looking far ahead enables one to
choose truths for emphasis in relation to one another, to
avoid over-much duplication, and to make provision for
cumulative effect from lesson to lesson.

In the third place, the haphazard plan may result from a practice all too common among Christian teachers, namely, that of making poor use of a ready-made plan of organization taken from a periodical or a book in which the lesson is treated. As indicated earlier, many lesson series for Bible teaching are admirably well organized, but no plan is a good one except that one which is best adapted to the particular class being taught. Outlines of content, data, prepared questions, and all other valuable material and teaching aids lose their effect if they are used in a purely mechanical way. Unplanned activity based on random ideas gathered from lesson helps will make only for ineffective teaching.

Finally, the haphazard plan may have its source in the incompetence of the teacher. It may be that he has had little or no general preparation for teaching, that he lacks knowledge of the principles of teaching, and that he does not know how to make an adequate plan for teaching a lesson. Such a teacher should not last very long, for either he should obtain the preparation necessary for good teaching or he should be replaced by one who can teach well. Any person called to do the work of a Christian teacher, impressed with a sense of responsibility and willing to pay the price involved in becoming prepared for his task, can get adequate preparation. The various means affording opportunity for such preparations were discussed in Chapter V. Certain it is that a teacher who esteems his privilege seriously will make ready for his task by careful planning.

2. *The formal plan*

The teacher who realizes the importance of his work, conscious of the fact that some sort of organization is necessary, may turn to the use of certain mechanical aids. Devices such as acrostics, organization of content around central points such as the questions, When? who? why? what? or a series of words with the same initial letter are illustrations of things that may be used as basic plans for organization. Herbart and his followers, with a view to providing a better basis for planning, devised the "five formal steps" in teaching. These are preparation, presentation, comparison, generalization, and application. If the pupil is regarded as a mere passive receptacle to be filled with knowledge poured in by the teacher, the formal plan is the one to use. But if the pupil is a vigorously active being who learns under the direction and guidance of a teacher who controls the situation, altering all or part of it so that the pupil's responses are modified and his learning directed, then the formal plan of presentation will not suffice.

Some of the faults of the formal type of lesson plan are: it does not recognize that life cannot be made to fit into molds predetermined by the teacher; it gives too little heed to the growing, emerging needs of pupils; it is too much concerned with imposing subject matter and not enough with responding pupils who should develop thinking, initiative, and resourcefulness; it would make the presentation the same for all types of subject matter regardless of the fact that different approaches must be used with different kinds of content; and it is wasteful of the teacher's time in that it requires too much writing.

3. *The chronological plan*

For much material, the chronological plan of organization is the easy and the natural one to use. The point of emphasis in this plan is the content of what is to be taught rather than the preparation of method for teaching. The order in which certain events took place, the relationships between them, and the ways in which some events grow out of others seem to demand the chronological plan. When the material itself is chronological in order, the main task of the teacher in preparation might logically seem to be that of so mastering this material as to be able to deal adequately with the events of the lesson in this order. Some teachers teach thus, enlarging upon the content by giving illustrations and by making applications, and do quite effective work.

However, since telling is not teaching, the teacher who uses the chronological plan might do much more effective work by using some other form of organization. For little children especially, the time order is unsuitable because they lack both an understanding of periods of time and the social experiences necessary for an understanding of the lives of people distant in either space or time. Even adults may find appreciation of long periods of time a difficult achievement. In teaching children for the first ten or twelve years of life, therefore, it is most important to deal with the event, the character, or the incident, making it real and vital in terms of attachment to the child's present instead of trying to give it meaning in its past setting.

By the age of nine or ten, the average child begins to develop some sense of actual chronological changes in terms of their relations to his present life and situation. From this point the chronological connections may gradually be given more and more emphasis, but the teacher needs always to remember that relations of events remote in time cannot be made clear even to adults without special effort on the part of the teacher.

4. *The logical plan*

The use of this plan necessitates the fitting together of the different parts of the content in the way best suited to its logical relationships. Large divisions down to minute details are organized strictly in terms of their interrelations. The logical organization of material is the most natural, convenient, and useful form of organization for one who already knows the content. Anyone who knows all the facts and details perceives that they belong together in some sort of orderly arrangement in which each item has its particular place in the outline of the total content, this place being determined by the relation of the particular element to other elements.

But this vision of the total cannot be seen by one who is just beginning a voyage of discovery into areas new and strange to him. The general and the abstract can have no meaning except in terms of the particular and the concrete. Knowledge and understanding of the parts that make up the whole must be obtained before logical connections among parts can be perceived. Complete mastery of content demands that one be able to see elements in their relationships, but this does not mean that the pupil can learn these elements in the order in which they will appear when the learning is completed. To present general truths before the pupil has had concrete experiences and contacts to give them meaning is an excellent way to make content perplexing and uninteresting.

Accordingly, the teacher must beware of organizing materials in terms of the order suitable to the adult mind or to the mind of one who knows the entire field. Much by way of mere factual information may be passed out to pupils by use of the logical plan of organization. Even small children may, through its use, be led to a point where they are able to delight the heart of an undiscerning teacher or a superficial observer with mere repetition of great and important truths. But to what avail is any manifestation of complete mastery of the greatest truth if that truth is without fulness of meaning to the heart and the life of him who utters it? One thought grasped and understood and applied by a pupil to his own experience is worth far more than any number of things obtained from mere passive absorption of what someone else has said out of the fulness of his knowledge and understanding.

5. *The psychological plan*

To organize material psychologically means simply to follow the order that is determined by the way in which the pupil learns most easily and naturally. It means that the content taught must be adapted to the learner's experience and ability, appeal strongly to his interest, and be related to his present life and conduct. Usually, it is possible to harmonize content with these three factors — capacities, interests, and needs of the pupils — together because they overlap and integrate quite typically. At times, however, it may not be possible to work out a plan satisfying all three requirements. A pupil might, for example, need an understanding of some part of the material at a time when he was not interested in it; or he might be interested in something at a time when his background of experience is not sufficient for mastery of that part. However, it may be stated very definitely that any plan of organization that does not take into consideration these three conditions fails to make provision for most effective learning.

Consideration of the experience level of the pupil will lead the teacher not only to select in terms of his background but also to choose the particular phase of material and the avenue of presentation most closely related to his immediate experiences. Interest is naturally related closely to experience, for pupils can generally be most readily interested in that with which they have had recent experience. In planning, the teacher should adapt material and approach so as to connect effectually with something that will appeal to the pupil's interest. As has been emphasized heretofore, learning takes place only in connection with felt need. Abstract materials or materials unrelated to present life and conduct make for pupil attitude unfavorable to good learning. One characteristic, then, of good order in planning is provision that each element be brought in when the need for it appears. Not only does this make for more rapid learning but it also insures clearer understanding and better retention of the content learned.

The Christian teacher who would teach in a vital way must always organize the teaching materials in a psychological manner; that is, in such a manner as to fit the mind and needs of the pupils. The Bible is so rich in materials that meet the needs of pupils of any and all ages that any portion may be adapted and presented in a truly helpful manner. The task of the teacher is to ascertain in advance what there is in the particular portion that will best fit the needs of the pupil in his particular life situation.

Next, some point of contact must be established between the materials and the present life experience of the pupil. Frequently the pupils, especially younger ones, will need to have their minds refreshed in regard to earlier experiences in order to make these vital at the present moment. That which may not be understood in the material will need to be explained or made clear in some other way. Finally, the pupil must be stimulated to respond, assimilate, appropriate, and apply, through the use of his experience, the ideas and truths presented in the new material. Obviously, the procedure in planning a lesson will vary according to the situation and the aim in view; so no set rules can be followed but the suggestions given in this paragraph may be found valuable as a basis.

The teacher who desires to present spiritual facts and truths most effectively can do no better than to study the method Jesus used in His teaching, which was always related to the experience and the needs of those whom He taught. In dealing with both friends and enemies, He demonstrated great skill in establishing a point of contact. He made frequent reference to the Old Testament, knowing that those to whom He spoke were very familiar with its content. To the woman of Samaria, whom He would give living water to drink, He talked first of the water in Jacob's well. Frequently, He used parables to make a point of contact. In dealing with enemies, the point of His teaching was most painfully evident even to them (Luke 20: 19).

Always He adapted His teaching to the capacity and needs of His hearers. His approach, material, method, questions, stories, and illustrations varied according to the individual or the group. The teaching about prayer (Luke 11: 1-13), the discourse with Nicodemus (John 3: 1-13), the conversation with those who sought a sign (Matt. 16: 1-4), the warning of the disciples against the teachings of these seekers (Matt. 16: 5-12), the leading of the disciples to an acknowledgment of His Messiahship (Matt. 16: 13-20), and a number of other simple, direct approaches to great facts and truths evidence the skill with which Jesus used the psychological plan of teaching.

6. *The written plan*

From the point of view of the form they may take, lesson plans are of two kinds, the memorized and the written. A good plan of the first kind is held in the mind of a teacher who has, in thought, seen the activities of the class hour from beginning to end. Though nothing is put on paper, all the details of the lesson are formulated and every provision is made for the meeting of all problems, questions, and situations that are likely to arise. While it is possible, especially for experienced teachers, to work out plans of this kind and to use them quite effectively, the written plan tends to make for greater accuracy and completeness of statement and, at the same time, it does not depend upon memory which may fail to function aright. The memorized plan requires less time to prepare, it is not subject to misplacement, and it allows for greater spontaneity in that the teacher need not be referring to it while conducting the recitation.

However, written plans are to be preferred for several reasons. For one thing, a written plan necessitates greater exactness in thinking. "Writing maketh an exact man," said Bacon. The very attempt to commit one's thoughts to writing causes one to clarify them and to be more definite in his thinking. Again, the writing of a plan makes for a unity that is at least more difficult to obtain otherwise. By writing, revising, and supplementing, the teacher can get an orderly sequence, leading to one unified and harmonious impression. Third, the written plan allows for freedom in teaching. The teacher, with the written plan in hand, can give individual attention to the matter under consideration without fear of forgetting some essential point. Also, when a digression is made, there need be no difficulty in getting back to the place of departure from the planned course of procedure. The beginning teacher will likely tend to follow his notes too rigidly but, as experience is gained, more freedom will be realized. No teacher should ever be a slave to his preparation. As soon as sufficient freedom is developed, the teacher may well leave the plan book at home even though he still uses it in preparation for each recital.

A further advantage of the written plan lies in the

use that may be made of it for the improvement of teaching. Each lesson plan should be made as if for repeated use and then preserved. A plan worth making is a plan worth saving. No wise teacher will use a plan a second time without change; he will find it a convenient stepping stone to a new and a better plan. Frequently, a teacher teaches a series of lessons a number of times from year to year. To build new lesson plans each time is not only a waste of time and energy, but it is also unwise from the standpoint of proper utilization of experience gained from the use of preceding plans. Furthermore, much that is learned from the teaching of one series of lessons may be used to advantage in the teaching of a different series.

Soon after a lesson is over, the teacher will do well to take the plan that was used and go over the lesson in retrospect. Judgment of weaknesses should be made honestly and impersonally. Notations of faults and suggestions for improvement should be written in the margins. If these impressions are not recorded while they are fresh, it is likely that they will be lost entirely with the consequence that little or no benefit will be derived from them. Then the lesson plan should be filed so as to be ready for prospective revision if and when another occasion for its use comes.

When such an occasion arises, examination of the plan several months later, from a fresh viewpoint, will provide the teacher with a still better basis for evaluation. Re-examination of the plan, rechecking it in the light of the inadequacies discovered earlier, and revising it in the light of another lesson will lead to the formulation of a much better plan than was the first one. Thus, each plan may become a foundation for better teaching.

STEPS IN LESSON PLANNING

To no small degree, success in teaching depends on ability to produce a good, flexible teaching plan. The teacher who knows what he wants to happen in the lives of his pupils and who has a workable plan of procedure for accomplishing that purpose will be successful in the performance of his task. Planning a lesson is equivalent to living through the classroom situation in advance. In the measure that the teacher can envision the class in action, anticipating all the factors involved, can he plan the lesson for the needs of the class. Anticipation of factors includes a working analysis of the materials to be used, the method of their use, probable difficulties the pupils will encounter, the manner in which these difficulties are to be met, and the desired and probable pupil reactions.

Obviously, lesson plans should vary in content and in form in accordance with the conditions that are to be met. To outline a single pattern for the making of all lesson plans is, then, something that cannot be done. Teaching is not a mechanical matter to be carried on in a purely routine way. What serves a given teacher most effectively should be considered best for his purpose in teaching. Exactly the same procedure will never be used twice, even by the same teacher. Nevertheless, there are certain steps all good teachers would likely take in pretty much the same order when planning a lesson. The principal steps are treated below in about the order they should come. The fact that they are so given does not mean that one step in planning is completed at a time; often two or more may be going on simultaneously.

1. *Becoming familiar with the lesson series as a whole* should be the first step in lesson planning. No lesson of a unit or series can be planned effectively except in the light of its relationship to the general volume of ma-

terial. The teacher should be entirely familiar with the general content to be taught, its theme, its purpose, and the general method which should be followed in teaching it. Special attention should be given to the lesson preceding and to the one following. The plan should definitely relate the lesson to the previous work of the unit or series. Since the pupil's experiences do not give him proper perspective or enable him to use recent experience properly in interpreting present situations, the teacher must provide for his conscious recognition of the connection between past and present experiences in order to insure integrated learning.

2. *Examination of the lesson to be taught* is the second step in planning. Not intensive study but a preliminary scanning to get a general idea of the content is the purpose of this step. Every passage of Scripture was written for a purpose and the teacher should ascertain the purpose of the lesson for the day. The idea of the writer and not the teacher's idea is the important thing, for the office of the teacher is to interpret truth, and he cannot do this truly except as he understands the original aim. This may vary little or much from what the teacher's own purpose for the class is, as determined by the needs of the pupils. If it varies greatly, perhaps a different lesson will have to be chosen; if the variation is not too great, supplementation from other sources may be sufficient to bring about adaptation for the present teaching purpose. Whatever is done in this step is done in the light of the teacher's knowledge of the capacities, the interests, and the needs of the pupils.

3. *Determination and statement of the aim of the lesson* comes next. The aim of a particular lesson will have to be formulated with reference to the content thereof and in terms of pupil experience. Any lesson material may suggest a number of purposes subsidiary to the general aim of the Bible passage as a whole.

Each of these may have good teaching value but all cannot be used in good teaching. Accordingly, the teacher should determine the one aim or purpose that is to be adhered to resolutely in the teaching of the lesson. Teaching is done for the sake of learning, and the learning process is centered in the pupils; so the aim of each lesson must be determined in the light of their needs. It is important that the aim of each single lesson be conceived in reference to the objectives of the unit or series and also in terms of the inclusive aim of all the teaching. The aim should be stated in specific terms; it should be a definite statement of the exact thing the teacher would like to accomplish.

4. *Providing for the organization and use of materials that will be needed in teaching* is an important matter. Materials must be selected, organized, and used in accordance with the aim sought. Usually this has to do with Biblical references or stories, extra-Biblical stories, reference material, poems, music, pictures or models, equipment for handwork, and activity to be engaged in to enrich and supplement the lesson content of a series. Full provision for pupil initiative and activity should be made, because it constitutes the medium of learning. Most careful consideration should be given by the teacher to the question of what materials to use as well as to the way in which they are to be organized for use.

5. *A statement of methods and procedures to be used in the lesson must be worked out.* This will include both those to be employed by the teacher and others that will be used by the pupils. In this step, the aim of the lesson must be kept very clearly in mind. The teacher should select those methods that will best lead to the attainment of the aim. Usually several methods in combination will be used and these will have to be chosen not only in the light of the aim of the lesson but also

with good understanding of the needs of the pupils if those needs are to be met successfully. It is especially important that a good way of approach be planned, because the start of a lesson has much to do with the results of the teaching. The approach must be made in terms of the experience of the pupils and should so discover needs and appeal to interest as to prepare the way for the presentation. Usually it is well to secure active participation on the part of the pupils from the very beginning rather than for the teacher to make the approach in terms of his own activity. In some effective way a point of contact must be established between the past experiences of the pupils and the new material that is to be presented.

After this point of contact is well established, the new material may be presented. As indicated, the particular method to be used will depend upon the aim of the lesson, the needs of the pupils, and the nature of the materials. A limited number of leading questions, or of key words or expressions touching upon vital phases of the lesson will be set down in the plan, as will also suggestions for illustrations, explanations, and applications at appropriate points. Notations concerning any expression work that is to be used and provision for carrying it out will be made. The plan will provide for a maximum of pupil participation in class discussion, in the making of reports, in motor activity, and in other ways, depending on the type of teaching that may be used in presenting the lesson. The problem to be met in connection with presentation is: How may the thought of the pupils be best stimulated and guided toward a conclusion ?

6. *Provision must be made for the formulation of working conclusions.* That which was taken as the fundamental thought, or the aim of the lesson, will determine the nature of the conclusions. Good planning necessi-

tates provision of means for the making of the final impression the pupils are to carry away and of applications to daily living that may be made by them later. Here, as in the presentation, pupil participation should be secured; hence the conclusions may well be stated in the form of stimulating questions related to the fundamental thought and its development during the period. These may bear upon something to plan or to do or they may lead to a statement of truth to be used to guide thought or action. Usually it is better to concentrate on two or three conclusions, often on a single one flowing directly from the main thought, rather than to present four or five different ones.

7. Having thought through and planned the lesson thus, *the teacher should now be ready to build a teaching plan so organized as to constitute a good guide to the conduct of the class session.* Of course, pencil and paper may well have been freely used from the very beginning of the preparation but now the whole should be put down in better form. The details of such an outline will depend upon variations in terms of many factors such as the level of the pupils, the lesson content, the teacher's predilections, the time limits for teaching, and the type of teaching. The important thing is that the teacher use some plan of logical organization for relating purposes, data, and procedures. What should be included in a written plan is that which will enable the individual teacher to do his best work. The main divisions of a plan might be the following: (1) the class or group to be taught; (2) the lesson topic; (3) the aim or purpose of the lesson; (4) a list of the teaching materials to be used; (5) the procedures to be followed; and (6) the conclusion or the summary. The fifth section is the heart of the plan; it may well have the following subdivisions: (1) the plan of approach; (2) teacher activities; (3) pupil activities; and

(4) notations concerning illustrations, questions, and discussions.

8. *Revision and review of the lesson plan* will need to be made. The plan should provide for every step in the learning process. It should help the teacher to move forward constantly and unhesitatingly throughout the classroom period to thorough accomplishment in teaching. Therefore, after it has been made with the greatest care, it should be subjected to most searching scrutiny to be sure that everything is as it should be. A good plan is invariably the outcome of at least several revisions in which the statement of the aim or purpose is reconsidered, modification of material to be used is made, the technique of teaching that gives promise of best results is subjected to further examination, and more consideration is given to anticipated situations that may arise during the class period, with determination of the possible procedures to be used in meeting them. Reviewing may also be done a number of times, for the teacher will wish to be so familiar with every part and detail of the plan as to be able to use it in the freest way during the teaching period. As a rule, it will be found wise to make a last review just before the class period begins.

Further Considerations on Lesson Planning

A lesson plan is a means to an end. The only justification for existence that it has is in its results in improved teaching. It should conserve the time and energy of the teacher and be a definite aid to him. The plan should, therefore, be specific and practical. Words used in the written plan should be meaningful and as few in number as are needed to express the thought adequately. On the other hand, the plan should be sufficient in content to make it a valuable aid. Vagueness and generality of statement should be avoided as well as all unnecessary formality. In short, the written plan should be a good, workable means for bringing about positively good results by way of promoting the effectiveness of the teaching.

A good lesson plan is flexible and adaptable to changing requirements and situations. There may even be times when good teaching demands the total abandonment of the plan in order to meet an emergency. The teacher should never be a slave to the plan, however good it may be. In building the plan, consideration may well be given as to what might be eliminated or reduced if necessary. Any teacher knows that unexpected situations may arise at any time; it is impossible to predict pupil reactions except as the teacher may too completely dominate the class period. Pupil response coming in a very unique or unexpected way may throw the lesson into a channel quite different from that of the plan. It may be that a pupil will bring up some problem important to solve at the moment and thus give the teacher a golden opportunity to do some teaching that was not at all foreseen when the plan was made.

The true aim of teaching may be furthered by digressing, in such a situation, from the formal teaching plan. As to whether or not this will be the case is a matter that will have to be judged by the teacher. It is important in this connection for the teacher to remember that he must keep the lead and decide, if he has led the class in the exploration of some tributary, when they have gone far enough and it is time to return to the main stream. The real teacher will keep in touch with the class rather than with his lesson plan, using the latter as something to depart from if his constant alertness for opportunities to meet the actual needs of pupils indicates that this is the wise thing to do. The purpose of the teacher may well be to develop habits of independence of the lesson plan, not habits of sub-servience to it.

Under the stimulus of a classroom situation, the teacher may have flashes of insight that could not have been experienced during the making of the plan. It may be well also to act upon these even if they do lead the class far from the planned route of travel. If present knowledge and understanding show that a certain direction is the best to take, it would be foolish to continue in another merely because one had previously decided to go that way. The necessity for flexibility and adaptibility of plan should never cause the teacher to excuse himself from most thorough preparation in planning. As was said in the beginning of this chapter, a lesson plan is not necessarily important, but planned lessons are. The teacher, as anyone else, will get nowhere if he has no idea as to where he wants to go or how he may get to where he wants to go. The wise teacher will plan with all the intelligence, knowledge, and foresight that he can muster, but he will keep his plan flexible so that it may be adapted to circumstances as occasion requires.

Another desirable characteristic of lesson plans is that they should provide for individual differences and individual problems. That no two pupils react exactly alike is a fact the teacher must keep in thought at every point in teaching. Consequently, it is impossible to prepare all questions and illustrations in advance. The plan should include pivotal questions and some basic illustrative data, but the teacher will need to be ready with a much larger store of good questions and illustrative material to meet the opportunity of the moment. On occasion, even these may not suffice, and recourse must be had to original and spontaneous production. However, the more thoroughly a teacher prepares and plans the less will be the need for the use of aids drawn upon on the spur of the moment—aids quite likely to be imperfect at best.

Two considerations about time come in connection with the planning of lessons. The first has to do with the time when the planning should be done. Too often the plan is made the night before the lesson is to be taught. No teacher can do most effective planning on such short notice because it gives too little time for looking up materials, thinking through the lesson, and living oneself into it. Best planning is done weeks and even months in advance of the time of teaching. A good teacher may well carry with him constantly a notebook with an outline of the lessons for a year where he can record illustrations, thoughts, and observations. The kind of teachers who succeed best are those who take their work seriously enough to begin to plan long in advance so that the final result is a plan that has been revised, thought through, and most thoroughly adapted to teaching needs.

A second factor in regard to time has to do with the determination of content in relation to the length of the teaching period. It is not easy, especially for an inexperienced teacher, to estimate the time that will be required to complete a given task. A common fault in teaching is to attempt to cover more ground than the time at the disposal of the teacher permits. Sometimes teachers find that they have done all that was planned and the period has not come to an end. Few teachers can estimate the time exactly. However, continued planning, if well done, with a careful estimate of the time and accurate checking afterwards will enable the teacher to develop in proficiency in estimating the time for lessons.

Finally, the Christian teacher will recognize his utter dependence on God in planning as in every other phase of his teaching. Here, as elsewhere, he will realize that the work is God's and that he, while a worker with God, is a channel through which the Holy Spirit operates to accomplish the purposes of God in the lives of the pupils whom he teaches. Accordingly, he will make constant use of prayer from the very beginning of his planning, seek the guidance of the Holy Spirit at every point, and trust from beginning to end in the wisdom and power that God alone can give to enable him to plan aright. No amount or quality of preparation made without these will avail to make Christian teaching or bring about Christian results, but careful, conscientious planning by a consecrated Christian teacher will make for a much more effective presentation of the Word of God as the Holy Spirit operates to make the truth clear to the hearts of those taught.

Questions and Problems

1. Comment on the relative importance of the three kinds of planning that must be done.
2. Why is a planned lesson more important than a lesson plan?
3. Show that teaching without a plan is impossible.
4. Do you agree with the statement to the effect that Christian teachers do too little planning? Why do they not plan more?
5. Can you add to the list of values that lesson planning gives?
6. What are the chief forms which haphazard planning assumes?
7. State the essential weaknesses of the formal plan.
8. Give illustrations of materials or lessons that would have to be organized chronologically.
9. Why is the chronological plan of organization unsuitable for use with children?
10. Does the logical plan suffice to meet the needs of children? Can it be adapted to their needs?
11. What is meant by the "psychological plan" of organization?

12. Are there portions of the Bible that cannot be taught according to the psychological plan? If so, what are some of them?
13. Give further examples illustrative of Jesus' use of the psychological approach.
14. Why should lesson plans be put in written form?
15. Does it minimize against the effectiveness of his teaching for a teacher to use a written plan when he is before his class?
16. How should a written plan be used after it has once served the purpose of use in teaching the lesson for which it was made?
17. What is the effect of using over and over again a plan once made?
18. Can lesson plans for all types of teaching have the same general form?
19. Show the importance of the teacher's being familiar with the entire series of lessons.
20. Why is it essential that the aim of the lesson be stated?
21. Select a Bible lesson and follow the eight suggested steps in preparing a plan for teaching.
22. How can the teacher stimulate and guide thought to satisfactory working conclusions?
23. To what extent can a teacher anticipate the unexpected? How may he provide for unexpected situations?
24. Should a teacher digress from his plan as a general rule, or seldom? Explain.
25. How will the conscientious Christian teacher make his lesson plans?

References

Betts, G. H., **How to Teach Religion** (New York: The Abingdon Press, 1919)

Burton, W. H., **The Nature and Direction of Learning** (New York: D. Appleton and Co., 1929)

Dobbins, G. S., **How to Teach Young People and Adults in the Church School** (Nashville: Sunday School Board of the Southern Baptist Convention, 1930)
Working with Intermediates (Nashville: Sunday School Board of the Southern Baptist Convention, 1926)

Freeland, G. H., **The Improvement of Teaching** (New York: The Macmillan Co., 1925)

Lotz, P. H., and Crawford, L. W., **Studies in Religious Education** Nashville: Cokesbury Press, 1931)

McCoy, C. F., The Art of Jesus as a Teacher (Philadelphia: The Judson Press, 1930)

Plummer, L. F., The Soul Winning Teacher (New York: Fleming H. Revell Co., 1934)

Roberts, S. L., Teaching in the Church School (Philadelphia: The Judson Press, 1930)

Schmauk, T. E., How to Teach in Sunday School (Philadelphia: The United Lutheran Publishing House, 1920)

Shaver, E. L., How to Teach Seniors (Boston: The Pilgrim Press, 1927)

Stormzand, M. J., Progressive Methods of Teaching (Boston: Houghton Mifflin Co., 1927)

Suter, J. W., Creative Teaching (New York: The Macmillan Co., 1924)

Thayer, V. T., The Passing of the Recitation (Boston: D. C. Heath and Co., 1928)

Vieth, P. H., How to Teach in the Church School (Philadelphia: The Westminster Press, 1935)

CHAPTER XIII

THE IMPROVEMENT OF TEACHING

THE preceding chapters represent an attempt to deal with a few of the elements essential to good teaching. Quite likely those who have read thus far are already engaged in teaching. It is probable also that these readers have a desire to do their work well. Every true teacher has the wish to improve his teaching. But wishing alone will never bring about improvement. He who would become a better teacher must become such not by wishing but by dint of hard work. Improvement will come only as the teacher constantly gives thought to making his teaching better, as he studies to improve, and as he works diligently to produce better results. No amount of wishing will avail as a substitute for work. The purpose of this final chapter is to present a few ideas that may be helpful to any teacher who sincerely desires to improve his teaching.

IMPROVEMENT CAN BE MADE

First of all, it can be stated that teaching is never done so well as to eliminate possibility of improvement. After the very best teaching has been done, it may be said most truthfully, "It might have been done better." As was shown in the first chapter, teaching is a very complex and subtle enterprise. Being such, it is subject to refinements of skill and technique without end. No perfect teaching can ever be done by a being as imperfect as man is.

Obviously, there are natural variations in the capacity to develop teaching ability, but any person of average intelligence who is given the opportunity to teach can become a better teacher if he will but use properly the means for improvement at his disposal in any normal situation in life, provided always that he is willing to pay the price. Success will come only as a result of painstaking effort in dealing with weaknesses, in careful study of results, and in ceaseless correction of errors. Only by long-continued perseverance in the face of discouragements can anyone become a really successful teacher. A good teacher is not made in a few short years. But improvement is bound to result if serious, conscientious effort in the direction of betterment is perseveringly made.

The growing teacher is the one who is making improvement in teaching. This one knows the worth of putting each phase of the teaching act in the crucible of critical self-evaluation to ascertain wherein it is inferior in quality. He subjects every teaching activity to rigid retrospective examination for the purpose of seeing whatever there may be of merit or fault, viewing all in a dispassionate, objective manner in order to have an adequate basis for better effort in the future. He makes intense dissatisfaction with results a starting-point for something better in the next teaching situation. Never content to rest on the thrill of feeling that something has been accomplished, he pushes on to higher attainments.

But the teacher who feels that he has learned all that is to be learned about teaching never attains the highest measure of success. Neither does he who is so conceited as to be content with the thrill of success once attained in a measure, be it large or small. Likewise the lazy teacher, the careless teacher, and the unfaithful teacher, fail to attain true success. Improvement can be made, and improvement must be made if the teaching is to accomplish its true end and purpose. The price of good teaching is the constant improvement of one's teaching. Not to improve means stagnation and ultimate failure while rightly directed effort at improvement pays high dividends in increased richness of quality in teaching.

IMPROVEMENT MUST BE CONSTANT

One important secret of successful accomplishment in teaching is unremitting attempt to improve. Working at anything by fits and starts seldom produces desirable outcomes. In perfecting any act or skill, conscious holding of oneself to the best possible performance is what counts for most. As soon as one becomes satisfied with anything less than his best, that soon does the quality of the work become less perfect. And in teaching as well as in many other kinds of activity, a bit of retrogression may be the beginning of lines of action that find ultimate expression in bad habits so fixed as to be almost impossible to break.

The long, steady pull is what counts. Great enthusiasm for perfection of accomplishment today will lose all or a good part of its value if tomorrow finds one yielding to the temptation of laziness or discouragement. In the daily round of common tasks, one experiences a tendency to let down a bit, but it is just here that one's level of attainment is determined. Doing less than one's best in the common task makes it impossible for one to do his best at some other task. The truly successful teacher sets his face like an adamant, as it were, and goes along making constant effort at improvement regardless of temptation, trial, discouragement, failure, success, or whatever experience he may meet.

Unceasing effort is the price that must be paid if one would become a better teacher.

As intimated in the preceding section, improvement is a long and gradual process. Teachers who fail are invariably those whose interest in improvement does not last over a long period of time. On the other hand, teachers who become superior strive continually over many years of time. At no point, regardless of how long one has been teaching, can he rest on past laurels, for many years of experience are not enough to eliminate the necessity for continued advancement. Gradual advancement along several lines of intelligent, persistent, well-directed effort is the secret of good teaching. This kind of teaching is largely a matter of development. The good teacher grows steadily as long as he teaches. He may make great progress in one year, but best teaching comes after years of effort.

BASIC ACTIVITIES OF TEACHING

Very commonly, teaching is interpreted to mean the work that is done by the teacher in the classroom. However, this is comparatively a small part of the effective teacher's work because the planning necessary for good teaching may take far more time and energy than the actual classroom teaching does. An essential component of planning is the study of pupil's needs and interests in order to determine what and how to teach so that their needs will be met. Planning is, therefore, the first basic activity of teaching. The second is the classroom teaching itself. The effective teacher will plan most carefully and afterward carry out the plan as skilfully as possible in the actual classroom teaching. Then will come a third activity, viz., the analysis and critical evaluation of this teaching in order to ascertain wherein it could be improved.

Teaching, then, is more than classroom work; it is

a unit activity with three major divisions: the planning, the teaching itself, and the diagnosis and improvement of the teaching. The teaching itself is the central phase; the others exist for the purpose of making this as effective as possible. Any teacher desirous of improving the quality of his teaching needs, therefore, to evaluate the planning, the teaching itself, and the procedures he uses to bring about better results in his teaching. In other words, the growing teacher will be concerned with improvement of planning, of teaching, and of his techniques for diagnosis and improvement of teaching. The three activities do not always follow one after the other in the order given. Any one may be used when it is expedient to do so. For example, diagnosis and improvement may very well be made in connection with the planning before any teaching is done, and planning may make for much better analysis and critical judgment of the quality of the teaching process.

These, then, are the basic activities of teaching. The teacher who does these well will be a good teacher. They are not easily done though some teachers will accomplish them more easily and effectively than will others. The teacher in all efforts at improvement needs always to see these activities as separate elements and also as component parts of the larger activity. Also, the teacher should keep very clearly in mind the fact that the teaching is done for the sake of the learner; his growth and his development constitute the reason for the teaching. This is the criterion by which the success of the teaching is always to be judged. An attempt at improvement of teaching means only that some better way for bringing about pupil growth and development is being sought. Only as the highest welfare of the pupil is promoted is there any point or value to the improvement of the activities of teaching.

The Christian teacher will, then, be concerned primarily with so planning the work that the learning activities of the pupils will result in that knowledge of the Word of God which will be effective in their lives, bringing them to Christ and building them up in Christ as perfect men of God, "throughly furnished unto all good works." This planning will be subjected to critical diagnosis and improvement both before and after the teaching has been done. Next, the teacher will carry out the plan in the classroom teaching, keeping his eyes open as he goes along for ways in which improvement might be made and, after the class is over, he will make a searching evaluation of the quality of the process to determine how well it may or may not have met the needs of the pupils. Finally, the planned procedures for betterment of the instruction will themselves be subjected to critical examination and evaluation in order to make them more perfect in the future.

The good teacher always keeps in the background. He will never do all the work while the class looks on because he knows that it is the learner who must do the learning. Only as he participates can any teaching succeed. The teacher will, consequently, refrain from taking exercise he does not need and direct the pupils in exercise they do need. This is a good point at which to begin the improvement of teaching. Most teachers will find it possible to improve their work by learning to talk less and to devote more time to the study of the reactions of the pupils. Less physical and verbal activity on the part of the teacher and more mental activity, directed intelligently and properly, will result in better teaching. The work of a good teacher is a matter of thoughtful analysis at every step. The influence upon the pupils of the facts and truths taught is the important thing and the work of good teaching consists in learning to wait while the pupils grow and develop. The successful teacher plans his work well, studies his pupils collectively and individually, provides each pupil with all possible opportunity for the exercise of desirable functions, and makes himself a wholesome, stimulating force in the development of the pupils.

IMPROVEMENT THROUGH SELF-SUPERVISION

Unless a teacher studies himself constantly, he will not improve as he should. The basic essential to improvement of teaching is such a strong desire to improve as will cause the teacher to criticize himself constructively and effectively. In the final analysis, it is the teacher himself who must improve; no other person and no other means avail except as the individual works upon himself with a sincere desire to do better work. Any person can do much, without aid of any kind, to better himself as a teacher and to improve greatly the quality of his work. Such self-improvement necessitates that one be a severe but just critic of his own teaching. Neither an overweening self-confidence that causes one to take groundless satisfaction in results nor such a harsh judgment as leads to a discouraged attitude of hopelessness will count in this connection. One should neither overestimate nor underestimate his worth but pass fair and thoughtful judgment upon his work with the very definite purpose to improve it.

Improvement of the teacher himself. Since the teacher himself is the most important human factor in Christian teaching, an important way to improve teaching is to improve the teacher. "Perfect schools are the result not so much of good methods as of good teachers, teachers who are thoroughly prepared and well-grounded in the matter that they have to teach; who possess the intellectual and moral qualifications required by their important office; who cherish a pure and holy love for the youths confided to them, because they love Jesus Christ." As was emphasized in Chapter IV, perfection

of Christian life and personality is the ideal. But as
no person can ever reach the standard of absolute per
fection in this world, it follows naturally that any
teacher can improve himself.

The teacher worthy of the name Christian will be in
vital touch with his Lord and earnest in his effort to
lead others into fellowship with Him. As a person
responsible for the spiritual welfare of those whom he
teaches, the Christian teacher will feel the need for continuous cultivation and deepening of his own spiritual
life. He will be faithful in prayer, in study of the
Word for the sake of his own spiritual life, and in
meditation on the things of God. He will avail himself
of the best privileges afforded in his environment for
development in grace. He will, like Chaucer's parson,
be most careful to practice in his own daily living the
teachings of Christ he is seeking to have his pupils
reduce to practice in their lives. The standard presented
to Titus by Paul may well be his standard: "In all
things showing thyself a pattern of good works: in doctrine showing uncorruptness, gravity, sincerity, sound
speech, that cannot be condemned; that he that is of the
contrary part may be ashamed, having no evil thing to
say of you" (Titus 2: 6, 7).

Improvement through experimentation. A second line
along which the teacher may work to improve the quality
of instruction is that of trying out things he has learned.
As the alert teacher studies his own teaching critically,
as he observes others in their teaching, as he reads, and
as he hears other teachers talk, he gets new ideas and
knowledge of better ways of working. At the first opportunity, he should try these. Teaching is an art that
must be learned. Every Christian teacher should have
training before he begins to teach though the training
can provide nothing more than a foundation. One can
progress faster and avoid many serious blunders if his

first teaching has been preceded by study of the prin
ciples of teaching, but every teacher must learn in the
school of experience.

The teacher who grows is the one who uses his classroom as a laboratory in which to gain new and better
experience. Of course, the careful teacher will not be
a hair-brained experimenter who makes pupils suffer
the effects of rushing in headlong to try things that just
happen to come to his attention. On the contrary, he
will be a painstaking worker who varies his methods
of procedure intelligently in order to advance. With
the understanding that the work is difficult, with the
very best training that it is possible to obtain, with a
willingness to work and to capitalize his experience as
he goes, and with a persistence that will not yield, he
will go forward, ever finding new and interesting things
to put into practice, grudging no effort that gives promise
of producing better results in the lives of his pupils.

A program for improvement. A third element in
improvement through self-supervision is a program for
self-improvement. One may get a just estimate of his
own worth and of the quality of his work by use of
his own unaided judgment or that of others with whom
he is in contact, but usually self-improvement comes
better through working with a definite plan. To improve, a teacher must have definite purposes vital to
him, and he must be moving along lines of well-balanced
progress. An otherwise intelligent teacher who lacks
ideals, who works without definite purpose, or who is
fitful and one-sided in enthusiasm will not make much
advancement. On the other hand, he who determines
specifically where he wants to go and continues per-
sistently along the same lines of progress for several
years will grow provided that his program for improvement is a good one.

While a considerable number of self-rating sheets

and score-cards have been devised for secular teaching, not many good standards have been formed for measuring the results of Christian teaching. With suggestions from secular sources and with the aid of such cards and scales as are given by Roberts,[1] Vieth,[2] Chave,[3] or Betts and Hawthorne,[4] any teacher sincerely desirous of highest improvement may formulate a standard of measurement that will be of great value to him.

No plan for improvement should be regarded as perfect or final nor should any standard of measurement be taken too seriously. A good plan once established will need to be modified by the teacher as he grows, though the general scheme that has been well thought out may never be entirely done away with by progress. The point is that any good standard of measurement will be found helpful as a definite means for realizing improvement. It will give the teacher something against which to check himself and his procedures so that he can learn where to place emphasis in bettering his teaching. The value of a standard lies not so much in its exactness as in what it suggests to him who uses it intelligently.

The conscientious teacher who sincerely desires to improve may well take note of the fact that perfection in all phases of teaching is something that is approached by few teachers. With a good plan for improvement well worked out, a teacher has at hand something that will challenge his best effort for years. It takes time to improve. A single year of rightly directed effort in the use of a good plan will result in improvement, but

[1] S. L. Roberts, **Teaching in the Church School** (Philadelphia: The Judson Press, 1927), page 148

[2] P. H. Vieth, **How to Teach in the Church School** (Philadelphia: The Westminster Press, 1935), pp. 167-170

[3] E. J. Chave, **Supervision of Religious Education** (Chicago: University of Chicago Press, 1931), pp. 315-317

[4] G. H. Betts and M. O. Hawthorne, **Method in Teaching Religion** (New York: The Abingdon Press, 1925), pp. 253, 255-258

during this period, one's standard for himself will have raised. Consequently, he will be ready to start on another lap of the endless race toward the ever-advancing goal of perfection. To the true teacher, the exhilaration of the race and not the attainment of the goal brings the thrill that prompts to ever better results.

IMPROVEMENT THROUGH STUDY

While the Christian teacher should get all the training possible before he enters upon his work, it is yet true that some of the best values that any growing teacher ever realizes are those coming from his training while in service. A successful and conscientious teacher must always be a learner; the training of a good teacher is never completed. Whatever he may have learned concerning teaching before entering upon his work, constitutes a foundation upon which he may build while he teaches. That which he has learned will make the true teacher so eager for further learning that he will continue to read and study in order to learn more.

Acquaintance with the reading habits of a teacher constitutes a good basis for predicting his success. No one will get far through the reading of the daily newspaper, the average magazine, and popular fiction. As the body is affected by the kind and quality of the food that is eaten, so the mental and the spiritual life are moulded by what they feed on. "Reading maketh a full man," said Bacon. The growing teacher will wish to read according to a plan that will include two types of reading: general and professional. The plan makes for systematic, persistent reading along well-conceived lines. Even if the plan is not followed throughout, the fact that it is in existence makes for advantage such as would not be realized were the reading done in a purely haphazard way. Furthermore, a plan will be of assistance in keeping one at reading that he might not get done if he had no plan.

General reading constitutes a good source of continued growth. Each teacher may well keep a notebook in which he jots down the titles of books and articles that he hears of or finds. From this and other sources, he can then make up reading lists. It is well to make a list of books to be read during a year and then use it as a guide to one's reading. Such a list aids greatly in the doing of some regular reading which, without the list, may never get done. Besides, it enables one so to plan his reading as to make for more complete and better rounded development, thus making for enlarged experience of life, which will be found useful in guiding others.

In his reading for development in teaching more specifically, the Christian teacher should also work according to a plan. The fields that he, as a growing teacher, will need to enter into more and more are: knowledge of the Bible and ways of studying it; knowledge of the pupils whom he teaches; understanding of the principles of teaching; knowledge of the church school, its curriculum, organization, and administration; and knowledge of himself. Each year the teacher may well read at least one or two books in each of these several fields. As he finds opportunity to do so, he may glean much that will be of value to him from some of the few magazines that deal with the work of the church-school teacher. A kindred source of much good information is the literature that is published for teachers in connection with many of the lesson series put out for the use of pupils.

A very effective means for further training is the teachers' meeting or workers' conference of the local church, though most church schools do not utilize it as such. Usually it is a business meeting rather than an educational one. However, regular meetings for the improvement of the teachers in service may well take the place of the customary irregular teachers' meeting for business. The alert teacher will lend his support to this change in complexion of the meeting and will also profit much from attendance thereupon.

The teacher who wishes to study for the purpose of improving his work will find further opportunity along some of the lines indicated in Chapter V. Courses given in local teacher training classes, correspondence courses, work in colleges and Bible institutes that give such training, summer training schools, etc., are some of the sources the teacher eager to improve through study may use in order to become capable of better teaching.

IMPROVEMENT THROUGH OTHER PEOPLE

One of the best ways in which a teacher may better his teaching is through learning from other people. Often it is said that experience is the best teacher, and frequently he who makes the statement hastens to add, "but it is the most costly." What one learns from the experience of other people does not cost the learner much. Wise is the teacher who profits from what others have gained through their experience.

Superintendent. A person from whom the Christian teacher may learn much is his superior. In most schools, this will be the superintendent of his department. Usually the superintendent is one who has had a considerable amount of experience in teaching and is, therefore, in position to pass on to the teachers in his department the benefits thereof. Any teacher, especially the young, inexperienced one, may well draw upon this store of experience in order to improve the quality of his work. The attitude of the successful teacher toward his administrative superiors will always be one of co-operation to the fullest extent. He will welcome their suggestions and criticisms and work wholeheartedly with them for the general improvement of the work of the whole department and of the entire school.

From another point of view, the superintendent of a department is in position to render aid to the individual teacher. His is the responsibility for an overview of the work of the entire department and of the work of each class in the department. As one who has this larger responsibility, he sees things in a perspective unlike that from which the teacher views even his own individual work and he is, consequently, able to render assistance that the teacher might not even be conscious of needing. The teacher who would grow is not likely to be disappointed if he makes it a point to understand the ideals of his superiors and tries conscientiously to follow these ideals. Many successful teachers owe much to the guidance of some superintendent of a department or a school under whom they worked.

Fellow-teachers. The growing teacher coöperates not only with superintendents but also with fellow-teachers. Among the most valuable lessons that any alert teacher ever learns are those picked up from fellow-teachers during informal conversation about their work. Sometimes two or more teachers work together, with mutual profit, on the solution of some problem. Informal observation, as opportunity permits, of the work of colleagues can give a teacher understanding of techniques and best ways to use them. No teacher can afford to show disrespect for the work of his colleagues because it is a most fruitful source for better ideas, larger understanding and more perfect knowledge of how to proceed.

Observation of teaching. Another avenue of improvement through others is observation of good teaching. Let the teacher who desires to improve visit public-school teachers, some of the best teachers in his own church school, or good teachers in other church schools. He can learn from watching others teach, both from their lacks and their mistakes and from their good qualities and their successes. When observing, it is well to use some objective standard of measurement such as a score-card and to make it a point to observe definite things. To observe in general does not count for much. Going to observe a teacher who excells in a particular phase of teaching such as leading a discussion or in the use of questions, makes for specific attention and more effective observation.

Observation of a class conducted for the purpose of demonstrating good teaching has splendid possibilities of value. The burden for originating such a class rests upon a supervisor, but if no supervisor exists or if one who exists does not provide a demonstration class, it is possible for a teacher to take the initiative. Let several teachers who are desirous of learning more about a certain phase of teaching technique get their heads together, gather a few pupils, and let one of their number conduct a teaching exercise, demonstrating that particular phase while the rest of them observe. After the teaching is over, the group of teachers can confer together concerning the manner in which it was done, commending, criticizing, and suggesting. All will receive profit from the exercise.

THE SUPREME MODEL

No teacher, be he a Christian teacher or not, is without a model to imitate. There is one teacher who is the model for all, one whom histories of education once described as "The Great Teacher," though modern histories do not usually mention Him. Jesus Christ was the Master Teacher. So effective was His teaching that officers sent by His enemies to arrest Him, coming back empty-handed, reported to those who had sent them,

"Never man spake like this man." Let any teacher who would become a better teacher give his days and nights to the study of His methods and his best energies to doing as He did. "The way Jesus taught is a model for all Christian teachers. As nearly as we can we are to teach as He taught."

"Modern pedagogy has used some new names for some old ways of teaching, but the pedagogy of Jesus, so far from having been surpassed, has not yet been attained." No other teacher has ever been so adept as He in going from the known to the unknown. He knew how to bring His subject, divine truth, and His pupil, man, together so that man could receive the truth. He used the simplest things of every-day life—the sower, the net, the lamp, the lilies of the field, and a host of others with which His hearers were familiar, to lead them to see the great eternal truths He wished them to know.

No other teacher has ever been so expert in motivating his pupils. No other has ever used better the principle of self-activity. None ever set more problems before the minds of his hearers. None ever used the question, "the universal instrument of all teaching," so effectively. What other told stories that have lasted so long and become so fraught with meaning? Which other was such a master of discussion? Can it be said of any other that he so fully and completely exemplified in his own practice the truths he taught? The Christian teacher has in His teaching an ideal way to teach that gives the widest scope for improvement.

But let the Christian teacher realize that the method of Jesus and the message of Jesus were one and the same thing. For Him, it was not a content on the one hand and a method on the other; the two went together as an inseparable unity. The all-important thing was the message of love and grace that He came to teach, and the method He used was merely a means to the end of so bringing that message to those whom He taught as to meet their deepest need for time and for eternity.

THE GUIDANCE OF THE HOLY SPIRIT

First, last, and always, the truly Christian teacher will realize his utter dependence upon the Spirit of God. The work that he is doing is God's work; he himself can never be other than a channel through which God operates. One outstanding characteristic of Jesus was His recognition of the fact that He was utterly dependent upon God for all that He did and taught. The deeds that He did were but the expression of God's working through Him; the words that He spoke were the words God had given Him.

When He committed God's work of teaching to the church, He said, "And, lo, I am with you alway, even unto the end of the world." As God had worked in and through Him while He was in the world in the form of man, He meant that He, as God, would work in and through Christian teachers as they do God's work. Previous to His departure, Jesus told His disciples that He would send the Holy Spirit and what the work of the Spirit would be (John 16: 7-15). So the Christian teacher can put his trust in the Holy Spirit to guide and to work through him, making him more and more nearly perfect in teaching God's truth to man.

QUESTIONS AND PROBLEMS

1. What kind of a teacher do you think would one be who had no desire to do his work better?
2. State the one thing that is always essential to improvement.
3. Do you agree with the statement which says teaching is never so well done that it might not be done better?
4. Is it possible that any one who can teach at all might not improve in his teaching?
5. Is it true that every teacher meets discouragements?

6. How would you explain, The growing teacher is the one who is making improvement in teaching? Do you accept the statement as true?
7. What types of teachers do not improve?
8. Why must improvement be constant?
9. Why is it "a long and gradual process"?
10. How long should a teacher continue to improve?
11. Show that actual teaching is relatively a small part of the work of a teacher.
12. Indicate how improvement may be made in the other two basic activities.
13. Does the bettering of each take place independently of the other two phases? Explain.
14. Why is teaching done?
15. Show the meaning of the statement, The teacher labors always to make himself useless.
16. In what three ways may a teacher improve himself through self-supervision?
17. In what sense is the training for teaching obtained before one enters his work, nothing more than a foundation?
18. Show the dangers of experimentation in teaching. How may they be prevented?
19. Outline what you consider would be a good plan for the improvement of teaching.
20. What kind of reading materials should a teacher use? Not use?
21. Distinguish between general reading and professional reading. In which field should a teacher read most?
22. Characterize a really good teachers' meeting in a local church. Have you had contact with such an one?
23. Indicate how other people may help a teacher to improve. Can you suggest people other than those mentioned who might help?
24. How may observation be used as a means of improvement?
25. Can you suggest further respects in which Jesus was a model for Christian teachers?
26. Is there any sense in which a teacher may be too dependent on the Holy Spirit? Explain your answer.

REFERENCES

Betts, G. H., *Teaching Religion Today* (New York: The Abingdon Press. 1934)

Betts, G. H., and Hawthorne, M. O., **Method in Teaching Religion** (New York: The Abingdon Press, 1925)

Chave, E. J., **Supervision of Religious Education** (University of Chicago Press, 1931)

Freeland, G. E., **The Improvement of Teaching** (New York: The Macmillan Co., 1925)

Garrison, N. L., **The Technique and Administration of Teaching** (New York: American Book Co., 1933)

Horne, H. H., **Jesus—the Master Teacher** (New York: The Association Press, 1920)

McKibben, F. M., **Improving Religious Education Through Supervision** (Chicago: Methodist Book Concern, 1931)

Richardson, N. E., **The Christ of the Classroom** (The Macmillan Co., 1931)

Roberts, S. L., **Teaching in the Church School** (Philadelphia: The Judson Press, 1930)

Smith, R. S., **New Trails for the Christian Teacher** (Philadelphia: The Westminster Press, 1934)

Vieth, P. H., **How to Teach in the Church School** (Philadelphia: The Westminster Press, 1935)

Teaching for Christian Living (St Louis: The Bethany Press, 1929)

INDEX

Adjustment and learning, 139.

Advantages, of story method, 245; of question-and-answer method, 253; of the lecture method, 272-275; of discussion, 281, 282; of project, 290; of dramatization, 294; of handwork, 296; of lesson planning, 304, 305.

Aim, nature of, 45, 46, 239; functions of, 47-51; inclusive, 51, 221; knowledge of Bible not the inclusive, 53; Bible the true source, 53; the perfect man of God, 54; conversion of pupil, 61; in relation to method, 239.

Aimlessness a curse, 42.

Aims, need for, 43; in New Testament, 44; nature of, 45; function in teaching, 47-51; value for measurement, 49; concrete statements of, 52; of Jesus, 55 ff.; subordinate, 60 ff.

Approval, desire for, 192.

Art, teaching as an, 17.

Athearn, W. S., 11, 100.

Attitudes, learning of, 166; of pupils toward learning, 240.

Axioms basic to Christian teaching, 9; supremacy of God, 9; need of personal Savior, 11; Bible the textbook, 13; teaching an art, 17.

Babson, Roger, 37.

Background of pupils, 210.

Behavior, nature of, 156; and teaching, 158.

Benson, C. H., 33, 52, 55.

Betts, G. H. and Hawthorne, M. O., 247, 287, 337.

Bible, textbook in Christian teaching, 13; Biblical versus non-Biblical materials, 15, 106, 112; teaching in the, 22; teaching necessary, 38; the true source of aim, 53; subject matter of teacher, 105; effective conditions of study, 108; methods of studying, 109 ff.; states the inclusive ideal, 201.

Books and teaching, 72.

Briggs, T. H., 168.

Burton, W. H., 156.

Character education, 14, 89; development of Christian, 64; Christian, 65; place in teaching personality, 89.

Characteristics, of good questions, 256-259.

Charters, W. W., 199.

Chave, E. J., 337.

Christian, defined, 70.

Christian teacher, inclusive aim of, 51 ff.; described, 71; essential marks of, 74-78; a growing personality, 78, 79; and preparation, 96 ff.

Christian teaching, contrasted with religious, 12; defined, 16; need for, 34-39; aims of, 51 ff.; and ideals, 169; building on past experience, 229; need for planning, 304.

Church, teaching in the, 28-33; school, 74.

Climax of story, 248.

Coe, G. A., 169.

Commins, W. D., 139

Commission, The Great, 26, 344.

Competition and rivalry, a primary desire, 194, 195.

Conduct, originates in the organism 149.

Confession, of Christ, 17, 61.

Consecration, to God, 17, 61.

Control, teaching as, 12.

Conversion, necessary, 11; emphasized by Jesus, 57; aim of teaching, 61, 142; work of Holy Spirit, 170.

Cope, H. F., 168.

Dangers, in use of story, 251, 252; of discussion method, 285, 286; of dramatization, 294; in handwork, 297-298.

Desires, primary, 188, 190, 195, 197.

Discussion method, 279 ff.

Dobbins, G. S., 52, 82, 93, 107, 240.

INDEX

Dramatization method, 292 ff.
Drives, use of native, 137, 145, 151, 212; dependent on tissue needs, 188; bodily condition as, 189.

Education, religious, 12, 13, 168; Christian, 12, 13; secular, 13, 167; character, 14, 89.
Effort, and learning, 173, 174.
Environment, 145 ff.; and teaching, 152.
Evangelist, work of in relation to teaching, 32, 34.
Experience, and learning, 176; desire for, 191; past, 207, 211; use of, 209; inadequate as basis, 221; building on past, 228.
Expression, and learning, 173; desire for, 192.

Factors to consider in choosing method, 238.
Facts, mastery of, 157.
Feeling, 225, 227.
Fellow teachers and self-improvement, 341.
Fergusson, E. M., 69.
Functions of aim, 47-51.

Gardener, teacher like a, 9, 129, 183.
Garrison, N. L., 76.
Gladstone, William, 37.
Growth, means of spiritual, 62 ff.; and service, 65; of teacher, 321; reading for, 339.
Guidance, law and spiritual, 19; of growth, 62; teaching as, 135, 226; of Holy Spirit, 344.

Handwork, 295 ff.
Heredity, in relation to teaching, 18; and personality, 80.
Holy Spirit, guidance of, 19, 39, 90, 152, 344.

Ideals, 166, 193, 199; necessity for, 200; building of, 217.
Illustration, 165, 230.
Improvement, of personality,

92; of method, 119; of teaching, 328 ff.; through self-supervision, 334; planning for, 336; through study, 338; through other people, 340.
Individual differences, 103.
Instinct, 132; teacher use of, 137, 145, 151; blindness of, 200.
Instruction, importance of concrete, 229.
Interest, as outcome of motivation, 183, 197; and attention, 186; kinds of, 187.
International Curriculum Guide, 236.

Jesus, as teacher, 24, 73; means by which He did His work, 25; aims in teaching, 55 ff.; and method, 299; the supreme model, 342.

Kilpatrick, W. H., 141, 168.
Knowledge, of Bible not inclusive aim, 53; needed by teacher, 101 ff.; alone not sufficient, 116, 128; and mind, 134; acquisition of, 138; and learning, 138.

Language, teacher understand pupils', 104; used by teacher, 162, 223; teacher understanding of, 179
Leader, the teacher as, 75.
Learner, the teacher as, 76.
Learning, and teaching, 127; physical basis of, 129; and acquisition of knowledge, 138; an aspect of mental development, 139; as adjustment, 139; as modification, 140, 156; as change in life, 141; pupil the center of, 141; factors that condition, 142 ff.; and environment, 145 ff.; place of purpose, 149 ff.; self-activity in, 151, 159, 166, 171, 215; no magic in, 152; meaning of, 155; not a result of reciting, 163; ideals and attitudes, 167; as goal seeking, 175; and experience,

INDEX

responsibility for, 100, 123; teaching as, 158; motor phase, 218; mental phase, 220; feeling phase, 225.

Price, J. M., 137.

Primary desires, use of in teaching, 195, 196; insufficiency of, 197.

Principles, basic to teaching, 9 ff., 233; and method, 117, 128; seven principles of teaching, 118; teaching must follow, 233.

Problem, of method, 234.

Project method, 286 ff.

Pupil, teacher learning to know, 101 ff.; unlearned tendencies of, 136; the center of learning, 141; expression necessary, 173; unification of effort, 174; and varied effort, 174; importance of pupil, 209; maturity of pupil a factor in method, 239; questioning, 264.

Purpose, 149 ff.; in relation to interest, 187; key to interest and effort, 226.

Question and answer method, 252 ff.

Raffety, W. E., 81, 97.

Reagan, G. W., 270.

Recitation, no evidence of learning, 163.

Reflex action, 132.

Religious education, 12, 13, 168.

Roberts, S. L., 46, 337.

Roosevelt, Theodore, 38.

School, changes in school life, 36; and teaching, 72; church, 74; importance of teacher knowing the, 97; teacher's knowledge of, 119.

Self-activity, and learning, 14, 151, 159, 166, 171, 215, 333; in learning ideals and attitudes, 167; as inhibition, 179; and motive, 198.

Service, and growth, 65.

Sin, fact of, 169; conviction of, 170.

Smith, R. S., 9.

Social, behavior of teacher, 88; life of pupil, 102.

Spirituality, dominant in Christian teacher, 91; education no substitute for, 150; essential, 202.

Stalker, J. H., 25.

Story, use of in teaching, 244 ff.

Structure, of nervous system, 131; of the story, 247-248; of the discussion, 282, 283.

Study, and teacher, 106 ff.; rules for, 107; study of the Bible, 108; plan of, 113; improvement through, 338, 340.

Success, in teaching, 19, 208.

Superintendent, teacher learning from, 340.

Teacher, like a gardener, 10; born or made, 18; Jesus as, 24; Paul as, 27; training, 31; call of, 31; every Christian a, 69; definition of Christian, 71; marks of a Christian, 74 ff.; as leader, 75; as learner, 76; as growing personality, 78; preparation of, 97, 121, 123; importance in school, 97; knowledge needed by, 101 ff.; understanding language of pupils, 104; and Bible, 105; and study, 106; need for knowing principles, 117; knowledge of school, 117; understanding how pupil learns, 128; and talking, 162, 178; recognizing principle of self-activity, 171; function of activity, 177; understanding pupil needs, 185; finding motives, 204; a limitation on method, 243; a constant student of method, 244; keeps in background, 335.

Teacher training, 31; necessary, 98.

Teaching, as self-activity, 11; as growth, 11; as control, 11; Christian vs. religious, 12, 13; an art, 17; success in,

INDEX

18; laws in, 19; in the Bible, 22; the Great Commission, 26; effects of in Early Church, 28; in Later Church, 29; ministry of, 32; of aim, 47; definition of, 70; and books, 72; and schools, 72; observation as preparation for, 120; and learning, 127; as guidance, 135, 179, 224; and behavior, 158; as preparation, 158; not telling, 160; self-activity in Christian, 169; and mind set, 217; complexity of, 233; and planning, 302; basic activities of, 331-332.

Technique, of questioning, 259-264; of lecturing, 275-277; of handwork, 296, 297.

Telling, not teaching, 160; the story, 249.
Temperament and disposition of teacher, 86, 87.
Thayer, H. H., 25.
Thomas, F. W., 214.
Thorndike, E. L., 179.
Thurstone, L. L., 149.
Time, for teaching, 242; for planning, 324; length of for class period, 324.
Training, necessary for teaching, 98; teacher training class, 122.
Trumbull, H. C., 29, 104, 170.

Vieth, P. H., 169, 337.

Wieman, H. N., 138.
Worship, a means of spiritual growth. 62